ABROAD

By the same author

Theory of Prosody in Eighteenth-Century England

Poetic Meter and Poetic Form

The Rhetorical World of Augustan Humanism: Ethics
and Imagery from Swift to Burke

Samuel Johnson and the Life of Writing

The Great War and Modern Memory

Editor

English Augustan Poetry

The Ordeal of Alfred M. Hale

Co-Editor

Eighteenth-Century English Literature

ABROAD

British Literary Traveling
Between the Wars

PAUL FUSSELL

OXFORD UNIVERSITY PRESS
Oxford   New York   Toronto   Melbourne

Copyright © 1980 by Paul Fussell
First published by Oxford University Press, New York, 1980
First issued as an Oxford University Press paperback, 1982
Library of Congress Cataloging in Publication Data
Fussell, Paul, 1924-
Abroad.
Bibliography: p.
Includes index.
1. English prose literature—20th century—History
and criticism. 2. Voyages and travels in literature.
3. Authors, English—20th century—Journeys.
4. British in foreign countries. I. Title.
PR808.V68F8 1980 820'.9'355 80-12810
ISBN 0-19-502767-1
ISBN 0-19-503068-0 (pbk.)
UK ISBN 0-19-281360-9 (pbk.)

Grateful acknowledgment is made to the following for permission to quote material in copyright:
B. H. Blackwell Ltd., for excerpts from "When It's Over," © 1917 from *A Lap Full of Seed* by Max Plowman. Jonathan Cape for excerpts from *The Road to Oxiana* by Robert Byron, © 1937; for excerpts from *One's Company: A Journey to China* by Peter Fleming, © 1934. Chatto & Windus Ltd., for excerpts from "It was a Navy Boy, so prim, so trim," © 1974 from *Wilfred Owen: A Biography* by Jon Stallworthy. James A. Decker, Publisher, for excerpts from "Your Passport Picture," © 1931 from *The Crannied Wall* by Laura Simmons. Gerald Duckworth & Co., Ltd., for excerpts from *Labels: A Mediterranean Journal* by Evelyn Waugh, © 1974. Faber & Faber Ltd., for excerpts from "The Waste Land," © 1936 from *Collected Poems* by T. S. Eliot; for excerpts from "The Dry Salvages," and "Little Gidding," © 1943 from *Four Quartets* by T. S. Eliot. Farrar Straus & Giroux for excerpts from *They Were Still Dancing* by Evelyn Waugh, © 1932. Harcourt Brace Jovanovich for excerpts from "The Waste Land," © 1936 from *Collected Poems* by T. S. Eliot; for excerpts from "The Dry Salvages," and "Little Gidding," © 1943 from *Four Quartets* by T. S. Eliot. *Harper's Magazine* for "The Stationary Tourist" and "Border Crossings" by Paul Fussell, reprinted from the April 1979 and July 1979 issues of *Harper's Magazine*; all rights reserved. William Heinemann Ltd., for excerpts from *Sea and Sardinia* by D. H. Lawrence, © 1956. Henry Holt and Co., for Poem XL ("Into My Heart an Air that Kills"), © 1940 from *Collected Poems* by A. E. Housman. Houghton Mifflin for excerpts from "Cinema of a Man," © 1952 from *Collected Poems: 1917-1952* by Archibald MacLeish. John Lehmann Ltd., for excerpts from *The Station* by Robert Byron © 1949. New Directions Publishing Corp., for excerpts from "Hugh Selwyn Mauberley," © 1926 from *Personae: The Collected Poems of Ezra Pound* by Ezra Pound. Oxford University Press, Inc., for "The Passport Officer," © 1978 from *Collected Poems* by Basil Bunting; for excerpts from "Autumn Journal," © 1967 from *Collected Poems* by Louis MacNeice; for excerpts from "It was a Navy Boy, so prim, so trim," © 1974 from *Wilfred Owen: A Biography* by Jon Stallworthy. Random House, Inc., for excerpts from "Dover," © 1976 from *Collected Poems* by W. H. Auden, ed., Edward Mendelson; for excerpts from "In Memory of W. B. Yeats," and "Passenger Shanty," © 1977 from *The English Auden: Poems, Essays, and Dramatic Writings, 1927-1939*, ed., Edward Mendelson. Illustrations from *The Valley of the Assassins* by Freya Stark, John Murray, London, copyright Freya Stark. The Viking Press for "Giorno dei Morti," and excerpts from "The Middle Classes," "Snake," and "Bavarian Gentians," © 1964 from *Complete Poems of D. H. Lawrence*, ed., Vivian de Sola Pinto and Warren Roberts.

Printing (last digit): 9 8 7 6 5 4 3 2

Printed in the United States of America

To Betty
fellow-traveler

PREFACE

This book is about travel writing, but it is also about travel, so I have dealt not just with books but with ships and trains, passport photographs and national borders and small French seaport towns, hotels and cafés and beach resorts, architecture ancient and modern, food and drink, nude sunbathing, and sex, both procreative and recreational. I have dealt with icy trenches and sunny patios, West African and Brazilian chiggers, touts of all nations, suntan oil, oranges and palm trees, the symbolic status of weather, the psychology of the sense of place, the spatial dislocations characterizing "modern" writing, and the once indispensable vade mecums of Baedeker and Tauchnitz. I have even had to talk about the difference between 15- and 18-inch coast-artillery guns. But I have done all these things to imply the context of travel writing from 1918 to 1939, to suggest what it felt like to be young and clever and literate in the final age of travel. Because the most sophisticated travel books of the age are British, I have focussed largely on them, although now and then I have considered an American example as well. And I have not scrupled to include occasional personal reflections on travel, so that the book aspires at once to the condition of literary criticism, social and cultural history, and autobiography.

I have talked about "the 20's" and "the 30's" without reposing much faith in the intellectual usefulness of such designations. More important than discriminating those two decades from each other is understanding the whole age's sense of having barely squeaked through one war and its gradually augmenting awareness of the approaching menace of another. It seems to matter less that an event occurred in

1921 or in 1936 than that it did not occur in 1912 or in 1963. The period I want to illuminate is the whole time between the wars.

For their advice, interest, and other favors I am grateful to Kingsley Amis, Malcolm Bradbury, Jeffrey Burke, Alfred Bush, Peter Conrad, Vivienne Crawford, Edwin Fussell, Daniel Garrison, Samuel Hynes, George Kearns, Norman Klein, Suzanne Mantell, John McPhee, Jeanette Mirsky, Harry T. Moore, John P. Pattinson, Richard Poirier, Peter Quennell, James Raimes, Edward Said, John Shakeshaft, Roderick Suddaby, and Christopher Sykes. John Saumarez Smith, of Heywood Hill, Ltd., has been so assiduous in locating out-of-the-way books that he has been a virtual research associate. Mrs. Lucy Butler has given generous assistance. Steven Helmling has kindly read the proofs. As usual, I am grateful to Rutgers University for many kindnesses. I must thank the John Simon Guggenheim Memorial Foundation for a year's Fellowship, and the Harris Foundation of Northwestern University for inviting me to present some of these materials as lectures under its auspices. And I want to thank the editors of the *Spectator* and *Harper's* for permission to re-appropriate those parts of this book that first appeared in their pages.

Rutgers University   P. F.
January 1980

Contents

ILLUSTRATIONS

ABROAD

FROZEN ORANGES

IN 1916 oranges, like other exotic things that had to travel by sea, were excessively rare in England. If you could find them at all they cost the shocking sum of 5d each. Wilfred Owen could locate no more precious image than oranges to register his delight at the golden hair and golden character of a "Navy boy" he met in a train compartment:

> His head was golden like the oranges
> That catch their brightness from Las Palmas sun.

To Owen the sailor seems everything the war is not. He is fresh, noble, and clean, and

> His words were shapely, even as his lips,
> And courtesy he used like any lord.
> "Was it through books that you first thought of ships?"
> "Reading a book, sir, made me go abroad."

Owen is ravished, and the only image adequate to his pleasure is that of the rich and rare conveyed by ship from a Mediterranean island neither northern, nor cold, nor restricted, nor Puritan, nor, like the trench world, destined to destruction, for Spain is neutral territory.

A year later, after the disastrous Battle of the Somme had attenuated in the cold mud, the winter was one of the most severe for a century. "Last night at mess the ginger ale was frozen," a young British officer wrote from his dugout in January, 1917. "We thawed some a bit but when we poured it out it froze into the glasses. The perrier water froze as soon as we opened the bottle. A little ginger ale spilled on the table and froze there." And as if this weren't enough,

3

"Two oranges this morning were as hard as cricket balls." Those frozen oranges stick in the memory as an emblem not just of the terrible winter of 1917 but of the compensatory appeal of the sun-warmed, free, lively world elsewhere, mockingly out of reach of those entrenched and immobile, apparently forever, in the smelly freezing mud of Picardy and Flanders. "Far, far from Ypres I long to be," they sang, and if for some the land of their dreams at the end of the long trail was simply "home," for others it was distinctly "abroad." The fantasies of flight and freedom which animate the imagination of the 20's and 30's and generate its pervasive images of travel can be said to begin in the trenches.

One who sought ever after the warm world somewhere else was ex-Captain Osbert Sitwell of the Grenadiers, who had been thoroughly chilled on the Western Front and almost destroyed at the Battle of Loos. A few years after the Armistice it was his delight to celebrate the orange in his travel book *Discursions on Travel, Art and Life* (1925). Riding on a train through the orange groves of Sicily, he is moved to celebrate the "orange-tree and the fruit it bears." Wherever the orange grows, he asserts, "you will find the best climate, the most beautiful of European buildings"; and he is pleased to realize that, unlike the apple, the orange, although golden, has never been associated with evil, only with warmth, civility, taste, beauty—everything the war was not. At the same time Sitwell was dilating on the orange in these terms, D. H. Lawrence was installing it at the center of his short story "Sun." It is an orange the mother rolls across the terrace to her infant boy whom she has just introduced to the therapeutic practice of nude sun-bathing. Her desire for him to accept it ("Bring Mummy the orange") signals an equation she makes between the sun, warmth, oranges, and full humanity. "He shall not grow up like his father," she decides, "like a worm that the sun has never seen."

It was at Ypres in 1917 that Gerald Brenan, later a distinguished traveler and resider abroad, matured his plans for escape—both from his parents and from the war—by reading, as he puts it, "a number of" travel books about Central Asia. "The things I had been dreaming of all through the war," he remembers, "my plans for the future were all of travel—to cross the Sahara, to live among the Taureg or the Bakhti-ari of Persia, to explore Guatamala and Ecuador"—all hot places, we notice. "It was very cold," Alec Waugh remembered of the trenches in the winter of 1917, and thirteen years later he made good his escape and recorded it in *Hot Countries,* an account of his travels to Tahiti, Siam, Ceylon, and other venues of the palm tree, a silhouette of which adorns both front and back covers. Waugh's *The Loom of Youth,* his novel of public-school emotional life which was thought scandalous in 1917, was being read in the trenches that year by Captain H. W. Yoxall. He was also reading two other new books everyone was passing from hand to hand, Barbusse's *Le Feu,* which registered the French soldiers' disgust with the war, and Norman Douglas's *South Wind.* Barbusse's novel recommended itself not least because of its authenticity about the cold of the trenches: the men of the narrator's company wear over their uniforms "the skins of animals, bundles of blankets, Balaklava helmets, woollen caps, furs, bulging mufflers (sometimes worn turban-wise), paddings and quiltings, knittings and double-knittings, coverings and roofings and cowls. . . ." Read in proximity to Barbusse, what an appeal *South Wind* must have extended to these trapped and freezing trench rats, what fantasies it must have triggered of unconstrained movement within a caressing warmth. If we wanted to designate a setting entirely opposite to the trench scene in northern France and Belgium, we could hardly do better than specify Douglas's island of Nepenthe, loosely identifiable with Capri. There the "broiling" sun shines daily, the cause of "paganism and nudity and laughter," and the benign climate is specifically contrasted with that of the northern countries, "lands adapted only for wolves and bears."

The "tropical" motif becomes a widespread imaginative possession of all in the trenches who were cold, tired, and terrified. A favorite greeting-card to send home was one to be bought at shops behind the line. Its message on the front, "Greetings from the Trenches," is worked in embroidered silk below a frieze of green and brown embroidered palm trees disposed on each side of an immense sun with the bright rays of its nimbus extending to the very edges of the design. Opened, the card reads,

> *My heart is with you*
> *And my thoughts every day*
> *For the Past, Remembrance*
> *For the Present, Good Wishes*
> *For the Future, Bright Hopes.*

(Imperial War Museum)

The hope that someday the war would end and the cold, fear, and exhaustion become only a memory prompted Max Plowman to lodge his wishes in a poem he called "When It's Over." In seven stanzas seven soldiers are asked what they will do when the war's over. Two of the seven indicate that "travel" or something very like it is on their minds. One, designating himself "a bit of a rover" (to rhyme with *over*), lusts "to get out and across the sea," where he can reside abroad in some place like Australia or New Zealand. (He is like the actual Ivor Gurney, the poet and composer. Discharged from the army in October, 1918, gassed and shell-shocked, the very first thing he does is to set out on foot from his home in Gloucester to find a ship sailing anywhere.) The fourth of Plowman's seven soldiers, who knows he will be very tired when the war's over, indulges in imagery of a warm tropical beach. He says:

> "I shall lie on the beach
> Of a shore where the rippling waves just sigh,
> And listen and dream and sleep and lie
> Forgetting what I've had to learn and teach
>   And attack and defend."

One reason this man's reveries may sound familiar to the literate is that they anticipate the "imaginary / Audition of the phantasmal sea-surge" and other images of tropical repose entertained by Pound's Hugh Selwyn Mauberley as appropriate to his longed-for flight from corruption and defeat. Pound was working on *Mauberley* in London during the war. It is remarkable the way his details of "the coral isle," "the unexpected palms," the "scattered Moluccas," "thick foliage," and "placid water" parallel those of the front-line mind. Pound derived some of his more outré tropical details, like the flamingos and the Simoon, from Flaubert's *Salammbô* (1862); the others could have come directly from conversations with wishful cold soldiers on leave, soldiers whom Pound's poem memorializes unforgettably:

> There died a myriad,
> And of the best, among them. . . .
> Charm, smiling at the good mouth,
> Quick eyes gone under earth's lid.

Pound's "scattered Moluccas" are the same Spice Islands that will attract H. M. Tomlinson, once all but frozen to death at Ypres and the Somme, who executes his own "farewell to London" in 1923 and records it in his travel book *Tidemarks* (1924). The hot Moluccas invited the former soldier who recalled the winter of 1917 on the Somme and wrote, "Nobody at home ever knew what the actions of that winter were like on the hills of the Ancre before the village of Miraumont, when the earth was marble, and every shell scattered frozen marl which flew like splinters of masonry." Six years later Tomlinson sails off to the South Seas with the tune of *Tipperary* in his head. In Borneo he encounters a legendary fellow-countryman named "Maguire" and fully understands when Maguire tells him, "The Somme told me all I wanted to know of Europe—that and the Vimy Ridge and some odd corners. If you smart city people arrange a show like that again, don't worry about me. I shall be fine here with the orang-utans." On the volcanic island of Ternate, one of the Moluccas, Tomlinson happens upon a stack of just-postwar British popular magazines. He finds them crammed with articles about the hot tropics and with stories set there.

After the United States had been in the war over a year and a half it was possible for an American as well as a British imagination to understand the compensatory principle by which trench sensibility finds itself propelled vigorously toward the tropics. Reviewing William Beebe's travel book *Jungle Peace* in the *New York Times Review of Books* in October, 1918, Theodore Roosevelt (no less) perceives that Beebe's travels to Guiana constitute, like Tomlinson's and "Maguire's," a specific recoil from the world of the trenches. As he says, "This volume was written when the author's soul was sick of the carnage which has turned the soil of Northern France into a red desert of horror. To him the jungle seemed peaceful . . . he gives cameos of what one sees sailing southward through the lovely islands where the fronds of the palms thrash endlessly as the warm trade blows." And in the Mauberley tradition, images of war and of the South Seas were juxtaposed in Edward Marsh's *Rupert Brooke: A Memoir* (1918), which depicted that young person with his "good mouth" now swimming in the warm Tahiti waters or loafing in a lava-lava, a flower behind his ear, now dying on a hospital ship off Gallipoli.

Between the wars, Guy Chapman, who had experienced the whole of the Great War, traveled extensively with his wife Storm Jameson. "We went to . . . obscure ruined monasteries," she says, "small provincial art galleries, the house in which a dead philosopher spent his life, salt marshes, trout streams, some turn in a rough nameless road which offered a view of a smiling valley and a line of hills, because, although he had not seen them, he knew they were there." Some of the most assiduous travelers of the 20's and 30's were those whose wanderlust and all else the war had nearly extinguished. Sensing their predicament and understanding the urgency of their precious images of compensation, we will find nothing absurd in Chapman's intense, irrational happiness in travel, even though he says, "I suppose there is something absurd about the intense happiness I get out of the simplest travel abroad." His reason is simple and sufficient: "I must say I enjoy being alive."

Nowhere to go

"WE thought that after the war we would quit the monotonous life at home and we would go adventuring." Thus one Private Willcox and his mate Ira in the trenches. From the misery of the Somme in July, 1916, Robert Graves sent his friend Siegfried Sassoon a rhyming letter dilating, as he says, on "the time that we were going to have together when the War ended; how, after a rest . . . , we were going for a visit to the Caucasus and Persia and China." But at home as well, among those exempted from the grosser threats of the war, the desire to travel abroad augmented as the war proceeded. "What I want to do when peace comes," wrote Harold Nicolson, whose war was spent in Whitehall, "is to motor in a two-seater through France and Spain." He finally got his wish, and when the war was over tooled around the Continent with as much pleasure as literary travelers like Hemingway and Patrick Balfour and Robert Byron.

The Defense of the Realm Acts of 1914 and 1915 effectively restricted private travel abroad. The main travelers were the hapless soldiery shipped to France and Belgium and Italy and Mesopotamia. The travel books appearing while the war lasted were by official travelers like the mendacious war correspondents. Other civilians were fixed in the British Isles for the duration. That meant four years, three months, and seven days of no traveling. And although of course not as nasty as life at the front, life at home was as constricted and unpleasant as regulations could make it, with a scarcity of all desirable things like meat, sugar, beer, and spirits. Food was so precious that throwing rice at weddings was prohibited, and it was unlawful to feed pigeons and stray dogs. By the winter of 1917 coal was tightly rationed, and most people were cold all the time. Museums were closed down, newspapers were smaller, and the muffin-man had long disappeared. The Food Ministry came up with the slogan, "Eat Slowly: You Will Need Less Food." If travel abroad was virtually prohibited, even domestic travel was limited. Trains were often cancelled, and the few civilians who managed to squeeze aboard were lectured by placards reading

> UNNECESSARY TRAVELING
> USES COAL REQUIRED TO
> HEAT YOUR HOMES.

It was not only in England that travel of any kind gave offense. John Williams tells us that in Germany when the war started, returning travelers encountered a hostility conveniently combining patriotism with envy: "Trains were seized and luggage unceremoniously thrown out, leaving wayside stations strewn with holiday trunks. . . ."

But the main loss in England was a loss of amplitude, a decay of imaginative and intellectual possibility corresponding to the literal loss of physical freedom. The very theater of thought and feeling contracted; the horizons closed in. In 1915 E. M. Forster observed that England felt "tighter and tinier and shinier than ever—a very precious little party, I don't doubt, but most insistently an island, and there are times when one longs to sprawl over continents, as formerly." The tone of England turned stuffy, complacent, cruel, bullying, and small-minded—as one should expect during any war, which as Osbert Sitwell perceives is necessarily co-incident with a hatred of poetry and art and a contempt for beauty: "The chipped plate, the banging door, the maimed animal, the bombed cathedral, are each, though different in degree, part of the constant rebellion against perfection. War, which is the crowning of chaos, war, with its squalid virtues of blackout and jealousy ('. . . he has more jam than me!'), and of skinflint thrift, always intensifies the innate Philistinism of every race." It is no surprise that in November, 1915, Augustine Birrell, Chief Secretary for Ireland, declared that "he for one would forbid the use, during the war, of poetry."

War intensifies the innate Philistinism of the British especially, D. H. Lawrence thought. There is no doubt that he was put upon more than most during the war, and hardly any British civilian could equal him in intensity of perception, emotional violence, and the conviction that he had been deeply wronged. Yet for all his special white-hot outrage, Lawrence's experience in wartime England and his almost continuous flight from it thenceforth—he returned only three times for brief visits—are emblematic of the behavior of many others propelled on their post-war travels as if by a wartime spring tightly compressed. Lawrence can be seen as merely the vanguard of the British Literary Diaspora, the great flight of writers from England in the 20's and 30's which deposited Gerald Brenan in Spain and Robert Graves in Majorca; Norman Douglas in Capri, Naples, and Florence, and Lawrence Durrell in Corfu; Aldous Huxley in California, Christopher Isherwood in Berlin and California, and W. H. Auden, finally, in New York; Bertrand Russell in China and Russia; Somerset Maugham and Katherine Mansfield on the Riviera; V. S. Pritchett in Paris; John Lehmann and Stephen Spender in Vienna; Basil Bunting on Tenerife, as well as in Paris, Rapallo, Berlin, the United States, Persia, and Afghanistan; Osbert Sitwell in Italy, and Edith, from 1932 to 1939, in Paris; and the Far Easterners—Edmund Blunden in Tokyo, Harold Acton and I. A. Richards in Peking, Julian Bell at Wuhan University, William Empson in Tokyo and Peking. On Corfu in 1936, Durrell, writing home for news, asked the pressing question, and in capitals: "IS THERE NO ONE WRITING AT ALL IN ENGLAND NOW?" This diaspora seems one of the signals of literary modernism, as we can infer from virtually no modern writer's remaining where he's "supposed" to be except perhaps Proust—we think of Pound in London, Paris, and Italy; Eliot in London; Joyce in Trieste and Paris; Mann ultimately in the United States. The post-war flight from the Middle West of Hemingway, Fitzgerald, and Sinclair Lewis is the American counterpart of these European flights from a real or fancied narrowing of horizons.

Lawrence's troubles in England during the war would constitute a sufficient motive for flight even for a saint. Already under legal pressure for his divorce costs, in autumn of 1915 he found that *The Rainbow*, the novel on which he reposed so much hope, was in trouble with both the press ("a monotonous wilderness of phallicism"—*Daily News*) and the law. In November the book was found legally obscene and the edition was destroyed. He was not just married to a German, who, although a naturalized British subject, was under surveillance by the Home Office as "a person of hostile origin"; he was wildly outspoken in his contempt for the war and its restrictions. During 1916 and 1917, when he and Frieda lived in sad poverty in Cornwall, they were clumsily persecuted by the local military, who suspected them of signalling to German submarines off the coast. Throughout, Lawrence was harassed and humiliated by repeated crude physical examinations for the army. In the twelfth chapter of his novel *Kangaroo* (1923) he memorably records his anguish in wartime England, his torture by "the whole spirit of the war, the vast mob-spirit, which he could never acquiesce in."

Like the troops in their cold holes, Lawrence spent a lot of time indulging imagery that expressed his own desire to "go"—anywhere. Having just heard of the death of Rupert Brooke, he writes Ottoline Morrell in April, 1915: "I wish I were going to Thibet—or Kamschatka—or Tahiti—to the ultima, ultima, ultima Thule. I feel sometimes I shall go mad, because there is nowhere to go. . . ." Since 1914 he had been projecting a colony of perhaps 20 fed-up exiles from England, who would escape to Florida, perhaps—the heat and palm trees were surely a draw—and there establish a sensible community, which he wanted to call *Rananim*. He even naively exhorted Forster to join, "with his woman." Reminding us a little of Mauberley, he tells Lady Ottoline in 1916: "The only thing now to be done is either to go down with the ship, sink with the ship, or, as much as one can, *leave* the ship, and like a castaway live a life apart." He stoked his anxious restlessness with books of travel and adventure. In his Cornish retreat in 1916 he read Richard Henry Dana's *Two Years Before the Mast*, as well as *Moby Dick*; and he asked a friend to send him *Omoo* or *Typee*. The same year he regaled himself with a Baedeker for Italy (probably *Central Italy and Rome*), and wrote his friend S. S. Koteliansky: "The Baedeker is *very* nice: I love its plans and maps and panoramas. . . . Would God we were all in Italy, or somewhere sunny and war-less." His desire to get out was such that he suddenly announced to Kot in 1917: "We will go to Russia. Send me a Berlitz grammar book. . . ." Finally the war was over, and the Lawrences were issued passports to leave. He wanted to go to America to lecture, but Amy Lowell dissuaded him. They sailed for Italy instead, in November, 1919, and thus they began their unremitting journey which for the next ten years took them generally southeastward, through the Mediterranean and on to the hot countries of the Pacific and the American southwest and Mexico and back to the Mediterranean, where Lawrence died, in Vence, in 1930.

The year after the Lawrences made good their escape, a play opened in London which could be thought a subtle stimulus to others to take the road. Of course there's no reason to explain the appeal of Gay's *Beggar's Opera* at any time. Yet there seems something special in the popularity of Nigel Playfair's 1920 revival at the Lyric Theater, Hammersmith. The production ran for 1,463 nights, or over four years. Considered—as its war-exhausted audience couldn't help considering it—in proximity to the straitened, puritanical England of wartime, the play could be received virtually as John Gay's merry retort to the Defense of the Realm Act. It overflows with images of irresponsibility and freedom, not to mention such appealing gestures of geographical escape as Macheath and Polly's duet "Were I Laid on Greenland's Coast," with its hummable romantic ending fusing the motifs of eroticism and flight:

> MACHEATH: . . . I would love you all the day,
> POLLY: Every night would kiss and play,
> MACHEATH: If with me you'd fondly stray
> POLLY: Over the hills and far away.

"Over the hills and far away": that line must have made many eyes water and directed many imaginations to ships' timetables. What a contrast to the wartime constriction of horizons, the depressing conviction that there is nowhere to go. Anthony Powell testifies that "the influence of *The Beggar's Opera* quickly entered every branch of daily life." The eighteen-year-old Evelyn Waugh, who had not yet traveled abroad, went to the play in 1921, and although neither then nor later given to outbursts of unalloyed critical enthusiasm, he pronounced the experience "simply perfect."

A convention of the travel books of the 20's and 30's is for the traveler to pay his respects to the Great War by implicitly recalling that time when travel was impossible, or when "going abroad" was a murderous parody of the real thing. Thus Peter Fleming, who was only eleven when the war ended. On the journey rendered in *Brazilian Adventure* (1933), perhaps the most popular travel book between the

wars, he finds himself searching for the "Serra do Roncador," a mountain range marked on the maps, all right, but actually non-existent, "a
figment of the fevered imagination of Brazilian cartographers." He
goes on: "Our horizon remained empty; we might as well have
searched for the Angels of Mons." And in *News from Tartary* (1936),
Fleming designates his Part Four as "No Man's Land." Waugh performs similar gestures in his first travel book, *Labels* (1930). His cruise
ship is approaching the Gallipoli Peninsula, and Waugh is on deck
with an American woman who insists on reciting John Masefield's
"Cargoes" and asking Waugh, "Can't you just see the quin-quē-
remes?" "I could not," writes Waugh, "but with a little more imagination I might easily have seen troopships, full of young Australians,
going to their death with bare knees."

Robert Byron seems as careful not to let us forget the relation between the pleasures of postwar traveling and the agonies by which
they have been purchased. Traveling to India and Tibet in 1929, he
is careful to tell us that at Corfu, during lunch, "Sir Geoffrey Salmond
said that he might be old-fashioned, but that *All Quiet on the Western Front* was not a book to leave in the drawing-room." Later, near
Gaza, he visits the former British trenches and finds them "still lit-
tered with bones and shredded clothing." Back in Calcutta after touring Tibet, he conducts two friends, "a Tibetan couple in full regalia,"
to the local opening night of R. C. Sherriff's *Journey's End:* "The
dialogue proved unintelligible to them, and they were further mystified
by the bursting shells." All this while Byron is registering the "pure
enjoyment which became known to me during my first visit to Asia
Magna."

In the same way, J. R. Ackerley, in his *Hindoo Holiday* (1932),
cannot deliver an account of his six months' farcical residence abroad
as private secretary to an eccentric Indian maharajah without occasional quasi-elegiac reversions to the war, whose remembered trench
horrors give dimension and meaning to the anomalous pleasures he
now enjoys. As if careful to enclose his Indian adventures within an
envelope suggesting memories of the war, he adverts to it at both
beginning and end. At the beginning as he wanders in a remote quarter of a town, he notices the similarity between the look of the Indian
streets and the look of the former trench walls; and at the end, as his
time in India is about to run out, the gruesome spectacle of a swatted

fly with twitching legs, devoured by ants on the floor of his room, reminds him of the feebly waving arms of a wounded German officer
dying between the lines in 1917. Except for these two moments
which embrace it, the bulk of Ackerley's text dwells on scenes of delight and freedom and comfort and comedy, but the reader will not
forget what Ackerley has not forgotten.

I HATE IT HERE

AFTER the war something new and recognizably "postwar" surfaces
in British intellectual and imaginative life. Browning and Symonds
and Ruskin and Pater could transfer much of their affection to the
Mediterranean without experiencing a correlative contempt for home.
Arnold could assault British Philistinism without the impulse to flee
and then to rationalize flight by melodramatic exposures of British
defects. Robert Louis Stevenson and Rupert Brooke were pleased to
journey away from England and equally pleased to return. But with
Lawrence and Douglas and Huxley and Graves ("I went abroad, re-
solved never to make England my home again"), and later, Durrell,
Isherwood, and Auden, departure is attended by the conviction that
England is uninhabitable because it is not like abroad. In 1972, a year
before the end of his life, Auden was presented in an interview with
this proposition: "In your early works, there seems to be a fierceness
towards England. There's a sense of being at war with where you are."
To which Auden answered crisply, "Yes, quite." Typical of the myth
figures of this period is Lawrence's miner Aaron Sisson, in *Aaron's Rod*
(1922), who like Joyce's Stephen in *A Portrait of the Artist as a
Young Man* (1916), takes flight to escape something hateful at home.
Freud has perceived that if one motive for travel is curiosity, a stronger

motive is that which impels adolescent runaways. "A great part of the pleasure of travel," he finds in 1937, "lies in the fulfillment of these early wishes to escape the family and especially the father." Auden seems to have been aware specifically of this point in his poem "The Capital," written in 1938, presumably about Brussels: "Far from your lights," he says, resides "the outraged punitive father." Isherwood's father had been killed in the war. He was thus obliged to conceive that it was his mother and her England he was rejecting by traveling far away with his friend Heinz, who in 1933 had been turned back by British immigration on suspicion of sexual undesirability. The impulse to flee will be the stronger when the father (or mother) is one who closes pubs, regulates sexual behavior, devises the British Christmas (a strong propellant of Osbert Sitwell to Italy), contrives that the sun shall seldom be seen, and finds nothing wrong with the class system and the greedy capitalism sustaining it. An insistent leitmotif of writing between the wars, for both successful and would-be escapees, is I Hate It Here.

The war was widely blamed for ruining England, for bringing on, as Pound puts it with characteristic vigor, "the state of utter dithering deliquescence into which England slopped in 1919." Returning from India in 1922, Forster describes his homeland as "a person who has folded her hands and stands waiting." Four years of repression, lies, casualty lists, and mass murder sanctioned by bishops have done their damage: "I do think that during the war something in this country got killed." Cyril Connolly writes his boyhood friend Noël Blakiston in 1929: "I have plumped against England. . . . I am tired of the country. . . . I do feel it is a dying civilization—decadent, but in such a damned dull way—going stuffy and comatose instead of collapsing beautifully like France." Basing his inferences on recent conversations with the inhabitants of Wigton, Cumberland, Melvyn Bragg says of the 20's that "the feeling and fact which comes through is of exhaustion, silted lives, numbness"; "the weight of . . . oral evidence supports the notion that England was in some way paralyzed and trapped." Paralysis is what Lawrence objectifies in Clifford Chatterley's service-connected disability, and Connie Chatterley becomes a perceptive critic of all in British life that is cramped, lifeless, and dim. What strikes her as she wanders through a town in the Midlands is "the utter negation of natural beauty, the utter negation of the gladness of life, the utter absence of the instinct for shapely beauty which every bird and beast has, the utter death of the human intuitive faculty." Horrors include "the stacks of soap in the grocers' shops, . . . the awful hats in the milliners'!"—details fleshing out Lawrence's perception that "our towns are *false* towns—every street a blow, every corner a stab."

What can one do but hate a place which is

dingy	fly-blown
leprous	defaced
faecal	discolored
verminous	stinking
lousy	smelly
moth-eaten	filthy
evil-looking	malformed
squalid	monstrous
bleak	gaunt
dull-colored	slimy
greasy	musty
grey	dead
sickly	sooty
stale	damp?

Where life is

moribund	malignant
dull	desolate
graceless	ruinous
vile	repugnant
frightful	mean
dreadful	spurious
horrible	appalling
sinister	sickening
dim-witted	mingy
meager	sordid
dismal	joyless
despondent	sneaking
godless	Canadian
Scotch	[and in 1936] pro-German?

All these adjectives are applied by Orwell to aspects of British life from 1919 to 1939. One could make a fairly representative poem of

The slums of Salford, in the Midlands. (Popperfoto)

the 20's and 30's by arranging them, after the manner of Auden or C. Day Lewis or MacNeice, to modify favorite I Hate It Here nouns: *gas-works, trains, sewers, vacant lots, new towns, power stations, housing estates, entryways, allotments, cities, streets, factories, canals, hoardings, chimneys, bridges, tramlines, wharves, alleys, slums, railway-arches, Woolworth's.* And that vision of the postwar British scene is not just Orwell's and Graham Greene's and the fellow-traveling poets'. It is shared by most of the nonpolitical, though sometimes reactionary, bright young "society" people. In Waugh's *Vile Bodies* (1930), Nina looks down from an airplane and sees "factories, some of them working, others empty and decaying; a disused canal." As the plane hits a bump "the scene lurched and tilted."

"I think I'm going to be sick," said Nina.

(Freud's *Civilization and Its Discontents* was about to burst on London, in translation from the Hogarth Press.)

Postwar London itself could be seen as a powerful stimulus to movement abroad. Five years after the war Tomlinson perceived that

The beach at Cannes in the 1930's. (Bettmann Archive)

every travel agency constituted evidence of secret disaffection, just as every travel poster was really an implicit satire on the local scene. "No wonder it pays," he says, "to decorate the walls of the capital with romantic but seditious pictures of palms, midnight suns, coasts of illusion, and ships outward bound. Nothing could so plainly indicate our revolt from the affairs we must somehow pretend to venerate." And ten years after the war it is specifically London stimuli that invite Allen and Philip, in Isherwood's *All the Conspirators*, to vacate London: "A poster seen in the Warren Street tube station had released sensory and motor images of gulls, passing, repassing. And from the greasy filth of Paddington goods siding one false overpowering breath of rotten seaweed. . . . Can't we start *now?*"

At Oxford around 1926 Louis MacNeice and his poetic friends would hire a canoe and "partly because of *The Waste Land*," spend days "paddling beneath the gas works, a fine place, we decided, for reading Webster." At such moments, he remembers,

> The foreign was calling strongly. I sat in my canoe and watched
> a goods train lumbering over the railway bridge and marked the

names on the vans to insert in a disillusioned sketch: "Hickleton—Lunt—Hickleton—Lunt—Hickleton—Longbottom—the placid
dotage of a great industrial country." . . . I did not want placid-
ity, or dotage, or industry; I wanted certain new worlds which
really meant old worlds, the Mexico of D. H. Lawrence or the
Capri of Norman Douglas. . . . Travel! Travel must be "experience" at its highest.

(In contrast, poets of the 1950's, like Donald Davie, Philip Larkin,
and Kingsley Amis, "conscious of the consequences of the decline of
empire," as Spender has said, stubbornly re-installed themselves in
England and became "in an almost literal sense 'little Englanders.'
Such poets were extremely conscious of the Englishness of their work,
hostile to the whole idea of 'abroad.' They were anti-foreign." Amis's
novel *I Like It Here* [1958] registers the attitude.)

Norman Douglas of Capri, and of Naples and Florence, was formerly of England, which he fled during the war to avoid prosecution
for kissing a boy and giving him some cakes and a shilling. Douglas
spent the rest of his life procuring revenge, first in *South Wind*
(1917), which, while celebrating easy-going Mediterranean ways, is
implicitly and sometimes explicitly about how awful England is. The
British ambition to regulate the moral conduct of others is an expression merely of envy, says Douglas's spokesman Count Caloveglia, "the
envy of the incomplete creature for him who dares express himself."
The Count concludes that "a plague has infected the world—the
plague of repression," but we are to understand that it is most virulent
in England, which during the war has contrived new ways of strangling
pleasure under the color of patriotism. The happy drunk of *South
Wind*, Miss Wilberforce, is there largely to ridicule the British laws
regulating drink, especially those established at the outset of the war
by the Defense of the Realm Act. Its very acronym D.O.R.A. suggests
the British auntie or nannie with pursed lips and wagging finger. As
Douglas's Mr. Keith tells Thomas Heard, D.D., "All mankind is at
the mercy of a handful of neurotics," wielding catchwords like *duty*
and *sobriety*. "Sobriety! In order that Miss Wilberforce may not come
home drunk . . . , all we other lunatics forgo the pleasure of a pint
of beer after ten o'clock. How we love tormenting ourselves!" Later,
Mr. Heard, now converted, catches the style and descants on British
monotony: "Everything fireproof, seaworthy. Kindly thoughts ex-

pressed in safe unvarying formulas. . . . The monotony of a nation intent upon respecting laws and customs. Horror of the tangent, the extreme, the unconventional. God save the King." (Mr. Heard now sounds like Forster.) As Douglas puts it in *Experiments* (1925), "Britons never shall be slaves. . . . [But] what else are we?" In *How About Europe?* (1930) he resumes his ridicule of Britons and their licensing laws ("What a pack of masochists!") and in addition mounts a spirited attack on British hotels, cooking, and Sundays. British customs examinations are "the most brutal and ferocious"; London's parks have been ruined by anti-sex patrols; blackmail flourishes because of preposterous sex laws; the income-tax is the most offensive in Europe; and the climate is loathsome.

It sometimes seems that it is only after the war that the British weather becomes a cause of outrage and a sufficient reason for departure. Before the war one had been rather proud of the fogs and damps and pleased to exhibit staunchness and good humor in adapting to them. Hardy and Hopkins and Housman and Robert Bridges had notated British winters and London snows with equanimity and sometimes even with satisfaction. But after 1918 it is as if the weather worsens to make England all but uninhabitable to the imaginative and sensitive. Actually England is a very habitable country. The fact is that the post-war hatred of the weather was a convention of the lettered designed to advertise England's deficiencies in other ways, especially those resulting from D.O.R.A. and betokening chapel-morality and related Calvinisms. Indeed, British weather is more temperate than that of the northeastern United States. There one finds really frigid winters, with annual ghastly blizzards killing scores of people and occasioning total stoppage of activity for days at a time; and really torrid wet summers, when everyone who can afford it either flees abroad or moves to the seashore. Fall brings hurricanes; spring, floods. The weather of Boston, New York, and Washington is so bad that if the United States had been colonized from west to east instead of the reverse, the northeastern United States today would be populated as sparsely as North Dakota. The main cities would be somewhere else, and the northeastern area would be planted out in soy beans. Yet the weather of the United States has not become a joke or a byword, which means that it is not deployable as an emblem of grey Puritan repression and the conventicle spirit the way British weather is. Or the way British food is. Connolly finds it useful to associate the weather with the food in *The Rock Pool* (1936) as images indicating Naylor's uneasiness about returning from the Mediterranean: "He thought of the scabby winter landscape that the close heaven seemed to cover; thin soup under a greasy tureen." And in Orwell's *Coming Up for Air* (1939), it is on "a beastly January morning, with a dirty yellowish-grey sky" that George Bowling enters a London milk-bar and orders coffee and frankfurters, only to find when he grinds a fissure in the frankfurter skin with his temporary false teeth—but let George Bowling tell it:

> I can't honestly say that I'd expected the thing to have a pleasant taste. . . . But this—well, it was quite an experience.
> The frankfurter had a rubber skin, of course. . . . I had to do a kind of sawing movement before I could get my teeth through the skin. And then suddenly—pop! The thing burst in my mouth like a rotten pear. A sort of horrible soft stuff was oozing all over my tongue. . . . I just couldn't believe it. . . . It was fish! A sausage, a thing calling itself a frankfurter, filled with fish!

"It gave me the feeling," says Bowling, "that I'd bitten into the modern world and discovered what it was really made of. . . . Rotten fish in a rubber skin." What else could one expect, really, on a beastly January morning?

After the war it was found that in addition to puritanical weather and revolting food, another part of the British heritage was a terrible awkwardness of body, largely unnoticed except by those able to invoke the yardstick of abroad. India was a favorite gauge. In *A Passage to India* (1924) it is because the punkah-wallah is beautiful and graceful that we sense so fully that Adela Quested is not. In the same way Robert Byron, in his *Essay on India* (1931), brings into juxtaposition the women of Sind and the women of London, to the latter's disadvantage: the Indian women walking to the water point and back balance jars on their heads "with such aristocracy of movement, such evidence of measureless tradition, such absolute control over every muscle, yet with such absolute flexibility" that they seem a ballet or a group from the court of Louis XIV. They are a useful measure: "Just a year later I attended a charity ball in a London hotel, at which the beauties of contemporary London consented to exhibit themselves in procession upon a raised platform. One by one they too came forward, but staggering and strutting like marionettes on a string, their arms and legs flying this way and that, their bodies propelled with jerks and starts, their eyes goggling and their lips wriggling." At that moment, Byron says, "I remembered the women of Sind." Basil Bunting likewise remembers the beautiful "old women / straight as girls at the well" in Afghanistan, and he proposes that travel vignette as a rebuke to the vile population of England, which includes "usurers, / cheats and cheapjacks, . . . boasters, / hideous children of cautious marriages," and "those who drink in contempt of joy."

If one could not escape this terrible place entirely, there was comfort in taking oneself to its very verge, ready to leap when possible into freedom and beauty and grace. Thus Connolly and his wife chose to live in South Devon and explained: "We must be able to get abroad at a moment's notice and Plymouth is the furthest place from London with fast boats to the Continent except Queenstown." And because it was a prominent jump-off stage for the Continent, Dover became popular in the mid-30's as a place to live, especially for Auden, Isherwood, Ackerley, William Plomer, Forster, and others attracted by the soldiers there, who, as Auden writes in "Dover,"

> crowd into the pubs in their pretty clothes,
> As pink and silly as girls from a high-class academy.

As the nearest "frontier" town to the Continent, Dover seemed almost within the jurisdiction of the Code Napoléon, and because it was so near Europe, there seemed less inhibition there than in, say, Glasgow in attending closely to what Plomer calls "the 'frou-frou' of kilts in the street."

The historian A. J. P. Taylor is puzzled over the reason so many postwar writers left England, both physically and in other ways. "To judge from all leading writers," he says, "the barbarians were breaking in. Civilized men could only lament and withdraw, as the writers did to their considerable profit. The writers are almost alone in feeling like this, and it is not easy to understand why they thus cut themselves off. . . . this was the best time mankind, or at any rate Englishmen, had known: more considerate, with more welfare for the mass of people packed into a few years than into the whole of previous history." Taylor's wet comment (dim-witted, Orwell would say) provides its own explanation of the phenomenon he cannot understand.

═══ THE PASSPORT NUISANCE ═══

THE phrase is Norman Douglas's. The passport was the novel instrument by which England restricted travel during the war and by which, like all other countries, it has interfered in it ever since. *Novel* because before 1915 His Majesty's Government did not require a passport for departure, nor did any European state require one for admittance except the two notoriously backward and neurotic countries of Russia and the Ottoman Empire. But after the war all Europe exhibited the state of mind which Baedeker takes as characteristic of pre-war Russia: "If a passport is not in order, its unhappy owner has to recross the frontier, the train by which he came waiting for this purpose." When the illicit lovers D. H. Lawrence and Frieda Weekley fled England for Metz in 1912, they simply went, leaving from Charing Cross Station and crossing to Ostend and thence proceeding to Germany. No one asked to see any passports, and they carried none. When in 1912 Gerald Brenan, propelled by disdain for his terrible family, ran away from home (that is, "set out on his travels"), he crossed the Channel to France without any passport. He simply went, and disguised as a gas-fitter at that. He did carry a (false) birth certificate, but only to produce if required at the Austrian border with Italy. (At the moment Austria was nervous about spies.)

Sophisticated British travelers of the 20's and 30's never tire of dilating on the pre-war joys of traveling abroad when, as C. E. Montague says, "Europe lay open to roaming feet. . . . All frontiers were unlocked. You wandered freely about the Continent as if it were your own country. Plenty of us had pervaded . . . France, Italy, Switzerland and the Low Countries for twenty or thirty years without knowing what a passport looked like." Twenty years after the war Patrick

Leigh Fermor was hiking around in Eastern Austria. "I was wandering across a field when a man in uniform began shouting from the dyke-road overhead. Where the devil did I think I was going? It was the Austrian frontier post. 'You were walking straight into Czechoslovakia!' the official said reproachfully as he stamped my passport."

What put a stop forever to passportless wandering was Regulation 14c of D.O.R.A., passed November 30, 1915: "A person coming from or intending to proceed to any place out of the United Kingdom as a passenger shall not, without the special permission of a Secretary of State, land or embark at any port in the United Kingdom unless he has in his possession a valid passport. . . ." It was a wartime emergency regulation, but like so many others—those closely monitoring pub-closing hours, for example—it was not repealed after the war but simply left standing: it was convenient for the government and no one complained very much. During the war a few "war passports" were issued, especially for transatlantic travel. Some of them were one-way, with return to England forbidden for the duration. The Lawrences tried to get even one of these but were refused.

As a fixture of the European scene since 1915, the passport now seems so natural that one forgets the shock and scandal it once occasioned. Robert Byron is one who treated his with a due contempt. In the space asking about "Any special peculiarities," he entered "Of Melancholy appearance," and in the square reserved for a photograph of bearer's wife he drew a ludicrous cartoon, "resulting," Anthony Powell recalls, "in the document being withdrawn." In Byron and Christopher Sykes's comic novel *Innocence and Design* (1935) Sir Christopher Bruce uses his passport, with its four blank visa pages, as a handy little notebook. The passport as an institution was an occasion for a laugh well into the 30's. In Waugh's *Scoop* (1938), William Boot and his boss Mr. Salter, of the *Daily Beast*, forget all about the need of a passport for Boot's journalistic visit to Ishmaelia until, ready to board his plane, his deficiency is belatedly discovered. He suddenly must move all his traps from the airport back to London, including his precious collection of cleft sticks, while Salter helps him acquire an emergency passport. "The Art Department will take your photograph and we have an Archdeacon in the Religious Department who will witness it." One of the Ishmaelian factions stamps its visa in Boot's passport, which, seen by the consulate of the opposing faction, causes them to burn the little booklet. Boot finally leaves England bearing two passports, both ridiculous.

An additional provision in Regulation 14c established for all time, as it proved, a further cause of comedy and embarrassment. "To every such passport . . . there must be attached a photograph of the person to whom it relates." This was something new. Literary theorists searching for the springs of "modernism" are likely to look too high, to inquire into subtle movements of the intellect or to go haring after Hegel and Nietzsche and Freud and Heidegger and Wittgenstein. There's another way of going about it, and that is to pay less attention to the presumed intellectual causes of unprecedented events than to the fact that they occur. Once they occur, people have to live with them, and living with them requires unique adjustments and reactions. To put it simply, the sum total of these adjustments and reactions produces what we recognize as "the modern sensibility." So small a phenomenon as the passport picture is an example of something tiny which has powerfully affected the modern sensibility, assisting that anxious self-awareness, that secret but overriding self-contempt, which we recognize as attaching uniquely to the world of Prufrock and Joseph K. and Malone. There are other unprecedented contributors to the modern neurosis: things like the numbers used in the modern world for personnel identification and coercion—social-security numbers, taxpayer numbers, driver-license numbers, license-plate numbers, and, on the Continent, identity-card numbers. But the passport picture is perhaps the most egregious little modernism. The subject of a passport picture knows in his heart of hearts the truth of Edward Weston's conclusion: "Only with effort can the camera be forced to lie: basically it is an honest medium." One truly "modern question" is: "Do I really look as awful as that?" (Before photography one could control the way one looked when not present: the portrait-painter would perform the will of the sitter.) That modern question especially disturbs because, as Susan Sontag observes, "All photographs are *memento mori*," testimonies of vulnerability. "Through photographs," she says, "we follow in the most intimate, troubling way the reality of how people age. To look at an old photograph of oneself . . . is to feel, first of all: how much *younger* I . . . was then. Photography is the inventory of mortality. A touch of the finger now suffices to invest a moment with posthumous irony." Eliot's "The Love Song of J. Alfred Prufrock" was written by 1910 or 1911, but it was not published, in Harriet Monroe's *Poetry*, until 1915. Was it perhaps the new "passport atmosphere" that made it seem to Pound especially worth sending to Monroe? Certainly a poem like Eliot's can be said to dramatize, among other things, the feeling attending an awareness of one's own passport picture. A low-down version of "Prufrock" would be Laura Simmons's poem "Your Passport Picture":

> *What though you hide it in your trunk—*
> *Ere sailing hour has set?*
> *Jammed down beneath your old blue serge?*
> *Don't think you can forget!*
> *The face within that passport book*
> *Will rise to haunt you yet.*

The tradition of the passport picture as a demeaning and shame-making corollary of modern experience has been constant since 1915. In 1938 the general editor of the *Daily Beast* speaks to Mr. Salter about Boot, a publishable photograph of whom is wanted:

> "There must be a photograph of him somewhere in the world."
> "They took one for his passport," said Mr. Salter, doubt-fully, "but I remember thinking at the time it was an extremely poor likeness."
> "I don't care if it looks like a baboon—"
> "That's just how it does look."

In Virginia Woolf's *Between the Acts* (1941) the final portion of Miss La Trobe's historical pageant concerns, as the program announces, "The Present Time. Ourselves." We know something absurd is going to happen, for "sounds of laughter came from the bushes." Without warning, out prances the entire cast, holding mirrors up to the audience, which thinks, "Ourselves? But that's cruel. To snap us as we are. . . . That's what's so distorting and upsetting and utterly unfair." The audience, "laughed at by looking-glasses," is as defenseless as the subject of a passport picture, who knows his picture is not merely on his passport but permanently on file somewhere, always available to be scrutinized and doubtless ridiculed by nameless but menacing civil servants. ("Look at the teeth on this one." "Yes, but I liked better the one without any chin at all. Do you suppose it's a congenital defect?") In Amis's *I Like It Here* Garnet Bowen compares his passport picture of 1946 with his new one of 1956; satiric analysis arrives finally at self-contempt:

> The lad in the 1946 one had looked back at Bowen with petu-
> lant, head-on-one-side sensitivity. Wearing a nasty suit, he had
> seemed on the point of asking Bowen why he wasn't a pacifist or
> what he thought of *Aaron's Rod*. The 1956 Bowen was twice as
> wide and had something of the air of a television panelist. His
> question about *Aaron's Rod* would have concerned how much
> money whoever wrote it had made out of it. It was odd how the
> two of them could differ so much and yet both look exactly the
> kind of man he would most dislike to meet or be.

Twenty years later a cartoon in the *New York Times* for Feb. 26, 1978, depicts a man at the rail of a liner (it must be a cruise ship merely, by this time) with a woman looking ill. He: "Are you O.K., Sylvia? Suddenly you look like your passport photo."

In addition to the photograph, the 1915 form of the passport required the bearer to indicate his "Profession." This open invitation to self-casting and social promotion, not to mention outright fraud, led of course to its own kinds of irrelevant or falsifying precision. "In my passport," says Graves in *Good-bye to All That* (1929), "I am down as 'University Professor.' That was a convenience for 1926, when I first took out a passport. I thought of putting 'Writer,' but passport officials often have complicated reactions to the word. [Kingsley Amis's current passport lists him as "Author."] 'University Professor' wins a simple reaction: dull respect. No questions asked. So also with 'Army Captain (pensioned list).'" WRITER is the profession Arthur Marshall designated for himself in applying for his passport, but he apparently wrote the R carelessly, for when he received the passport he found himself styled WAITER, a profession, he found, "which apparently is not very highly regarded at frontiers."

The 1915 passport also devoted one page to "Description of Bearer." Here were entered not just such particulars as age and place and date of birth but such physical data as height (but not, interestingly, weight), and color of hair and eyes. "Forehead" had to be described ("medium" was a favorite), like nose ("straight," "normal," "hooked," etc.), mouth ("medium," "normal": did anyone ever write "attractive" or "charming"?), chin ("small"), complexion ("fresh," "ruddy"), and face ("square," "round," "oval"). This was all so novel and startling in 1915 that it invited responses like this letter to *The Times:*

> Sir,
>   A little light might be shed, with advantage, upon the high-handed methods of the Passports Department at the Foreign Office. On the form provided for the purpose I described my face as "intelligent." Instead of finding this characterization entered, I have received a passport on which some official utterly unknown to me has taken it upon himself to call my face "oval."
>
> Yours very truly,
BASSETT DIGBY.

It would become a convention in the 20's and 30's that the passport, in addition to producing anxious self-consciousness and simplifying the self, falsifies as well by remaining static while the person changes. As early as 1922 Lawrence conceives of the passport as a handy metaphor of misapprehension and misrepresentation when in *Aaron's Rod* he sets Aaron to musing in northern Italy about which is the "authentic" Aaron, the one formerly married to Lottie at home, or the current single one, wandering abroad. "When I am formulated, sprawling on a pin, / When I am pinned and wriggling on the wall," says Prufrock. In Aaron's mind

> was pinned up a nice description of himself, and a description of Lottie, sort of authentic passports to be used in the conscious world. These authentic passports, self-describing: nose short, mouth normal, etc.; he had insisted that they should do all the duty of the man himself. This ready-made and very banal idea of himself as a really quite nice individual: eyes blue, nose short, mouth normal, chin normal: this he has insisted was really himself. It was his conscious mask.

But Aaron's flight abroad, the action that ironically has made the formulas of his literal passport so familiar to him, has changed that:

> Now at last, after years of struggle, he seemed suddenly to have dropped his mask on the floor, and broken it. His authentic self-describing passport, his complete and satisfactory idea of himself suddenly became a rag of paper, ridiculous.

Ideas like these are not thinkable in the same form before 1915. Likewise unknown before 1915 is that ritual occasion for anxiety so familiar to a modern person, the moment one presents the passport at a frontier. In 1920 Lawrence observes with fascination the half-gentleman and debtor Maurice Magnus's anxiety as he "passes" the "examination" of passports upon arriving at Malta. "Yes, he passed all right. Once more he was free." Having passed, Magnus's anxieties are temporarily stilled, and he becomes again "quite superb and brisk." In the modern travel experience, it is the moment of presenting one's passport to cross from one state to another that is the debased equivalent of the moment in romance when the outsetting hero defeats or conciliates, in Joseph Campbell's terms, the "shadowy presence" that guards the hero's passage out of his own land and lets him through the gate into his adventures. For the hero, it is a moment of triumph. For the modern traveler, it is a moment of humiliation, a reminder that he is merely the state's creature, one of his realm's replaceable parts. And returning is worse. It would be depressing to estimate the amount of uniquely modern anxiety experienced by the traveler returning to his own country when the passport officer slowly leafs through his book of pariahs searching for the name of the traveler there. The wartime atmosphere which nourished the passport as an institution hangs about it forever. It is an atmosphere in which human creatures are conceived as personnel units; it is a world unwittingly evoked by the language of Lord Sandhurst, who noticed in 1915 the many apparently fit young men lounging around London and, wondering whether conscription shouldn't be applied, spoke of them as "very good male material."

Here is a poem by Basil Bunting, written in the early 30's:

> This impartial dog's nose
> scrutinizes the lamppost. All in good order.
> He sets his seal on it and
> moves on to the next.

> (The drippings of his forerunners
> convey no information,
> barely a precedent.
> His actions are reflex.)

Is this about a dog peeing on a lamppost? No, it's titled "The Passport Officer," and it nicely registers the postwar sense of the nasty dehumanization of everyone touched by the passport nuisance, officials included. In *Black Lamb and Grey Falcon* (1942), Rebecca West's travel book (to give it the simplest name) about Yugoslavia, Hitler is considered a phenomenon more or less understandable once it is remembered that he was literally "the child of one of those parasites on our social system, a douanier."

===== ALL THESE FRONTIERS =====

IN 1930 two strangers meet by chance on a train crossing the Dutch-German border. One is young William Bradshaw, like his creator Christopher Isherwood fleeing England for the wider horizons of Berlin. The other is Mr. Arthur Norris, clad in a suit that looks costly and equipped with gold cigarette lighter and wig. If Magnus suffers passport anxiety, it is nothing to the fit of nerves which seizes Mr. Norris as the train approaches the frontier. The first sign of his apprehension is his "nervous recoil" when Bradshaw asks him for a light. "His fingers, nervously active, sketched a number of flurried gestures round his waistcoat."

" 'Do you know what time we arrive at the frontier?' " Bradshaw asks him.

" 'I'm afraid I couldn't tell you exactly. In about an hour's time, I believe.' "

"An unpleasant thought seemed to tease him like a wasp," says Isherwood. "He moved his head slightly to avoid it. Then he added, with surprising petulance: 'All these frontiers . . . such a horrible nuisance.' "

Bradshaw sympathizes: " 'They ought to be done away with.' "

" 'I quite agree with you,' " says Mr. Norris. " 'They ought indeed.' " By the time the train is crossing the frontier and slowing down at Bentheim, where passports will be examined, Mr. Norris has revealed that he is an extraordinarily experienced traveler. Indeed, he has "delivered a lecture on the disadvantages of most of the chief European cities." Bradshaw reports: "He had suffered from rheumatics in Stockholm and draughts in Kaunas; in Riga he had been bored, in Warsaw treated with extreme discourtesy, in Belgrade he had been unable to obtain his favorite brand of tooth-paste. In Rome he had been annoyed by insects, in Madrid by beggars, in Marseilles by taxi-horns."

But now the train has stopped, and in the corridor a dread voice is heard: " '*Deutsche Pass-Kontrolle.* All passports please.' " Mr. Norris is now almost sick with worry, which he covers by prattling in an unnatural voice about the topography of Athens. When the frontier guard takes his passport out into the corridor and after scrutinizing it holds a page against the light, " 'I was amazed,' " says Bradshaw, " 'to see what a state he was in; his fingers twitched and his voice was scarcely under control.' " But Norris somehow survives the test, and as his passport is returned he sinks back and calls for fresh air. " 'All this traveling . . . very bad for me.' " As *Mr. Norris Changes Trains* (1935) goes on to reveal, the "charming" Mr. Norris, nominally in the import-export business, has cause to be nervous at frontiers. He is a con-man and swindler, a pornographer and whip-collector, a pimp and frequent bankrupt and known to the police of many countries as a grossly mercenary spy and go-between. His consciousness of frontiers and the threat they pose is necessarily extreme. But even if exaggerated it suggests the general sense of frontiers as menacing which forms so large a part of the imagination between the two World Wars. The way to imitate an early Auden poem is to get as many frontiers into it as possible. Peter Stansky and William Abrahams' title for their book about Julian Bell and John Cornford, *Journey to the Frontier* (1966), perfectly catches the tonality, fusing as it does the title of Auden's and Isherwood's play *On the Frontier* (1938) with that of Edward Upward's novel *Journey to the Border* (1939).

The anomalous "front" of the Great War, that appalling line of wandering smelly ditches demarcating the border pro-tem between

Allies and Central Powers, helps establish for the succeeding two decades the idea that a frontier is not just absurd but sinister. The historian of the modern imagination could trace almost a direct conceptual tradition from the idea of the trenches to that of the Maginot Line and then to the division of Korea at the 38th Parallel and the Berlin Wall, all "iron curtains" marking strict geographical zones of malign, usually mortal, import. It is in this tradition that in 1938 Hitler's demands of Czechoslovakia took the form of talk about "the revision of frontiers," and that the Second World War begins for the British with Hitler's crossing the Polish frontier, a line originally devised by the remote, scholarly geographers of the Congress of Paris in 1919. Here numerous experts redrew the European frontiers to reward victors and humiliate losers, and for the next twenty years Europe became frontier-obsessed and, like Auden, map-mad.

As a result of the treaties not just of Versailles but of Neuilly, St. Germain, Trianon, and Sèvres, dramatic alterations were worked on the borders of Germany, France, Belgium, Italy, Austria, Denmark, Greece, and the former Ottoman Empire. The frontiers of Lithuania, Poland, Hungary, Romania, Yugoslavia, and Czechoslovakia were defined or re-defined. "Fiume" and "Danzig" were equipped with their own small frontiers in their new capacity as free cities or states. This multiplication and alteration of frontiers served to advertise the irrational nationalism that contributed so largely to the European tone between the wars, a nationalism borrowing vigor from the bullying vainglory of the Allied victors hot for reparations and the self-pitying whine of the Germanic underdog. At the end of his adventures Mr. Norris has had enough of Europe—he is about to be arrested again—and determines on flight to the New World. " 'I feel I need a complete change of scene,' " he tells Bradshaw. " 'One's so confined here, so restricted. As you get older, William, you'll feel that the world gets smaller. The frontiers seem to close in, until there's scarcely room to breathe.' " But the New World has its nasty frontiers too, as Graham Greene discovered in Mexico in 1938. Entering the Mexican state of Tabasco by boat at Frontera, he feels something of Mr. Norris's anxiety and observes, "It is before you cross a frontier that you experience fear." Try to imagine Wordsworth saying that, or even the proto-modern Matthew Arnold, and you have an idea of the uniqueness of "the modern," whatever exactly it is.

The British are singularly sensitive to land frontiers because (with the exception of the one embarrassing line separating Ulster from Ireland) they have none. This fact alone makes them special among Europeans. For the British, national boundaries which are not a matter of immemorial sea and shore but drawn by the hand of man are at best ridiculous and at worst monstrous. As Hector Bolitho says, "It is not easy for us to comprehend the warping influence of ever-changing frontiers upon European peoples. . . . Our frontiers are defined by nature and have not been subject to the caprice of any congress." It is not an Alsatian or an Austrian but the quintessential Englishman Robert Byron who asserts: "There is something absurd about a land frontier." Ironic, then, that it was the British themselves, saddled with the Balfour Declaration, who for two generations had to draw and police impossible land frontiers in Palestine.

The British conviction of the absurdity of the thing is what leads to the satiric high-jinks practiced by so many travelers of the 20's and 30's as they encounter land frontiers or experience the ludicrous parochialism these frontiers betoken and encourage. In the autumn of 1938, at Tabriz, Persia, Byron and his friend Sykes can't resist returning the frontier *fiche* filled out this way:

AVIS

Je soussigné { Robert Byron
{ Christopher Sykes

Sujet { anglais
{ anglais

et exerçant la profession de { peintre
{ philosophe

déclare être arrivé en date du { 13me octobre
{ 13me octobre

accompagné de { un djinn
{ un livre par Henry James.

For the British especially the idea of a frontier town is synonymous with fraud, greed, stupidity, and sadism. Thus Peter Fleming as he crosses from China into India and finds that "Tashkurgan was a frontier town if ever there was one. It had . . . the air of living on passers-by," and was therefore a great place for "trumped-up passport regulations, inspired by aimless malice."

One would not have to be British, or even notably sensible, to perceive that the frontiers attending the whole concept of "Fiume" constitute a scandal. In 1924 Osbert Sitwell sets a little passport farce on the border between Fiume and Italy. "Entering Fiume was no easy matter," he writes, the journey across the border resembling a scramble through "a thicket of passports and questions." Among the hazards is the special stupidity of the frontier guards. One of them, frowning over the first page of the absurd little booklet proferred by Sitwell, firmly mistakes the official granter of the passport, Lord Curzon, Secretary of State for Foreign Affairs, for "bearer," and in a fury of political self-righteousness asserts that Lord Curzon, notorious as an "enemy" of Fiume, is on no account allowed to enter. Sitwell's comic contempt for the guard seems somehow British, and so does the empiricism and moral outrage of Rebecca West's account of the miseries of Fiume in 1937. She and her husband find that unhappy place a town

> that has the quality of a dream, a bad headachy dream. Its original character is rotund and sunburnt and solid, like any pompous southern port, but it has been hacked by treaties into a surrealist form. On a ground plan laid out plainly by sensible architects for sensible people, there is imposed another, quite imbecile, which drives high walls across streets and thereby sets contiguous houses half an hour apart by detour and formality. And at places where no frontiers could possibly be, in the middle of a square, or on a bridge linking the parts of a quay, men in uniform step forward and demand passports, minatory as figures projected into sleep by an uneasy conscience.
>
> "This has meant," said my husband as we wandered through the impeded city, "infinite suffering to a lot of people," and it is true. Because of it many old men have said to their sons, "We are ruined," many lawyers have said to widows, "I am afraid there will be nothing, nothing at all."

That passage is acute in perceiving two "modern" facts at once: the inevitable association between passports and anxiety and the correlation between the idea of frontiers and the idea of ruin. And West's passage has further implications for an inquirer into the nature of "the modern." Her image of Fiume as "hacked by treaties into a surrealist form" suggests a relation between the literal frontier scene between the wars and the methods of the art and writing of those years aiming at a critical, and even satirical, refraction of modern actuality.

Fragmenting and dividing anew and parcelling-out and shifting around and repositioning—these are the actions implicit in the redrafting of frontiers. All these actions betray a concern with current space instead of time or tradition. All imply an awareness of reality as disjointed, dissociated, fractured. These actions of dividing anew and shifting around provide the method of collage in painting, and in writing they provide the method we recognize as conspicuously "modern," the method of anomalous juxtaposition. Think of *The Wasteland* and the *Cantos* and *Ulysses* and their reliance on disjoined "quotations" from others or from one's self. Think of David Jones's *In Parenthesis* and *The Anathémata,* and even of Connolly's *The Unquiet Grave.* "The taste for quotations (and for the juxtaposition of incongruous quotations)," says Susan Sontag, "is a Surrealist taste." In modern writing the expectations attaching to the old, readily understandable order of reasonable narrative sequence (cf. "modern European history") are defeated, and we see "spatial form," as Joseph Frank has called it, rather than traditional temporal form, governing the literature most eloquent of the anxious, troubled scene between the wars.

FROM EXPLORATION TO TRAVEL TO TOURISM

BECAUSE travel is hardly possible anymore, an inquiry into the nature of travel and travel writing between the wars will resemble a threnody, and I'm afraid that a consideration of the tourism that apes it will be like a satire.

Two bits of data at the outset. When you entered Manhattan by the Lincoln Tunnel twenty years ago you saw from the high west bank of the Hudson a vision that lifted your heart and in some measure redeemed the potholes and noise and lunacy and violence of the city. You saw the magic row of transatlantic liners nuzzling the island, their classy, frivolous red and black and white and green uttering their critique of the utility beige-gray of the buildings. In the row might be the *Queen Mary* or the *Queen Elizabeth* or the *Mauretania*, the *United States* or the *America* or the *Independence*, the *Rafaello* or the *Michelangelo* or the *Liberté*. These were the last attendants of the age of travel, soon to fall victim to the jet plane and the cost of oil and the cost of skilled labor.

A second bit of data, this one rather nasty. An official of the Guyanese government was recently heard to say that Jonestown might be turned into a profitable tourist attraction, "on the order of Auschwitz or Dachau." The disappearance of the ships from the Hudson, like the remark from Guyana, helps define the advanced phase of the age of tourism.

The rudimentary phase began over a century ago, in England, because England was the first country to undergo industrialization and urbanization. The tediums of industrial work made "vacations" necessary, while the unwholesomeness of England's great soot-caked cities made any place abroad, by flagrant contrast, appear almost mystically salubrious, especially in an age of rampant tuberculosis. Contributing to the rise of tourism in the nineteenth century was the bourgeois vogue of romantic primitivism. From James "Ossian" Macpherson in the late eighteenth century to D. H. Lawrence in the early twentieth, intellectuals and others discovered special virtue in primitive peoples and places. Tourism is egalitarian or it is nothing, and its egalitarianism is another index of its origins in the nineteenth century. Whether in the Butlin's Camps of the British or the National Park campsites of America or Hitler's Strength-through-Joy cruises or the current Clubs Méditerranée, where nudity and pop-beads replace clothes and cash, it is difficult to be a snob and a tourist at the same time. By going primitive in groups one becomes "equal," playing out even in 1980 a fantasy devised well over a century ago, a fantasy implying that if simple is good, sincere is even better.

It was not always thus. Before tourism there was travel, and before travel there was exploration. Each is roughly assignable to its own age in modern history: exploration belongs to the Renaissance, travel to the bourgeois age, tourism to our proletarian moment. But there are obvious overlaps. What we recognize as tourism in its contemporary form was making inroads on travel as early as the mid-nineteenth century, when Thomas Cook got the bright idea of shipping sight-seeing groups to the Continent, and though the Renaissance is over, there are still a few explorers. Tarzan's British father Lord Greystoke was exploring Africa in the twentieth century while tourists were being herded around the Place de l'Opéra.

And the terms *exploration, travel,* and *tourism* are slippery. In 1855 what we would call exploration is often called travel, as in Francis Galton's *The Art of Travel.* His title seems to promise advice about securing deckchairs in favorable locations and hints about tipping on shipboard, but his sub-title makes his intention clear: *Shifts and Contrivances Available in Wild Countries.* Galton's advice to "travelers" is very different from the matter in a Baedeker. Indeed, his book is virtually a survival manual, with instructions on blacksmithing, making your own black powder, descending cliffs with ropes, and defending a camp against natives: "Of all European inventions, nothing so impresses and terrifies savages as fireworks, especially rockets.

. . . A rocket, judiciously sent up, is very likely to frighten off an intended attack and save bloodshed." On the other hand, the word *travel* in modern usage is equally misleading, as in phrases like *travel agency* and *the travel industry*, where what the words are disguising is *tourist agency* and *the tourist industry*, the idea of a *travel industry* constituting a palpable contradiction in terms, if we understand what real travel once was.

"Explorers," according to Hugh and Pauline Massingham, "are to the ordinary traveler what the Saint is to the average church congregation." The athletic, paramilitary activity of exploration ends in knighthoods for Sir Francis Drake and Sir Aurel Stein and Sir Edmund Hillary. No traveler, and certainly no tourist, is ever knighted for his performances, although the strains he may undergo can be as memorable as the explorer's. All three make journeys, but the explorer seeks the undiscovered, the traveler that which has been discovered by the mind working in history, the tourist that which has been discovered by entrepreneurship and prepared for him by the arts of mass publicity. The genuine traveler is, or used to be, in the middle between the two extremes. If the explorer moves toward the risks of the formless and the unknown, the tourist moves toward the security of pure cliché. It is between these two poles that the traveler mediates, retaining all he can of the excitement of the unpredictable attaching to exploration, and fusing that with the pleasure of "knowing where one is" belonging to tourism.

But travel is work. Etymologically a traveler is one who suffers *travail*, a word deriving in its turn from Latin *tripalium*, a torture instrument consisting of three stakes designed to rack the body. Before the development of tourism, travel was conceived to be like study, and its fruits were considered to be the adornment of the mind and the formation of the judgment. The traveler was a student of what he sought, and he was assisted by aids like the 34 volumes of the Medieval Town Series, now, significantly, out of print. One by-product of real travel was something that has virtually disappeared, the travel book as a record of an inquiry and a report of the effect of the inquiry on the mind and imagination of the traveler. Lawrence's Italian journeys, says Anthony Burgess, "by post-bus or cold late train or on foot are in that great laborious tradition which produced genuine travel books." And Paul Theroux, whose book *The Great Railway Bazaar* is

one of the few travel books to emerge from our age of tourism, observes that "travel writing is a funny thing" because "the worst trips
make the best reading, which is why Graham Greene's *The Lawless
Roads* and Kinglake's *Eothen* are so superb." On the other hand, easy,
passive travel results in books which offer "little more than chatting,"
or, like former British Prime Minister Edward Heath's *Travels*, "smug
boasting." "Let the tourist be cushioned against misadventure," says
Lawrence Durrell; "your true traveler will not feel that he has had his
money's worth unless he brings back a few scars." (A personal note:
although I have been both traveler and tourist, it was as a traveler, not
a tourist, that I once watched my wallet and passport slither down a
Turkish toilet at Bodrum, and it was the arm of a traveler that reached
deep, deep into that cloaca to retrieve them.) If exploration promised
adventures, travel was travel because it held out high hopes of mis-
adventures.

From the outset mass tourism attracted the class-contempt of kill-
joys who conceived themselves independent travelers and thus superior
by reason of intellect, education, curiosity, and spirit. In the mid-
nineteenth century Charles Lever laments in *Blackwood's Magazine*:

> It seems that some enterprizing and unscrupulous man [he
> means Thomas Cook] has devised the project of conducting
> some forty or fifty persons . . . from London to Naples and
> back for a fixed sum. He contracts to carry them, feed them, and
> amuse them. . . . When I first read the scheme . . . I caught
> at the hope that the speculation would break down. I imagined
> that the characteristic independence of Englishmen would revolt
> against a plan that reduces the traveler to the level of his trunk
> and obliterates every trace and trait of the individual. I was all
> wrong. As I write, the cities of Italy are deluged with droves of
> these creatures.

Lever's word *droves* suggests sheep or cattle and reminds us how traditional in anti-tourist fulminations animal images are. (I have used
herded, above.) "Of all noxious animals," says Francis Kilvert in the
1870's, "the most noxious is the tourist." And if not animals, insects.
The Americans descending on Amalfi in the 1920's, according to
Osbert Sitwell, resemble "a swarm of very noisy transatlantic locusts,"
and the tourists at Levanto in the 1930's, according to his sister Edith,

are "the most awful people with legs like flies who come in to lunch in bathing costume—flies, centipedes."

I am assuming that travel is now impossible and that tourism is all we have left. Travel implies variety of means and independence of arrangements. The disappearance not just of the transatlantic lovelies but of virtually all passenger ships except cruise vessels (tourism with a vengeance) and the increasing difficulty of booking hotel space if one is not on a tour measure the plight of those who aspire still to travel in the old sense. Recently I planned a trip to the Orient and the South Pacific, hoping that in places so remote and, I dreamed, back-ward, something like travel might still just be possible. I saw myself lolling at the rail unshaven in a dirty white linen suit as the crummy little ship approached Bora Bora or Fiji in a damp heat which made one wonder whether death by yaws or dengue fever might be an attractive alternative. Too late for such daydreams. I found that just as I was inquiring, passenger ship travel in the Pacific disappeared, in April, 1978, to be precise. That month the ships of both the Matson and the Pacific Far East Lines were laid up for good, done in by the extortions of the oil-producing nations. In the same month even a small Chinese-owned "steam navigation company" running a regular service between Hong Kong and Singapore put away its toys. Formerly it had been possible to call at the remote island of Betio and Tarawa Atoll to pay respects to the ghosts of the United States and Japanese Marines, and an enterprising couple had built a small inn there. Now access to Betio and Tarawa is by air only and the plane flies on alter-nate Thursdays, which means you have to stay there two weeks if you go at all. No one will go there now. I did not go there but to the big places with big hotels and big airports served by big planes. I came to know what Frederic Harrison meant when he said, "We go abroad but we travel no longer." Only he wrote that in 1887. I suppose it's all a matter of degree. Perhaps the closest one could approach an experi-ence of travel in the old sense today would be to drive in an aged automobile with doubtful tires through Roumania or Afghanistan without hotel reservations and to get by on terrible French.

One who has hotel reservations and speaks no French is a tourist. Anthropologists are fond of defining him, although in their earnestness they tend to miss his essence. Thus Valene L. Smith in *Hosts and Guests: The Anthropology of Tourism*: "A tourist is a temporarily leisured person who voluntarily visits a place away from home for the purpose of experiencing a change." But that pretty well defines a traveler too. What distinguishes the tourist is the motives, few of which are ever openly revealed: to raise social status at home and to allay social anxiety; to realize fantasies of erotic freedom; and most important, to derive secret pleasure from posing momentarily as a member of a social class superior to one's own, to play the role of a "shopper" and spender whose life becomes significant and exciting only when one is exercising power by choosing what to buy. Cant as the tourist may of the Taj Mahal and Mt. Etna at sunset, his real target today is the immense Ocean Terminal at Hong Kong, with its miles of identical horrible camera and tape-recorder shops. The fact that the tourist is best defined as a fantasist equipped temporarily with unaccustomed power is better known to the tourist industry than to anthropology. The resemblance between the tourist and the client of a massage parlor is closer than it would be polite to emphasize.

For tourist fantasies to bloom satisfactorily, certain conditions must be established. First, the tourist's mind must be entirely emptied so that a sort of hypnotism can occur. Unremitting Musak is a help here, and it is carefully provided in hotels, restaurants, elevators, tour buses, cable-cars, planes, and excursion boats. The tourist is assumed to know nothing, a tradition upheld by the American magazine *Travel* (note the bogus title), which is careful to specify that London is in England and Venice in Italy. If the tourist is granted a little aware-ness, it is always of the most retrograde kind, like the 30's belief, which he is assumed to hold, that "transportation," its varieties and promise, is itself an appropriate subject of high regard. (Think of the 1939 New York World's Fair, with its assumption that variety, celer-ity, and novelty in means of transport are inherently interesting: "Getting There Is Half the Fun.") A current day-tour out of Tokyo honors this convention. The ostensible object is to convey a group of tourists to a spot where they can wonder at the grandeurs of natural scenery. In pursuit of this end, they are first placed in a "streamlined" train whose speed of 130 miles per hour is frequently called to their attention. They are then transferred to an air-conditioned "coach" which whisks them to a boat, whence, after a ten-minute ride, they are ushered into a funicular to ascend a spooky gorge, after which, back to the bus, etc. The whole day's exercise is presented as a marvel of contrivance in which the sheer variety of the conveyances supplies a large part of the attraction. Hydrofoils are popular for similar reasons, certainly not for their efficiency. Of the four I've been on in the past few years, two have broken down spectacularly, one in Manila Bay almost sinking after encountering a submerged log at sophomoric high speed.

Tourist fantasies fructify best when tourists are set down not in places but in pseudo-places, passing through subordinate pseudo-places, like airports, on the way. Places are odd and call for interpretation. They are the venue of the traveler. Pseudo-places entice by their familiarity and call for instant recognition: "We have arrived." Kermanshah, in Iran, is a place; the Costa del Sol is a pseudo-place, or Tourist Bubble, as anthropologists call it. The Algarve, in southern Portugal, is a prime pseudo-place, created largely by Temple Fielding, the American author of *Fielding's Travel Guide to Europe.* That book, first published in 1948, was to tourism what Baedeker was to travel. It did not, says John McPhee, "tell people what to see. It told them . . . what to spend, and where." Bougainville is a place; the Polynesian Cultural Center, on Oahu, is a pseudo-place. Touristically considered, Switzerland has always been a pseudo-place, but now Zermatt has been promoted to the status of its pre-eminent pseudo-place. Because it's a city that has been constructed for the purpose of being recognized as a familiar image, Washington is a classic pseudo-place, resembling Disneyland in that as in other respects. One striking post-Second War phenomenon has been the transformation of numerous former small countries into pseudo-places or tourist commonwealths, whose function is simply to entice tourists and sell them things. This has happened remarkably fast. As recently as 1930 Alec Waugh could report that Martinique had no tourists because there was no accommodation for them. Now, Martinique would seem to be about nothing but tourists, like Haiti, the Dominican Republic, Barbados, Bermuda, Hong Kong, Fiji, and the Greek Islands.

Today the tourist is readied for his ultimate encounter with placelessness by passing first through the uniform airport. Only forty years ago the world's airports exhibited distinctive characteristics betokening differences in national character and style. Being in one was not precisely like being in another. In Graham Greene's novel of 1935, *England Made Me,* the character Fred Hall, we are told, "knew the airports of Europe as well as he had once known the stations on the Brighton line—shabby Le Bourget; the great scarlet rectangle of the Tempelhof as one came in from London in the dark . . . ; the white sand blowing up round the shed at Tallinn; Riga, where the Berlin to Leningrad plane came down and bright pink mineral waters were sold in a tin-roofed shed." That sort of variety would be unthinkable now, when, as Bernard Bergonzi says, airport design has become a "ubiquitous international idiom."

Moving through the airport—or increasingly, being moved, on a literal endless belt—the tourist arrives at his next non-place, the airplane interior. The vapid non-allusive cheerfulness of its décor betrays its design and manufacture as Southern Californian. Locked in this flying cigar where distance is expressed in hours instead of miles or kilometers, the tourist is in touch only with the uniform furniture and fittings and experiences the environment through which the whole non-place is proceeding only as he is obliged to fasten or loosen his seat belt. Waugh was among the first to notice "the curious fact that airplanes have added nothing to our enjoyment of height. The human eye still receives the most intense images when the observer's feet are planted on the ground or on a building. The airplane belittles all it discloses." The calculated isolation from the actual which is tourism ("We fly you above the weather") is reflected as well in the design of the last of the serious passenger liners, the QE2. Here the designers carefully eliminated the promenade deck, formerly the place where you were vouchsafed some proximity to the ocean. Now, as John Malcolm Brinnin has said, "Travelers who love the sea, delight in studying its moods, and like to walk in the sight and smell of it, were left with almost no place to go." Except the bars and fruit-machines, doubtless the intention. As the ship has been obliged to compete in the illusion of placelessness with the airport and the jet, its interior design has given over its former ambitions of alluding to such identifiable places as country estates with fireplaces and libraries, urban tea-dance parlors, and elegant conservatories full of palms, ferns, and wicker, and instead has embraced the universal placeless style, eschewing organic materials like wood and real fabric in favor of spray-painted metal and dun plastic. I don't want to sound too gloomy, but there's a relation here with other "replacements" characterizing contemporary life: the replacement of coffee-cream by ivory-colored powder, for example, or of silk and wool by nylon; or glass by lucite, bookstores by "bookstores," eloquence by jargon, fish by fish-sticks, merit by publicity, motoring by driving, and travel by tourism. A corollary of that last replacement is that ships have been replaced by cruise ships, small moveable pseudo-places making an endless transit between larger fixed pseudo-places. But even a cruise ship is preferable to a plane. It is healthier because you can exercise on it, and it is more romantic because you can copulate on it.

Safe and efficient uniform international jet service began in earnest around 1957. That's an interesting moment in the history of human passivity. It's the approximate moment when radio narrative and drama, requiring the audience to do some of the work by supplying the missing visual dimension by its own imagination, were replaced by television, which now does it all for the "viewer"—or stationary tourist, if you will. Supplying the missing dimension is exactly what real travel used to require, and it used to assume a large body of people willing to travail to earn illumination.

But ironically, the tourist is not without his own kinds of travails which the industry never prepares him for and which make tourism always something less than the ecstasy proposed. The sense that he is being swindled and patronized, or that important intelligence is being withheld from him, must trouble even the dimmest at one time or another. In addition to the incomprehensible but clearly crucial airport loudspeaker harangues, the tourist is faced by constant rhetorical and contractual challenges. He meets one the moment he accepts the standard airline baggage check and reads, "This is not the Luggage Ticket (Baggage Check) as described in Article 4 of the Warsaw Convention or the Warsaw Convention as amended by the Hague Protocol 1955." The question arises, if this baggage check is not that one, what is it? If it is not that Luggage Ticket (Baggage Check), how do you get the real one? And what does the real one say when you finally get it? Does it say, "This *is* the Luggage Ticket (Baggage Check) as described in, etc."? "On no account accept any substitute." Or "Persons accepting substitutes for the Luggage Ticket (Baggage Check) as described in Article 4 . . . will legally and morally have no recourse when their baggage is diverted (lost), and in addition will be liable to severe penalties, including immediate involuntary repatriation at their own expense."

Another cause of tourist travail is touts. The word *tout*, designating a man hounding a tourist to patronize a certain hotel or shop, dates approximately from Cook's first organized excursion to the Paris Exposition of 1855. Some tourist brochures will gingerly hint at such hazards as sharks, fetid water, and appalling food, but I've never seen one that prepared the tourist for the far greater threat of the tout.

Tour guides are touts by nature, required to lead tourists to shops where purchases result in commissions. In Kyoto recently a scholarly guide to the religious monuments, full of dignity and years, had to undergo the humiliation of finally conducting his group of tourists to a low ceramics shop. He almost wept. Tour guides are also by nature café touts: "Let's rest here a moment. I know you're tired. You can sit down and order coffee, beer, or soft drinks." And souvenir-shop touts: "This place has the best fly-whisks (postcards, scarabs, amber, coral, camera film, turquoise, pocket calculators) in town, and because you are with me you will not be cheated." All kinds of tourists are fair game for touts, but Americans seem their favorite targets, not just because of their careless ways with money and their instinctive generosity but also their non-European innocence about the viler dimensions of human nature and their desire to be liked, their impulse to say "Good morning" back instead of "Go away." It's a rare American who, asked "Where you from, Sir?" will venture "Screw you" instead of "Boise."

Touts make contemporary tourism a hell of importunity, and many of my memories of tourist trips reduce to memories of particular touts. There was the money-changing tout at Luxor so assiduous that I dared not leave the hotel for several days, and the gang of guide-touts outside Olaffson's Hotel, Port au Prince, who could be dealt with only by hiring one to fend off the others. There was the nice, friendly waiter at the best hotel in Colombo, Sri Lanka, whose kindly inquiries about one's plans cloaked his intention to make one lease his brother's car. There was the amiable student of English in Shiraz whose touching efforts at verbal self-improvement brought him gradually to the essential matter, the solicitation of a large gift. There was the sympathetic acquaintance in Srinigar whose free boat ride ended at his canalside carpet outlet. There was the civilized Assistant Manager of the Hotel Peninsula, Hong Kong, an establishment so pretentious that it picks up its clients at the airport in Rolls-Royces, who, repulsed at the desk, finally came up to my room to tout the hotel's tours. There were the well-got-up young men of Manila who struck up conversations, innocently expressing interest in your children and place of residence, and then gradually, and in their view subtly, began to beg. Rejected there, they then touted for shops. They then turned pimps, and, that failing, whores. The Philippines is a notable tout venue, like Turkey, Iran, Mexico, Egypt, and India. All are in the grip of a developing capitalism, halfway between the primitive and the overripe. In London there are no touts: it's easier there to make a living without the constant fear of humiliating rebuff. On the other hand, there are none in Papua New Guinea either. It is not yet sufficiently "developed," which means it doesn't yet have a sense of a richer outside world which can be tapped. In the same way, your real native of a truly primitive place doesn't steal from tourists. Not out of primitive virtue but out of ignorance: unlike a resident of, say, Naples, he doesn't know what incredible riches repose in tourists' luggage and handbags.

As I have said, it is hard to be a snob and a tourist at the same time. A way to combine both roles is to become an anti-tourist. Despite the suffering he undergoes, the anti-tourist is not to be confused with the traveler: his motive is not inquiry but self-protection and vanity. Dean MacCannell, author of the anthropological study *The Tourist*, remembers a resident of an island like Nantucket who remonstrated when, arriving, MacCannell offered to start the car before the ferry docked. "Only tourists do that," he was told. Abroad, the techniques practiced by anti-tourists anxious to assert their difference from all those tourists are more shifty. All involve attempts to merge into the surroundings, like speaking the language, even badly. Some dissimulations are merely mechanical, like a man's shifting his wedding ring from the left to the right hand. A useful trick is ostentatiously not carrying a camera. If asked about this deficiency by a camera-carrying tourist, one scores points by saying, "I never carry a camera. If I photograph things I find I don't really see them." Another device is staying in the most unlikely hotels, although this is risky, like the correlative technique of eschewing taxis in favor of local public transportation (the more complicated and confusing the better), which may end with the anti-tourist stranded miles out of town, cold and alone on the last tram of the night. Another risky technique is programmatically consuming the local food, no matter how nasty, and affecting to relish sheeps' eyes, fried cicadas, and shellfish taken locally, that is, from the sewagey little lagoon. Dressing with attention to local coloration used to be harder before jeans became the international costume of the pseudo-leisured. But jeans are hard for those around sixty to get away with, and the anti-tourist must be careful to prevent betrayal by jackets, trousers, shoes, and even socks and neckties (if still worn) differing subtly from the local norms.

Sedulously avoiding the standard sights is probably the best method of disguising your touristhood. In London one avoids Westminster Abbey and heads instead for the Earl of Burlington's eighteenth-century villa at Chiswick. In Venice one must walk by circuitous smelly back passages far out of one's way to avoid being seen in the Piazza San Marco. In Athens, one disdains the Acropolis in favor of the eminence preferred by the locals, the Lycabettus. Each tourist center has its interdicted zone: in Rome you avoid the Spanish Steps and the Fontana di Trevi, in Paris the Deux Magots and the whole Boul' Mich area, in Nice the Promenade des Anglais, in Egypt Giza with its excessively popular pyramids and sphinx, in Hawaii Waikiki. Avoiding Waikiki brings up the whole question of why one's gone to Hawaii at all, but that's exactly the problem.

Driving on the Continent, it's essential to avoid outright giveaways like the French TT license plate. Better to drive a car registered in the country you're touring (the more suave rental agencies know this) if you can't find one from some unlikely place like Bulgaria or Syria. Plates entirely in Arabic are currently much favored by anti-tourists, and they have the additional advantage of frustrating policemen writing tickets for illegal parking.

Perhaps the most popular way for the anti-tourist to demarcate himself from the tourists, because he can have a drink while doing it, is for him to lounge—cameraless—at a café table and with palpable contempt scrutinize the passing sheep through half-closed lids, making all movements very slowly. Here the costume providing the least danger of exposure is jeans, a thick dark-colored turtleneck, and longish hair. Any conversational gambits favored by lonely tourists, like "Where are you from?" can be deflected by vagueness. Instead of answering Des Moines or Queens, you say, "I spend a lot of time abroad" or "That's really hard to say." If hard-pressed, you simply mutter "Je ne parle pas Anglais," look at your watch, and leave.

The anti-tourist's persuasion that he is really a traveler instead of a tourist is both a symptom and a cause of what the British journalist Alan Brien has designated *tourist angst*, defined as "a gnawing suspicion that after all . . . you are still a tourist like every other tourist." As a uniquely modern form of self-contempt, *tourist angst* often issues in bizarre emotional behavior, and it is surprising that it has not yet become a classic for psychiatric study. "A student of mine in Paris," writes MacCannell, "a young man from Iran dedicated to the [student] revolution, half stammering, half shouting, said to me, 'Let's face it, we are all tourists!' Then, rising to his feet, his face contorted with . . . self-hatred, he concluded dramatically in a hiss: 'Even *I* am a tourist.' "

Tourist angst like this is distinctly a class signal. Only the upper elements of the middle classes suffer from it, and in summer especially it is endemic in places like Florence and Mikonos and Crete. It is rare in pseudo-places like Disneyland, where people have come just because other people have come. This is to say that the working class finds nothing shameful about tourism. It is the middle class that has read and heard just enough to sense that being a tourist is somehow offensive and scorned by an imagined upper class which it hopes to emulate and, if possible, be mistaken for. The irony is that extremes meet: the upper class, unruffled by contempt from any source, happily enrolls in Lindblad Tours or makes its way up the Nile in tight groups being lectured at by a tour guide artfully disguised as an Oxbridge archeologist. Sometimes the anti-tourist's rage to escape the appearance of tourism propels him around a mock-full-circle, back to a simulacrum of exploration. Hence the popularity of African safaris among the upper-middle class. One tourist agency now offers package exploristic expeditions to Everest and the Sahara, and to Sinai by camel caravan, "real expeditions for the serious traveler looking for more than an adventurous vacation." Something of the acute discomfort of exploration and the uncertainty of real travel can be recovered by accepting an invitation to "Traverse Spain's Sierra Nevada on horseback ($528.00)."

But the anti-tourist deludes only himself. We are all tourists now, and there is no escape. Every year there are over two hundred million of us, and when we are jetted in all directions and lodged in our pseudo-places, we constitute four times the population of France. The decisions we imagine ourselves making are shaped by the Professor of

Tourism at Michigan State University and by the "Travel Administrators" now being trained at the New School in New York and by the International Union of Official Travel Organizations, whose publications indicate what it has in mind for us: *Factors Determining Selection of Sites for Tourism Development*, for example, or *Potential International Supply of Tourism Resources*. Our freedom and mobility diminish at the same time their expansion is loudly proclaimed; while more choices appear to solicit us, fewer actually do. The ships will not come back to the Hudson, and some place in Guyana will doubtless be selected as a site for tourism development. The tourist is locked in, and as MacCannell has pointed out, as a type the tourist is "one of the best models of modern man-in-general."

THE TRAVEL ATMOSPHERE

A part of the "cultural archeology" of the twentieth century: that's what John Pearson has called the Eiffel Tower Restaurant in London, once a haunt of the Sitwells and their retinue. Pieces of the same cultural archeology are the ships and trains of the 20's and 30's, together with their accessories and associations. What school child of the period can forget the hours wasted with colored paper and paste and poster paint on projects like "Transportation" or "Travel"? The ostentatiously "modern" mural devised in 1928 for the Bullock's Wilshire department store, in Los Angeles, conveys excitement in the form of an art-deco liner and train, and the artist has made the wave undulations resemble the smoke billows from the locomotive stack as if to suggest that the two means of "transportation" are romantic and wonderful in the same way. Two years later the decorators of the Chrysler Building in New York followed suit, making "travel" the theme of the painted ceiling in the lobby. Heady stuff. To travelers of the 20's like H. M. Tomlinson, the idea of travel is practically equivalent to the idea of ships, and the familiar spectacle of ships nearby—now, as we have seen, all but vanished—induced curious, subtle psychological ripples incident only to that time and place. "In New York, in the twenties and thirties," Alec Waugh remembers, "you were always conscious of the liners that you saw from your office and apartment windows. There was a feeling, in consequence, that you had very little time, that you had to make the most of every contact quickly."

Images of *sailing* and *sailing away* will assume a weight more than cliché-metaphoric when projected and received in a context in which real passenger vessels, "sailing days," "sailing parties," and even "sailing baskets" are a part. Once we look at the intercourse between literature and actuality this way, we sense that Hart Crane's "Voyages" (1926) is as rigorously of the period as things like Sutton Vane's popular play of 1923, *Outward Bound*, with its shipboard setting, or Osbert and Sacheverell Sitwell's play of the same year, *All at Sea: A Social Tragedy in Three Acts for First Class Passengers Only*. An American publishing enterprise of the 20's was called The Four Seas. Its now being defunct seems suggestive. Conrad Aiken published his novel *Blue Voyage* in 1927, the same year Yeats chose to title his poem not "Going" or "Proceeding to Byzantium" (one could get there overland, even in the early Middle Ages) but "Sailing to Byzantium." Noël Coward, not to mention Cole Porter, would have been virtually silent without ships, P & O as well as transatlantic, as devices and props and sets and occasions. Someday, and perhaps rather soon, Auden's lines

> You were a great Cunarder, I
> Was only a fishing smack,

are going to need annotation.

If a port like Dover was a magnet for homosexuals, ports attracted others as well. Harold Acton notices that in the 20's "the life of seaports held a fresh fascination for artists, poets and composers," composers like Erik Satie, a native of Honfleur, or Jacques Ibert, whose composition *Escales* (1924) is described by Nicolas Slonimsky in visual, indeed travel-book terms as "a triptych of geographic impressions." As Acton recalls, "Half the canvases at exhibitions were ar-

rangements of ships and sailors. Poetry and fiction were pervaded by a
tang of tar. Not the sea itself . . . , it was the port of call that excited
creative artists—the bar half open on the jetty, the sailors and their
molls." Acton's observation may do more than myth criticism can to
suggest why those sailors and fishermen and even fish-vendors are in
The Waste Land, why we hear there

> Beside a public bar in Lower Thames Street,
> The pleasant whining of a mandoline
> And a clatter and a chatter from within
> Where fishmen lounge at noon. . . .

Indeed, to read such modern masterpieces as *The Waste Land,*
Ulysses, and *A Draft of XVI Cantos,* all from the early or mid-20's,
with a renewed awareness of their "period" travel dimension is perhaps
to re-attach some meaning to them which has been largely adrift since
their time. I am thinking not only of things so obvious as the presence
of the *Odyssey* in both *Ulysses* and the *Cantos,* and the guide-book
obsession in *Ulysses.* I am thinking also of what a geographical work
The Waste Land is, and how concerned with topography it is, how it
is the work of an imagination stimulated by great presiding motifs of
movements between Germany, Russia, Greece, India, Switzerland,
Smyrna, Carthage, Phoenicia, Jerusalem, Egypt, and Austria, as well as
by shifts of perceived landscape and setting—sand, rock, water, mountains, plains, snow, sea, city, river, ship, even hotels. Eliot weaves into
his poem 31 different place-names or precise geographical locations.
The poem, like the works of Spengler and Frobenius, both registers
and stimulates the "travel" imagination. It is wonderful that a poem
so central to the age should be so geographical. And we can observe a
similar sensitivity to the topographical in another monument of the
20's, E. M. Forster's *Aspects of the Novel,* which originated as the
Clark Lectures at Cambridge in 1927. In his first lecture, Forster pays
homage to William George Clark, the Victorian Shakespearean
scholar, and observes that he also wrote two travel books, one on
Spain, one on Greece. And a couple of hundred words later we find
Forster imagining the novel in terms of *mountains, rills, swamps,* and
tumps of grass, the whole *spongy tract* "bounded by two chains of
mountains neither of which rises very abruptly—the opposing ranges
of Poetry and of History— and bounded on the third side by a sea—a

sea that we shall encounter when we come to *Moby Dick.*" Novelists
as well as novels can be conceived topographically, as Lawrence does
with himself when he tells a correspondent, "I am very conceited, but
not lofty. . . . I am like a bit of hummocky ground, with many little
amusing eminences—but Alpine—Oh dear No!"

To canvass merely the titles of works between the wars is to sense
their permeation by the "travel" spirit, from Conrad's *The Rover* of
1923 to Isherwood's *Goodbye to Berlin* and Anthony Powell's *What's
Become of Waring* of 1939. (Powell is alluding to Browning's poem of
1842, which begins,

> What's become of Waring
> Since he gave us all the slip,
> Chose land-travel or seafaring,
> Boots and chest or staff and scrip,
> Rather than pace up and down
> Any longer London-town?

Like Arnold "explaining" Clough's departure from England, Browning, here, at least, conceives that voluntary flight from London requires
some justification.) In 1919 there is Maugham's *The Moon and Sixpence,* in 1920, Pound's "Mauberley," in 1922 Lawrence's *Aaron's Rod*
and in 1923, *Kangaroo.* The year 1924 brings forth such "spatial" works
as Sacheverell Sitwell's *Southern Baroque Art,* Hemingway's *In Our
Time,* and Forster's *Passage to India.* In 1926 Lawrence is in Mexico
with *The Plumed Serpent* and Hemingway has gone to Paris and
Pamplona in *The Sun Also Rises.* In 1927 C. E. Montague's novel
takes the reader *Right Off the Map,* Eliot invites him to join the
"Journey of the Magi," and Elizabeth Bowen allows him to live in
The Hotel. (Hotel-consciousness is a largely unexamined feature of
the imaginative life of the period. Between 1927 and 1932 the Dor-
chester, Park Lane, Mayfair, Grosvenor House, and Strand Palace were
all built in London, and everyone seems to have been remarkably
hotel-minded. When young Anthony Carson arrived at his private
school in America, the first thing it reminded him of was a hotel: it
had "lifts, a ballroom, cinema and tiled swimming pool where you
could buy sundaes and sodas." A very popular easy read in the early
30's was Vicki Baum's *Grand Hotel,* which, if written today, would
have to be re-conceived as *Grand Motel.* The equivalent popular novel

of the 70's is, typically, *Airport*.) In 1928 Siegfried Sassoon gives the reader glimpses of *The Heart's Journey* and William Carlos Williams takes him along on *A Voyage to Pagany* (that is, Europe). R. C. Sherriff's play about trench warfare, produced in 1929, is called *Journey's End*, a title so familiar now that it's hard to get the original context back. To 1929 also belongs Sinclair Lewis's *Dodsworth*, which resembles not merely a travel book but, when it's treating Venice, a guide book. Aldous Huxley's well-known essay "Wordsworth in the Tropics" (1929) could hardly have been written without the travel atmosphere of its moment. For Huxley, Wordsworth is defective because "he never traveled beyond the boundaries of Europe," never "spent a few weeks in Malaya or Borneo," never took "a voyage." The result is an ultimate inhibition of imagination. The year 1929 is notable too for a very different sort of performance. One of the sensations that year was a book by one Joan Lowell, *The Cradle of the Deep*, widely bought and enthusiastically received: the first printing was 75,000 copies. It purported to record, with coy lubriciousness, the author's adventures on sailing ships in the South Seas. It was full of implausible situations and unbelievable gooey dialogue. In fact, it was a fraud, as Lawrence perceived—"The girl at sea is a feeble fake," he wrote a friend—but it indicates the avid market for anything approximating a narrative of travel or adventure personally attested. In 1930 Sassoon is *In Sicily* while John Dos Passos is surveying *The 42nd Parallel*. More hotel comedy surfaces in Rose Macaulay's best-seller of 1931, *Going Abroad*, while the same year Pearl Buck is getting off hundreds of thousands of copies of her "China" novel, *The Good Earth*. Hemingway is doing guide-book Spain again in 1932 with *Death in the Afternoon*, J. R. Ackerley is wondering at the attractively anomalous Indian scene in *Hindoo Holiday*, and Graham Greene is exploiting the Orient-Express railway fad in *Stamboul Train*. (J. B. Priestley angrily saw himself satirized in the character of Greene's complacent plebeian novelist Quin Savory, traveling to the Orient in search of material not for a travel book but for a novel, to be titled *Going Abroad*, "An Adventure of the Cockney Spirit.") The year 1933 brings Powell's comic novel *Venusberg*, which opens with Lushington being told by his editor, "Seeing the world broadens the outlook. You can learn a lot abroad"; the same year gives us Orwell's *Down and Out in Paris and London*, Michael Roberts's anthology of largely left-wing poetry titled *New Country,* and a stern warning by the now-reactionary Sassoon, *The Road to Ruin.* In 1934 Orwell publishes *Burmese Days,* Waugh *A Handful of Dust* (where we say farewell to Tony Last trapped in a quasi-Brazilian jungle), and H. V. Morton *In the Steps of the Master.* This last is forgotten today—just as well: it is gravely naïve—but in its day it was an important bourgeois devotional classic and sold 210,000 copies the first two years. The book assumes the precise historicity of Jesus and locates topographically all the events depicted in the Gospels. "I have attempted," says Morton, "to put down in this book the thoughts that come to a man as he travels through Palestine with the New Testament in his hands." The book is interesting here because it suggests the readiness of the 30's audience to receive essayistic views and improving exposition so long as they were attended by the décor of travel—the palm trees of the Holy Land can't have hurt—or seemed to issue harmlessly as an adjunct to geography. (In 1936 Morton repeated the performance, traveling to Greece and Turkey and delivering his homilies under the title *In the Steps of St. Paul.*) A very different kind of book, but still an "abroad" book, belongs to 1935, Connolly's *The Rock Pool.* The same year Hemingway published his *Green Hills of Africa* and Isherwood *Mr. Norris Changes Trains.* The later 30's will attach the conventional British sense of abroad to the war in Spain: 1937 is the year of Arthur Koestler's *Spanish Testament* and Elliot Paul's *The Life and Death of a Spanish Town,* 1938 of Orwell's *Homage to Catalonia* and MacNeice's *I Crossed the Minch.* At the same time it was being generally agreed that sympathizers with the U.S.S.R.'s external political policies in Spain and elsewhere should be named not *friends* or *approvers* or *supporters* but *fellow-travelers.* And then in 1939 the atmosphere begins to dissipate: Henry Green's *Party Going* enacts the abortion of travel just as Isherwood's *Goodbye to Berlin* notates the end of "residing abroad." Auden and Isherwood's *Journey to a War* (the Sino-Japanese one) plays out the sad if necessary action by which the travel book finally mutates into the book of war reporting.

Steinbeck's *The Grapes of Wrath,* of 1939, seems identifiably a work conceived within the travel atmosphere, with its "documentary" registration of what things are like in unfamiliar places. I find suggestive of the prevailing atmosphere even Eliot's titling the *Four Quartets* after places, as well as declaring, in "Burnt Norton," that

"The detail of the pattern is movement" and resuming that theme in "The Dry Salvages" while transforming the sense data of "travel" into metaphysics:

> When the train starts, and the passengers are settled
> To fruit, periodicals and business letters
> (And those who saw them off have left the platform)
> Their faces relax from grief into relief,
> To the sleepy rhythm of a hundred hours.
> Fare forward, travelers! not escaping from the past
> Into different lives, or into any future;
> You are not the same people who left that station
> Or who will arrive at any terminus,
> While the narrowing rails slide together behind you;
> And on the deck of the drumming liner
> Watching the furrow that widens behind you,
> You shall not think "the past is finished"
> Or "the future is before us."
> At nightfall, in the rigging and the aerial,
> Is a voice descanting (though not to the ear,
> The murmuring shell of time, and not in any language)
> "Fare forward, you who think that you are voyaging;
> You are not those who saw the harbor
> Receding, or those who will disembark. . . ."

And these paradoxes of travel as metaphysical perception of eternity return at the end of "Little Gidding":

> We shall not cease from exploration
> And the end of all our exploring
> Will be to arrive where we started
> And know the place for the first time.

But one can infer more about the spirit of the age from a pack-rat like Archibald MacLeish than from a master like Eliot. "Nimble at other men's arts how I picked up the trick of it," Edmund Wilson has him say, designating a talent that makes him both "A clean and clever lad / who is doing / his best / to get on" and a performer indispensable to the subsequent student of period themes. MacLeish's poems of the 20's and 30's encapsulate the public interests of the moment, and in nothing so much as their devotion to the travel—or perhaps even tourist—motif. Hear some lines from "Cinema of a Man" (1930):

> *He sits in the rue St. Jacques at the iron table*
>
> . . .
>
> *Now he sits on the porch of the Villa Serbelloni*
>
> . . .
>
> *Above Bordeaux by the canal*
> *His shadow passes on the evening wall*
>
> . . .
>
> *He wakes in the Grand Hotel Vierjahrzeiten*
>
> . . .
>
> *Now he is by the sea at St.-Tropez,*

et cetera. (Impossible to keep from thinking of the late-6o's film satirizing catch-all tourism, *If It's Tuesday, This Must Be Belgium.*) Even MacLeish's well-known poem "You, Andrew Marvell," which seems to be about Marvell's ability to imagine the whole planet at once, proves to be as well an exhibition of its author's familiarity with place-names and topographical features. And perhaps no poem of MacLeish's is more representative of its age than "Tourist Death," dedicated, if not addressed, to Sylvia Beach, where life itself is equated with travel-and-tourist actions until finally the addressee is presented with the question: "Do you ask to travel forever?" (It was a favorite conceit of the period: witness not merely Eliot's performance but Sassoon's "The Traveler to His Soul," a poem assuming that "traveler" will be understood specifically as "living person, moving from birth to death.") Regardless of his poetic merits, MacLeish superbly represents that between-the-wars generation which shared, as Robert Wohl has observed, "a mentality, a collective state of mind, that left its imprint on the language and literature of the 1920s." Sacred to this generation is the image not just of the traveler but of the wanderer, the vagabond, or even Chaplin's cinema tramp, all skilled in the techniques of shrewd evasion and makeshift appropriate to the age's open road.

The figure of the open road had of course been a staple of romanticism at least since Whitman, but between the wars it takes on renewed vigor. The American Schuyler Jackson, intimate of Robert Graves and Laura Riding, conceived the idea of a publishing enterprise called the Open Road Press devoted largely to issuing I Hate It

Here materials. J. B. Priestley's cheerful novel *The Good Companions* (1929) appropriates the open road theme for purposes of optimistic propaganda, while, as Charles Loch Mowat points out, "A. P. Herbert's *Water Gypsies* (1930) sent everyone vagabonding in imagination of the canals." Walter Starkie's *Raggle-Taggle: Adventures with a Fiddle in Hungary and Roumania* (1933) had much the same effect, although here the images were of roughing it around campfires. The image of the neo-medieval wandering minstrel or clerk, as in Villon, enticed more young people than Ezra Pound to Provence and environs. Looking back from 1977, Patrick Leigh Fermor locates the literary influences that impelled him to walk over Europe in the 1930's: "Set on the way by my Villon craze, I had discovered and devoured Helen Waddell's . . . *The Wandering Scholars* [1927] . . . and I wasn't slow . . . to identify myself with one of those itinerant medieval clerks." We should notice the way the titles even of scholarly works like Waddell's seize on the prevailing imagery. Thus, if we have Richard Halliburton's *The Royal Road to Romance* and Huxley's *Along the Road* in 1925, and Orwell's *The Road to Wigan Pier* and Robert Byron's *The Road to Oxiana* in 1937, between them we find John Livingston Lowes's source-study of the pre-eminently geographical "Kubla Khan," *The Road to Xanadu* (1927). In 1928 Van Wyck Brooks seems to recognize the travel atmosphere by choosing the title *The Pilgrimage of Henry James*, just as A. J. Symons does in 1934 with *The Quest for Corvo*. It seems appropriate that looking back from the 50's on his experiences in the 20's with Lawrence at Taos, Witter Bynner should title his malicious memoirs *Journey with Genius* (1951), just as it seems fitting for Jeffrey Amherst to title his memoirs of the 20's and 30's *Wandering Abroad* (1976). Indeed, there seems no literary place too high or too low for the travel obsession to show itself. Thus Emily Post's *Etiquette* (1922). The book illustrates its principles with playlets involving characters (usually depicted at table) like the Worldlys, Lucy Gilding (*née* Wellborn), Mr. and Mrs. Kindheart, and the distinguished Mrs. Oldname: she is a model of the "tactful hostess who never forgets to say to a lady guest, 'Mr. Traveler, who is sitting next to you . . . , has just come back from two years alone with the cannibals.'"

Perhaps the most pleasant relics of this lost age of travel to hold and handle are the little volumes of the Travelers' Library, which seem quite ordinary artifacts until we realize how unlikely it would be that any other age would produce them. Jonathan Cape began publishing the series in 1926, and by 1932 it included 180 titles with over a million copies in print. The volumes, smaller than 5 x 7 inches, bound in a fine light-blue, gold-stamped cloth and selling for 3/6 each (about a dollar), were "designed for the pocket"—of travelers, that is—and, the ad continues, "A semi-flexible form of binding has been adopted, as a safeguard against the damage inevitably associated with hasty packing." (*Hasty packing:* what excitement that phrase can still engender, even if those who hastily pack now are corporate persons sent to hurriedly called sales meetings or correspondents sent abroad in a crisis not to travel but to remit official copy.) By 1929 the Travelers' Library list included so many travel books that we must suppose that reading about someone else's travel while traveling oneself was an action widely practiced. It was assumed, indeed, to constitute a large part of what traveling was, which is to say that traveling was considered to be, *ipso facto*, literary traveling. Abroad, one traveled literally, but by reading, figuratively as well, making an exciting metaphoric relation between one's current travel and someone else's travel in the past. Stuck at home, one "traveled" too by reading about it; there, the act of reading easily became a substitute if not a trope for the act of traveling. Even for stay-at-homes a pinch of exoticism could be had for 3/6 to convey some romance, freedom, desire, and warmth into the chill Midlands evening well before the invention of television. Both travelers and non-travelers could regale themselves with such Travelers' Library titles as Henry Festing Jones's *Diversions in Sicily,* Constant Sitwell's *Flowers and Elephants* (travels in India; introduction by E. M. Forster), Edith Wharton's *Italian Backgrounds* and *In Morocco,* Marmaduke Pickthall's *Oriental Encounters,* D. H. Lawrence's *Twilight in Italy,* John Dos Passos's *Orient Express,* Max Murray's *The World's Back Doors* (a journey around the world), *The Travels of Marco Polo,* Maugham's *On a Chinese Screen,* Henry James Forman's *Grecian Italy,* Percy Lubbock's *Roman Pictures,* and even something nice to read specifically in a deckchair, Eugene O'Neill's *The Moon of the Caribees, and Other Plays of the Sea.* Of course W. H. Davies' *Autobiography of a Super-Tramp* is on the list: although published in 1908, it remained popular and influential throughout the 20's and 30's. We can be fairly sure that the author of *Down and Out in Paris and*

London and *The Road to Wigan Pier* knew it well. As Michael S. Howard has indicated in his account of Jonathan Cape as a publisher, that house was acute in sensing the postwar demand for travel books of all kinds—Lady Warren's *Through Algeria and Tunisia on a Motor Cycle* was on the 1922 list—and signing up some of the brightest stars, like Robert Byron, Peter Fleming, and Beverley Nichols.

If as a reading non-traveler of the 30's you wanted a more direct experience of literary traveling, there was the "Things Seen" series of pocket-sized guides, "so well written," says the *Bristol Times*, "that one may follow the writer in his lively description without the fatigue of the actual journey." The list of titles (*Things Seen In . . .*) suggests the places the between-the-wars British traveler took as his province: *Kashmir, Japan, China, Egypt, Northern India, Palestine, Constantinople, Bay of Naples, Sicily, Ceylon*. A pleasant feature, on the back end-paper, is a "Calendar for Readers Who Intend To Go Abroad," which suggests the best months for traveling in different places.

Close readers of Davies's *Autobiography of a Super-Tramp* couldn't help noticing that much of the book seems of doubtful authenticity, resembling a collection of short stories as much as anything else, or a series of extravagant episodes like those in Kafka's *Amerika*. The suspicion must occasionally have troubled readers that a thing proclaiming itself a travel book was sometimes not registering actual experience but was produced by an author like Powell's Waring, who has not bothered to undergo "the fatigue of the actual journey," preferring to work up his account in a library. Anxiety about the authenticity of travel experience seems to have troubled both the editors and readers of the *Wide World Magazine* ("The Magazine for Everybody"), a prominent popular manifestation of the travel vogue of the 20's. An editorial note invites submissions from "travelers, explorers, tourists, missionaries, and others" but insists that narratives must be attested to be "strictly true in every detail." When the magazine began in 1917 it contained half war anecdotes ("Across Germany to Freedom," "With the British Armored Cars in Russia") and half travel or adventure pieces ("Across Unknown Arabia in Disguise," "On Foot through South America"). Indeed, the cover of the number for December, 1917, announces the general contents with a significant parallelism: "Stirring War Stories, Adventures, Travel Articles, etc."

We can infer the psychic needs of the audience from the advertisements: "Be an Artist"; "What's Wrong with You? Pep! Nerve! Vigor! Gone?"; "Grow Tall"; "You Have a Beautiful Face: But your *Nose?*" From such ads we can also infer the distance of the *Wide World* from such genteel siblings as the American *National Geographic Magazine* and the British *Geographical Magazine*. The *Wide World* insisted that travel overlap adventure, and that it be honestly reported at the same time. Its travel-hungry audience demanded that narrative ("A Battle with Bears") be both credible and exciting, a stimulus to its own fantasies of adequacy and freedom. Reading the magazine while actually traveling could be especially gratifying. An elderly clergyman on the Orient Express in Greene's *Stamboul Train* tells all and sundry: "I always read a *Wide World* when I travel."

The traveler had frequent occasion to look with gratitude toward Leipzig, for that city was the origin of both the Baedeker guides and the Tauchnitz series of pocket-sized paperbacks in English available at most Continental railway-station bookstalls. The series was begun as early as 1837 by Bernhard Tauchnitz as a way for British and American authors to realize Continental royalties in the days before international copyright. Tauchnitz purchased authors' Continental rights and distributed their works only there, printing on the cover of each volume "Not to be introduced into the British Empire or the U.S.A." He was finally distributing the works of over 600 Anglo-American authors, and there's hardly a travel account between the wars that neglects to mention the convenience of these little books. Green paper bindings indicated works of travel, and Tauchnitz was conscious that his editions were aimed specifically at the British traveler. In 1883 John Addington Symonds was asked by Tauchnitz to prepare a one-volume selection of essays from his *Sketches in Italy and Greece* and *Sketches and Studies in Italy*. He prepared an abridged edition of 312 pocket-sized pages titled *Sketches in Italy* and indicated in a Prefatory Note that in his selection he has been aware that his reader will be a traveler. "I have been careful," he writes, "to include the more picturesque pieces . . . , in order that the present volume might assume the character of an Italian sketch book, and adapt itself to the use of travelers rather than of students." When brought home and bound in cloth or leather, the Tauchnitz volumes were thoroughly presentable. (My copy of Symonds's Tauchnitz *Sketches in Italy*, bound in half-leather, actually was presented—to the American painter Stuart Davis by Bernard Berenson—with the inscription: "To recall his first days in Italy—with the hope of many more to be spent there together.")

The very word *Baedeker*, now replaced by such words as Murray, Fodor, and Fielding, is alone almost sufficient to connote the special travel atmosphere between the wars. The Baedeker enterprise, which started with Karl Baedeker's first guidebook, to Coblenz, in 1829, was brought to a rude halt in 1944 when the Baedeker printing works in Leipzig were destroyed by bombers of the R.A.F. What seems to make the Baedeker guides so clear an expression of the period is their emphasis on seeing and learning, rather than, as in such successors as Fodor and Fielding, on consuming. Their very tone—secure, precise— suggests the poise, knowledge, and "inner-directedness" of the true traveler, who knows what he wants and what he's doing. "Hotels," says Baedeker, "which cannot be accurately characterized without exposing the editor to the risk of legal proceedings are left unmentioned." That witty, critical tone has all but disappeared from the guidebooks of the age of tourism, although there are occasional outcrops, made all the more attractive by their rarity, like this performance by Bob Green in *Fodor's South-East Asia*, 1978:

> *Cruise ships* [calling at Hong Kong] dock at the Ocean Terminal, one of the world's best facilities for cruise passengers. This modern, 30-acre, air-conditioned shopping center is the biggest in Hong Kong and perhaps in the entire region. . . . there are facilities for cabling or making overseas telephone calls, exchanging currency, mailing parcels or forwarding baggage, and hiring a car or launch.

And then:

> The traveler arriving by ship can also usually count on being welcomed to Hong Kong by a cluster of pimps and touts.

Green's delightful *count on*, *welcomed*, and *cluster* may suggest that we need a critical theory of guidebooks, whose literary character is easily overlooked in the contemporary decadent romantic atmosphere where, because they presumably offer pure fictions, the sorriest novelist is held to resemble an "artist" and the clumsiest small poet is readily canonized, even though neither is capable of producing a sentence as artistically satisfying as Green's. In the same way Baedeker is a better writer than the bulk of Victorian novelists.

"A Baedeker to a continent": that's the period metaphor Pound invokes to describe his survey essay on Henry James, written in 1918. And in the early 30's, Spender, writing the poem "Beethoven's Death Mask," requires a simile indicating the way Beethoven "moves" across his "vision." He does so, Spender decides, "like a ship." When Harold Acton surveys the panorama of Paris in a snow-storm from a high apartment window, he gazes "as from an ocean liner," and asks, "Why travel, with such a view as this at one's command?" In *Kangaroo*, Lawrence titles one chapter "Harriet and Lovat at Sea in Marriage," and like Pound telling a *"Femme"* that "Your mind and you are our Sargasso Sea," dilates on the ironies of marriage by means of the imagery of ocean voyages and ocean geography—Atlantic and Pacific, the Straits of Magellan, currents, narrows, hurricanes, and typhoons. His "travel" imagination works by means of railway figures as well. In *Lady Chatterley's Lover* he deploys an image of travelers' trunks with their self-satisfied labels denoting ownership when he makes Tommy Dukes guy Arnold Hammond about the smug little success-lust of married people:

> "That's what sex is to you . . . a vital little dynamo between you and Julia to bring success. . . . Married people like you and Julia have labels on you, like travelers' trunks. Julia is labelled Mrs. Arnold B. Hammond . . . just like a trunk on the railways that belongs to somebody. And you are labelled Arnold B. Hammond, c/o Mrs. Arnold B. Hammond."

As long as history can remember, life has been figured as a journey, and there's nothing unique in the traditional recourse to this cliché during the 20's and 30's. But it would be hard to designate another time when it was so conventional to conceive of life specifically as a journey by *rail*. No surprise, when we consider the railway consciousness of the age, the popularity of the *Railway Magazine* in the 20's, the tendency to admit that for all his faults Mussolini at least "made the trains run on time," the plethora of romantic railway films in the 30's: *Rome Express, Shanghai Express, The Phantom Ex-*

press, Orient Express, Streamline Express, Exile Express, and Hitch-cock's *The Lady Vanishes.* One of Ivor Novello's first film successes was his role in *The Sleeping Car,* and in the 20's a West End play by Arnold Ridley called *The Ghost Train* ran 655 performances, just as Maurice Dekobra's *La Madone des Sleepings* sold over a million copies in numerous translations. A quintessentially "modern" event was Lenin's arrival by train at Petrograd's Finland Station. Ever since Whitman's "To a Locomotive in Winter," trains had been possible themes for art, but it's only in the 20's and 30's, with things like Spender's "The Express" and Arthur Honneger's musical composition *Pacific 231,* that the train theme became a fad. Graham Greene is said to have written *Stamboul Train* while listening to *Pacific 231* on the gramophone. How dated Norman Douglas's joke about the Carrs sounds today. They were a couple he knew in Smyrna. The man, ex-cessively fond of eating, was called Dining Car; the wife, Sleeping Car. No wonder train journeys offered themselves as a ready trope for "life." Alma M. Karlin in *The Odyssey of a Lonely Woman* (1933) pleads for a relaxed, "Oriental" approach to life, which after all, she says, is "a journey, and is none the pleasanter for being passed in an express. The man who travels on a stopping train sees and enjoys more of all that lies along the railway line." But some people can't help being carried along fast. In *Mr. Norris Changes Trains,* Bradshaw and Arthur Norris celebrate the arrival of the New Year, 1931, at a night-club together with the sinister Baron von Pregnitz. At midnight, "a tremendous crash exploded from the band. Like a car which has slowly, laboriously reached the summit of the mountain railway, we plunged headlong downwards into the New Year." And having ar-rived at that new place and lived there long enough for it to grow familiar, Bradshaw finds that "like a long train which stops at every dingy little station, the winter dragged slowly past." Peter Quennell exploits the same imagery during his unhappy stay in Japan, where he has undertaken a teaching stint accompanied by his wife. They meet the Japanese professor in charge of them: "We shook hands; a deep silence immediately fell and, during the two days which we spent under his guardianship, long pauses and sudden fits of random small-talk alternated like bursts of gloom and sunshine on a journey through a succession of railway tunnels, the tunnels being longer than the lucid interspaces."

GRAHAM GREENE'S PARALLEL JOURNEY

ANYONE, thus, was likely to invoke easily this "travel" figuration, equating something in real life—reading, marriage, conversation—with ship or train travel and illustrating with the appropriate imagery. But not everyone was moved to reverse the process, to find in actual travel a palpable trope for something else and then to prosecute that resemblance for over 300 pages. This is what Graham Greene does in his *Journey Without Maps* (1936), his account of a rugged 200-mile trip on foot through a portion of West Africa. He made the trip in 1934, accompanied by his 23-year-old cousin Barbara. Beginning at Freetown, Sierra Leone, he journeyed with three native bearers inland to French Guinea and then back to the coast through Liberia. There were no places to stay but huts in villages of varying degrees of squalor, or, to use the term which Greene has made his trademark, seediness. And sometimes things were worse than seedy. They were downright nasty. Greene's supplies fell victim to great red ants and roaches, his person to chiggers and the worst kind of malarial mosquitoes. After he had acquired malaria, his whisky ran out. But there were a few moments of comedy: one "native" proved to be named Wordsworth, testifying to an earlier visit by a reading literary traveler; another was named Samuel Johnson.

Greene was fascinated by two West African fixtures: one was the cult of the Bush Devil, the local emblem of power in every village; the other was the Lightning Society, a country-wide sodality of gifted necromancers who create lightning on call, whenever it is needed for entertainment or décor at local functions. As Greene's title indicates, he had to travel (*explore* would be a better word) with virtually no

Graham Greene. (Keystone)

maps: the map of Liberia issued by the British General Staff featured "a large white space covering the greater part of the Republic," while the one published by the U.S. War Department leaned in the other direction, becoming quite "Elizabethan in its imagination" by fancifully noting "Dense Forest" and "Cannibals," and specifying "rivers which don't exist." The absence of trustworthy maps meant that at each village Greene had to negotiate directions for getting to the next. The journey was more than strenuous: it was dangerous. The Official Government Blue Book on Liberia warned: "As far as is known, the principal diseases of the interior include elephantiasis, leprosy, yaws, malaria, hookworm, schistosomiasis, dysentery, small pox and nutritional conditions. . . . In Monrovia itself malaria is practically universal." At the end, Greene was grateful to board the ship at Monrovia that conveyed him back to Dover: "Of course I was happy, I told myself, opening the bathroom door, examining again a real water-closet, studying the menu at lunch, while out of the porthole . . . Liberia slid away." But as his tone indicates, his reaction to the whole experience has been all but indefinably complex.

It was boredom, he says, that impelled him to make "this absurd and reckless trek," that same boredom that in his youth seduced him to neurotic games of Russian roulette. In West Africa he was searching for fear: not terror, which is sudden, but fear, which augments slowly and inexorably until it reaches a climax. "From terror one escapes screaming," he writes, "but fear has an odd seduction. Fear and the sense of sex are linked in secret conspiracy, but terror is a sickness like hate." He did experience "the agreeable ingredient of fear" (as he had when a child playing hide-and-seek in the dark), but what he found even more of was—boredom again, "a deeper boredom on the long forest trek than I had ever experienced before."

How was he to make anything but a boring book from a boring experience? "I was haunted by the awful tedium of A to Z." He had to write the book: he'd already spent on the trip his publisher's advance, and he could earn nothing more until he produced the book. The problem was that

> this book could not be written in the manner of a European tour; there was no architecture to describe, no famous statuary; nor was it a political work in the sense that Gide's Voyage au Congo was political, nor a book of adventure like those of Mr. Peter Fleming—if this was an adventure it was only a subjective adventure, three months of virtual silence, or "being out of touch."

The way out was to conceive the journey as a metaphor for something else. "The account of a journey," he perceived, "—a slow foot-sore journey into an interior virtually unknown—was only of interest if it paralleled another journey. It would lose the triviality of a personal travel diary only if it became more completely personal." Thus, he says, "I rashly proposed to make memory the very subject of this book," specifically, memory of the complicated delights of fear in infancy.

Literally, Greene's journey is a tour inland from the coast which returns, finally, to the coast again. Somewhat like Conrad's *Heart of Darkness*, it uses the action of the jungle trip as an immense metaphor of a return through adulthood back to adolescence and finally to the inland of early childhood. The corrupt settlements of "the Coast" are analogous to post-adolescent consciousness: they betoken self-

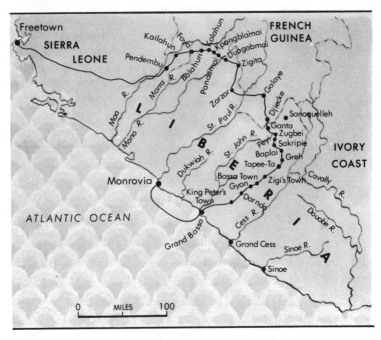

GREENE'S WEST AFRICAN JOURNEY

conscious primping sexuality, rapacity, aggression, bad faith. Along the noisome coast the favorite tipple is cane juice, a violent distilled spirit devised by pseudo-civilization as a rapid mechanical anodyne. By contrast, inland the tipple is a mild palm wine, productive of "a happy sleepy mellow state" approximating an adult memory of the condition of infancy. Inland, "one had the sensation of having come home, for here one was finding associations with a personal and racial childhood. . . ." Inland, the Bush Devils and the Lightning Society are agents less of terror than of power, and they carry Greene back to a childhood whose *frissons*, because uninterpretable, assumed a force more magical than terrifying. Inland, he says, "I had taken up the thread of life from very far back, from so far back as innocence." Even the boredom of life inland, he finds, is like the boredom not of adulthood but of childhood: a cosy, benign, happy boredom.

Thus Greene metamorphoses space into time, transforming his

journey into a virtual autobiography in little. The book is not distinguished for coherence, but what is impressive is the way Greene avoids a simplistic or conventional or automatically "romantic" conception of childhood "innocence." He recognizes that childhood is one's age of fear, but also that the fear, like the benign boredom, is attended by a vivacity and brilliance that fade with adolescence. The final paragraph of *Journey Without Maps* unites the two terms of the metaphor, fusing literal details with figurative import:

> After the blinding sunlight on the sand beyond the bar, after the long push of the Atlantic sea, the lights of Dover burning at four in the morning, a cold April mist coming out from shore with the tender. A child was crying in a tenement . . . , the wail of a child too young to speak, too young to have learnt what the dark may conceal in the way of lust and murder, crying for no intelligible reason but because it still possessed the ancestral fear, the devil was dancing in its sleep

—like the inland Bush Devils.

What inland Africa is made to mean is "The Lost Childhood" Greene laments in his essay of that title. There we find him projecting the figure of travel to assert that at his adolescence "life took a new slant in its journey towards death." One precious thing left behind as Greene's journey began accelerating was his childhood excitement over the witch Gagool, in Rider Haggard's *King Solomon's Mines* (1886), his favorite book as a child ("and without a knowledge of Rider Haggard would I have been drawn later to Liberia . . . ?"). Gagool connotes the excitement of perceiving that one is "alive," the thrill when one recognizes, half-fearfully, that one's life is "before one." Greene recovers the infant emotion appropriate to Gagool one night when his bearers "sat in their shuttered hut with their hands over their eyes and someone beat a drum and a whole town stayed behind closed doors while the big bush devil—whom it would mean blindness to see—moved between the huts." (The Bush Devil is "actually" the local blacksmith dressed up.)

Childhood is a non-cerebral, thus mapless, little journey. "One had lived for 14 years in a wild jungle country without a map, but now [in adolescence] the paths had been traced and naturally one had to follow them." Adolescence presents maps showing all too plainly the numerous routes to the coast, where there is abundance of cane juice and much else. Returning to the coast finally, Greene comes upon something he's not seen for months, sexual self-consciousness: "A young girl hung around all day posturing with her thighs and hips as suggestively as any 'tart.' Naked to the waist, she was conscious of her nakedness; she knew that breasts had a significance to the white man they didn't have to the native."

Speaking of such literary travelers as Fleming, Waugh, and himself, Greene says, "We were a generation brought up on adventure stories who had missed the enormous disillusionment of the First War; so we went looking for adventure. . . ." Restless, often neurotic, these travelers enacted a merely more vigorous version of the unceasing kinesis John Carswell finds typical of sub-Bloomsburians like J. Middleton Murry, Katherine Mansfield, Holbrook Jackson, A. R. Orage, Edwin Muir, and Lawrence. "Recruits from far afield, geographically and socially," once they have met in London they "explode again over the surface of the earth. They are in constant movement from cottage to cottage, from country to country, from one side of the Channel to the other, in search of new places to sense their emancipation. . . . Most of them pioneered a new form of travel—the unladen, intellectual kind." This new form was to last only a brief time, for very soon the travel sense of place was going to yield to the touristic phenomenon of placelessness. "No longer do we move through space as we once did," says Daniel J. Boorstin. "Moving only through time, measuring our distances in homogenous ticks of the clock, we are at a loss to explain to ourselves . . . where, or even whither, we are going." Greene had the advantage that the metaphor of real travel still carried sufficient weight to support, as it would for Eliot, something like a metaphysics of perception.

ONE OF THE CHEAPEST
WAYS OF LIVING

ALREADY I can hear the complaint, "What snobbery. These experiences are all right for the rich and leisured, but how about all the others?" But we may forget the way things have changed since the 20's and 30's. In our day the industrialization of travel, its transformation into tourism, has employed not only the jet pilot and the baggage handler and the tout and the builder of box hotels at the seashore and the purveyor of uniform "international" food, but the copywriter. Especially the one adept at suggesting a pleasing alliance between travel and wealth. To turn to tourist ads (I am looking at a recent Sunday's *New York Times*) is to be regaled with substantives like *millionaire, paradise, champagne, leisure,* and *luxury,* attended by such magical modifiers as *gourmet, ritz, elegant, spacious, lush,* and *pampered.* In the face of such contemporary fantasizing it may be a surprise to discover how little encounters with abroad used to cost. One could be conveyed "luxuriously," to be sure, but one could also travel very cheaply. It could cost less to be a traveler then than to be a tourist now. Clever young people could travel for years simply by writing about it. Like Alec Waugh, who says of his first round-the-world trip in 1926, "When people used to ask me how I could afford to do so much traveling, I replied that I spent far less abroad than in a London flat. Travel, by ocean liner, was indeed in those days one of the cheapest ways of living, certainly for a freelance writer who carried his office with him and could work in his cabin or in a saloon."

It is true that subsequent inflation makes prices between the wars seem ludicrously low by today's standards—you could rent a London flat for a hundred pounds (about five hundred dollars) a year. But it is also true that because labor was then not so well treated and fuel was cheap, things in which labor and fuel were important were not just relatively but actually much cheaper than today. V. S. Pritchett's lunches in Fitzrovia could cost as little as 11 pence, you could get a decent six-course meal in Soho for 2/6 (about 75 cents), a ready-made suit for 35/ (10 dollars), and an Atlantic round-trip, all included, for 20 pounds (110 dollars). (After every war ship travel is notably cheap for the victors. There is an excess of leftover troopships to be transformed into passenger carriers, and ships captured or seized as reparations are plentiful—passengers of the 20's went to and fro on the *Majestic*, formerly the German liner *Bismarck*, just as passengers of the 50's took the *Liberté*, formerly the German *Europa*. In the early 20's half the ships in the world were British.) In the States $260.00 bought you a Ford. One of the Greek monks Robert Byron met on Mt. Athos proposed to resign and flee to Canada. For his transatlantic passage, starting from Piraeus, he needed to save 7,000 drachmas— about 18 pounds, or 90 dollars.

If travel within the pound and dollar world was cheaper than today, travel on the Continent was melodramatically cheaper, especially in the early 20's, when the pound and the dollar were stronger than Continental currencies. Thus, as Malcolm Cowley has perceived, the seduction of so many young American writers by Europe. They were attracted, to be sure, by the absence there of Prohibition and Puritanism, women's clubs and Kiwanis, but they were attracted even more by the rate of exchange, which, Hemingway recalls, was so enticing that in the 20's "two people could live comfortably and well in Europe on five dollars a day and could travel." Visiting the German town of Kehl in 1922, he and his wife consumed a five-course meal at the best hotel for 120 marks, or 15 cents. And as the German inflation worsened, such scenes grew even more dramatic. In 1924 Hugh Walpole attended the Beyreuth Festival for ten days at a total cost of three shillings. Prices in France were almost as pleasant, especially in 1926, when the franc was at its lowest: bed and breakfast in Paris came to 2/6, and a meal with wine was ninepence, or 19 cents.

Things went on in this happy way until September, 1931, when Britain went off the gold standard. The trap dropped for the English on the Continent. Suddenly, they were impoverished. For the moment it became unpatriotic to travel and waste pounds abroad. But if you got far enough from the Continent you could still do very well. On Corfu Lawrence Durrell and his wife Nancy enjoyed a villa, with maid and sailboat, for four pounds a week, and it was in the early 30's that Waugh—and Hemingway—began to see the advantages of sating their appetites and curiosity outside of Europe: they went to Africa, while Robert Byron took off to India and Peter Fleming to Brazil and China.

These people made their money take them very far, less because they were equipped with capital than because they were equipped with intelligence, energy, and curiosity. They were secure in their values, which must make them seem anomalous to us.

===THE ENGLISHNESS OF IT ALL===

AS travelers and travel-writers the English are special. "Frenchmen travel with some definite end in view," says Peter Quennell, but "Childe Harold and Waring are peculiarly Anglo-Saxon types," exhibiting that "centrifugal tendency" notable at most times but most notable between the wars when all circumstances combined to solicit the English abroad. "The Gallic poet or novelist," Quennell observes, "once he has begun to make a name, usually abandons his native province and sets forth along the road to Paris; but no sooner has a literary Englishman read the notices of his first successful book than . . . he lays his plans for leaving London and, perhaps having tried a house in the country, next considers leaving England and is presently heard of among the Greek islands or as the lonely inhabitant of a Mediterranean village." Abroad is a picnic, but, as Rose Macaulay perceives, it is specifically an English picnic.

The geographical and linguistic insularity of the English is one cause of their unique attraction-repulsion to abroad, but another reason they make such interesting travelers is the national snobbery engendered by two centuries of wildly successful imperialism. I know of no other European culture which has devised so telling a registration of its half-disdainful awareness of outsiders as the British, with its folk-jest that "Wogs"—sometimes "Niggers"—"begin at Calais." It is the British of the 20's and 30's who devise the term *Dagoland* to embrace everything from Genoa to the Orient; and it is Cyril Connolly, irrecoverably British for all his touching attempts to be French, who says of the Portuguese that he is fond of them "because they have carried Dagoism to its highest point." And because of their thriving class system, the British do not always have to proceed abroad to do something very like traveling. Between the wars, Frances Donaldson notes, the upper- and middle-classes regarded the working-class as quasi-foreign, and when they moved among them with a view to improving their lot, "they did so as anthropologists . . . or missionaries, visiting a tribe more primitive than themselves." Exactly, in fact, the way Orwell confesses to have done in *The Road to Wigan Pier*. An upper-class education is a help here, as Stansky and Abrahams observe of Orwell, whose literary-classical (largely Latin) experience at Eton had the effect of turning him into "a keen social observer, aware of the nuances of social distinctions and practices" and thus nicely prepared for the related careers of both novelist and travel-writer.

Another reason for British distinction in both traveling and travel-writing is suggested by Christopher Sykes, who imputes these impulses to the complicated British sense of "residing on the outskirts of the Roman Empire" and thus of being teased by a Germanic suspicion that "we are not wholly satisfactory." One result of this little unease, Sykes says, is the British desire to escape from oneself (cf. gardening, stamp-collecting, crossword-puzzle working): the "easiest relief . . . is in foreign travel." But there are complications. While the English feel a special impulse to travel, at the same time, Sykes notes, they feel that "what happens outside their native land is the work of rogues." Hence the special comedy of British travel books: travelers like Flaubert or Gide or Lévi-Strauss are unthinkable in the British tradition. Waugh and Fleming and Byron are English.

Whatever the reasons, for the British, travel is not a luxury—it is

Peter Fleming playing
Patience in China, 1935.
(Bettmann Archive)

an essential, one of "The Essentials of Life," to use the title of a series
of books by Lt.-Col. F. S. Brereton, C.B.E., published in the 30's. His
volumes treat such indispensables as Shelter, Food and Cooking,
Clothing—and Travel. A whole section in the stacks of the London
Library, an institution very largely developed between the wars, is
designated "Hints for Travelers." If any other national literature contains a work so curiously travel-obsessed as J. P. Pearson's *Railways
and Scenery* (4 vols.; 1932), I don't know of it. A London clerk,
Pearson began making rail journeys in 1888, first to Calais. Some of
them lasted four months. The shapeless, rambling book in which he
recorded these travels runs to a million and a half words, but it is
hardly a book at all: rather, it is an empirical accumulation of all the
travel data and impressions that impinged on Pearson's magpie sensibility over the years. In his resolute empiricism and singlemindedness,
if not madness, he is, as Bryan Morgan suggests, identifiably British,
"the prototype of that particular type of railway enthusiast . . . most
commonly found, perhaps, in Britain." We recall Waugh's membership during the 20's in the Railway Club at Oxford, a society enrolling
also such devotees of abroad as Connolly, Acton, Patrick Balfour,

Mark Ogilvie-Grant, and Sykes. In the standing joke about the Englishman's love of privacy, it is not an empty drawing-room that is his idea of heaven, it is an empty first-class compartment on a train.

Significantly, there is no Travelers' Club in New York. There is one in London. Its original requirement for membership was an achievement of travel a thousand miles from London—not, one might say, a very strenuous prerequisite, since trips to Lisbon or Naples or Dubrovnik or Helsinki would suffice. But it's the idea of the thing that's important, the difficulty of imagining such an institution elsewhere. There is a Travelers' Club on the Champs Elysée; but it is British, not French. In Tierra del Fuego in the 1970's Bruce Chatwin met an Englishwoman who, upon the death of her mother in the 20's, got rid of all her possessions and purchased a suitcase. She then did nothing but travel for seven years, inspecting the U.S.A. and Canada, Australia, Japan, Hong Kong, and South America, where she finally came to rest in Patagonia to be discovered by Chatwin, another English traveler. We feel this would not be so comically in character if the woman were French or Austrian. In the same way, it seems unlikely that anyone but an Englishman would, at the age of 19, set off to walk from London to Constantinople, not for "publicity," as today, but because that's what one did. Patrick Leigh Fermor did that in 1933, and he didn't return until 1937. The impulse to walk to the East similarly seized Gerald Brenan. Headed for Asia, he got as far as Yugoslavia before giving up.

Perhaps we can agree, then, with Sykes that "delight in travel has for long been an English characteristic," and we perceive with him that "among the young men of the 'twenties the cult became an obsession." Curiously, the obsession seemed to grip Oxford preeminently. Cambridge can boast a few devotees of abroad, mostly homosexuals like Forster, Ackerley, and Isherwood, but it is Oxford that produced the bulk of between-the-wars literary travelers. Balliol is responsible for Greene, Patrick Balfour, Aldous Huxley, Peter Quennell, and Connolly, all perhaps encouraged to look abroad by Balliol's famous history don, "Sligger" (F. F. Urquhart), who regularly conducted his favorite youths to his long-vacation reading parties in the French Alps. Magdalen produced Alan Pryce-Jones; Christ Church, David Talbot Rice, Sykes, Fleming, and Auden; Hertford, Evelyn Waugh; and Merton, Robert Byron. Merged into a single type, these people project an image of a character "the age demanded," with Byron representing one extreme, Fleming the other. Byron was monomaniacal and doubtless slightly mad, carrying in him, as Anthony Powell remembers, "something of the genuine 19th century Englishman—a type even in those days all but extinguished in unmitigated form—the eccentricity, curiosity, ill temper, determination to stop at absolutely nothing." Fleming was different: the best-selling character he would learn to project in his works is that of the cheerful British amateur confronting the anomalies of abroad with unfailing pluck, intelligence, good-humor, and modesty. If Byron's character has the effect of making the reader proud of British resoluteness—*stubbornness* might be a better word—Fleming's makes the reader proud of British decency, a refreshing contrast to all those nasty "artistic" young people like Brian Howard. One thing happening in these travel books is a re-definition of the character of the British "young person": projecting, implicitly, various models of the post-war young man, these books are part of the contemporary debate about the value of the "younger generation." Should it be condemned for frivolity, or admired for resourcefulness?

Conscious of the Britishness of the characters they display, both Fleming and Byron are careful in their travel books to remind the reader of their origin in a particular British intellectual and emotional tradition. Fleming's is that of Whig optimism, as his reading suggests. On the trek from China to India narrated in *News from Tartary* (1936), he describes a day of rest: "The idle day was welcome. The sun shone, [Macaulay's] *History of England* was extremely exciting, and there was nothing to do except from time to time catch the camels before they strayed too far." Byron's different tradition is established by the reading he undertakes on *The Road to Oxiana* (1937): Crawley's translation of Thucydides, Gosse's *Father and Son*, and most conspicuously, Boswell's *Life of Johnson*. Lost in the Persian desert with only a disaffected guide for company, Byron settles down for the night:

> [The guide] would not even help me unload the luggage. Finally I shook him out of his despair and he consented to hobble the horses. Then he sank onto his tuft again, refused the food I offered him, and tried to refuse the blanket till I tied it round his shoulders. It was very cold; we were again in a thick damp cloud. I spread my bedding, dined off some egg, sausage, cheese,

and whisky, read a little Boswell, and fell fast asleep among the
aromatic herbs with my money-bags between my feet and my big
hunting knife unclasped in my fist.

British phlegm and uncomplaining competence could hardly be better
dramatized, and it is in part the allusion to Boswell which establishes
in British skepticism and empiricism the tradition of this intensely
British performance.

If we focus not just on Byron but on Norman Douglas, D. H.
Lawrence, and Evelyn Waugh as well, we can't help noticing something very British the four have in common, a powerful strain of lawless eccentricity and flagrant individualism. These traits will make it
seem almost inevitable that they will become travelers and produce
highly personal travel books. The character they jointly assume, for all
their differences, is that of the British traveler as outrageous person,
conducting his libertarian gesture against the predictable uniformity,
the dull "internationalism," of post-war social and political arrangements. The reason the English write richer travel books than, say, the
French, says Norman Douglas, is not just that the sense of genre is
looser in England, enabling the writer to toss in everything—essays,
autobiography, social criticism, statistics, homilies, complaints about
D.O.R.A. It is also the British "commendable distrust of authority"
and the tradition of "extremest individualism." These things are am-
ply available for contemplation in the achievement of Robert Byron.

SANCTE ROBERTE,
ORA PRO NOBIS

IN 1965, stuck in the Rome airport for seven hours with nothing to read, recoiling from the awful paperbacks on show—"dictionaries of sexology, lives of the First Ladies"—Nancy Mitford spent her time regretting the dead. She concluded that "except relations I miss Robert the most. . . . It's the jokes." And a year later, on All Souls' Day, again she gives herself up to recalling the dead, and again associates jokes with Byron: "It's people one has jokes with whom one misses. . . . Robert is still the person I mind about the most." He had disappeared beneath the ocean twenty-five years before, in 1941, when, aged 36, he was lost together with everyone else on a torpedoed transport. He was heading for Cairo, it was said, as a war correspondent. The destruction of this admirable man before his work was half finished furnishes yet another reason to execrate the Second World War. Deeply infused with his humanistic curiosity, the travel book in his hands becomes a vehicle of scholarship, but without forfeiting outrage and humor, and without forgoing a generous comic embrace of all the anomalies and dislocations synonymous with travel. His travel book of 1937, *The Road to Oxiana,* is his masterpiece, but all nine of his books dramatize the action of the disciplined moral intelligence beleaguered by stupidity, convention, received error, greed, provincialism, nationalism, and aggression. If we still believed that the souls of the dead could assist and comfort us, he would be venerated as the saint of all whose imaginations come alight at the thought of travel in the now obsolete sense. At unceasing war with pomposity and self-satisfaction, he is a hero among travelers. When Patrick Leigh Fermor

set out from London in 1933 on his walk to Constantinople, he carried
the very rucksack which had accompanied Mark Ogilvie-Grant, David
Talbot Rice, and Byron on their trip to Mt. Athos, a trip rendered by
Byron in *The Station* (1928). This rucksack, "weathered and faded by
Macedonian suns," was clearly a valuable relic, "rife with *mana*."

The upper-class Wiltshire family into which Robert was born in
1905 was very distantly related to Lord Byron, and Robert's wanderings in Greece were often eased by the instant excitement occasioned
by his surname. His family lived in Savernake Forest, near Marlborough,
in an atmosphere of heavy Victorian eccentricity. When Waugh and
Byron were yet speaking to each other, in October, 1928, Waugh went
to dinner at the Byrons' and found the scene "curiously barbaric":
"Rutting stags in the forest outside. Inside, long, uncarpeted, unlit
passages. Furniture unrelieved 1840." Dinner with Robert's parents
and his two sisters were likely to provide bizarre scenes. Peter Quennell
reports that Robert's father, angry at one of his daughters, once
plunged a fork into her thigh at table. Robert shared this tendency to
dramatic violence, but toward his parents, especially his mother, he
exhibited a very old-fashioned filial piety. He dedicated *The Byzantine
Achievement* (1929) thus: "In celebration of the past year, twenty-
fifth since the wedding of my father and mother." And eight years
later he concludes *The Road to Oxiana* with this gesture recording his
return to "a beloved home" after eleven months in Afghan Turkestan:
"Our dogs ran up. And then my mother—to whom, now it is finished,
I deliver the whole record." And then this generous tribute: "What I
have seen she taught me to see, and will tell me if I have honored it."
Perhaps we can infer something of his relation to his mother from his
characterization of the Byzantine woman Theodota as a "type of an
eternal verity, the mother anxious for her children's worldly advance."

Robert's family, though odd, was not rich, and once launched he
sustained himself by publishers' advances on his travel books. But his
family was able to send him to Eton and to Merton, from which he
issued in 1926 with a third-class degree in History. His intensely eccentric, almost "Byronic," character seems to have become fixed in its
adult form in early boyhood. "I was never adolescent," he once told
Christopher Sykes. "I cannot remember ever being younger than I
am." Boy or man, he seems to have looked remarkably the same: wide-
open eyes, long nose, a mouth tending to fall open with wonder or

outrage, straw-colored hair resistant to the brush. Although tending to stoutness, "he became fat or thin with great rapidity," Sykes remembers. "If he got what he wanted to eat he became fat in a matter of days, if not, he lost weight immediately." In England he was fussy about cleanliness, although abroad he would put up with anything. The man did differ from the boy in his tendency to doze off at evening social functions, as well as in his fondness for plebeian Gold Flake cigarettes, one of which almost always dangled from his lips. At Eton he was known already for his capacity for indignation, impelling what Acton calls his "provocative tirades"; and already he was skillful in evading authority for the sake of idiosyncratic adventuring, often sneaking out of school disguised as an old woman to attend the cinema. He loved dressing up, and often appeared at parties as Queen Victoria, whom he was persuaded he resembled.

At Oxford he knew Acton, Waugh, and Brian Howard, and despite the customary outrageous remarks and affectations, was perhaps less homosexual than neuter, despite having once said, in answer to a stupid question about what he would like best in the world, "To be an incredibly beautiful male prostitute with a sharp sting in my bottom." He was always in strenuous opposition: at Oxford he decorated his rooms with busy Victorian bric-a-brac—especially wax and shell flowers under bell jars—as a contemptuous reaction to the "purity" of the Winckelmann classicism officially ladled out at Eton. "The very words 'intellectual' or 'good taste'," Anthony Powell recalls, "threw him into paroxysms of rage." His later frenzied passion for Byzantine art and architecture was a reaction to both classical purity and the wax flowers. As Peter Quennell says, Byron held every idea with the utmost intensity and cast every opposing idea as "the enemy." He lived by means of frantic antipathies: to the tame, the tedious, the colorless—his forays into the Middle East were largely searches for "colored architecture" as a relief from the principle of greyness obtaining in England. The postwar emotional prostration was also one of his enemies. Acton considers that Byron thought it necessary "to discard the conventions of a mentality that will never finish recovering from the war." He is interpreting Byron's invitation for Acton to move to a more gamey, quasi-"Byzantine" part of London: "Come to Paddington! Paddington is the symbol of all that Bloomsbury is not. In place of the refined peace of those mausolean streets, here are public-houses, fun-fairs, buses, tubes, and vulgar posters. Also here are small brick houses, Gothic mews, and great tapering tenements in which to live."

Byron's quarrel with Waugh dates from autumn, 1930, when Waugh chose to be received into the Roman Catholic Church, an act of hostility, as Byron conceived, to his own Byzantinism. For his part, Waugh found Byron's Byzantinism bogus, "just a fad." At Oxford "he hadn't done his work and was sent down without a degree so he turned against the classics." In Sykes's view, "like Luther, he was convinced . . . that the Papacy was identical with Antichrist." Nor did this opinion exhaust his store of half-comic eccentric positions. Sykes recalls: "Certain ordinarily accepted ideas baffled him totally. It was to him partly a mystery, partly a horrible proof of the vileness of normal taste, that the Dutch and Flemish masters are considered with universal respect. That Rembrandt was thought to be one of the great artists of the world was a fact that administered to him an unremitting sense of disgust." The same with Shakespeare, a writer Byron thought vastly and superstitiously overrated. The reputation of *King Lear* puzzled him, and he stigmatized *Hamlet* as "that emotional hoax."

Byron's mock-Blimpish adversary habit is one source of his success as a traveler. One reason he enjoyed Russia so much, he confesses, was "the pleasant feeling of pugnacity that woke in my bosom." His lavish quarrels abroad, whether with *hôteliers* or with pomposities like the German archeologist Herzfeld, who sought to prevent photography at Persepolis as if he owned it, are generally occasioned by some mean assault on human freedom and dignity. At Darjeeling, a maître d'hôtel, he recalls, "requested me to share my dinner-table with others. 'We shall soon have everyone sitting at separate tables,' he complained. Observing that the dining-room held about a quarter of its full complement, and that half the waiters were standing idle, I rounded on him with such ferocity as to shatter his belief in good-fellowship among guests for good and all." And sometimes his rich collisions with the enemy arise both from general principles and from more utilitarian motives. A brief experience of Lebanon in 1933 persuaded him and his companion Sykes that in those parts "the cost of everything from a royal suite to a bottle of soda water can be halved by the simple expedient of saying it must be halved." A hotel at Baalbek provided an opportunity for employing "our technique," and

Byron renders the conversation with mingled pride and self-satire in *The Road to Oxiana:*

> "Four hundred piastres for *that* room? *Four hundred* did you say? Good God! Away! Call the car. Three hundred and fifty? One hundred and fifty, you mean. Three hundred? Are you deaf, can't you hear? I said a hundred and fifty. We must go. There are other hotels. Come, load the luggage. I doubt if we shall stay in Baalbek at all."
>
> "But, sir, this is a first-class hotel. I give you very good dinner, five courses. This is our best room, sir, it has bath and view of ruins, very fine."
>
> "God in heaven, are the ruins yours? Must we pay for the very air? Five courses for dinner is too much, and I don't suppose the bath works. You still say three hundred? Come down. I say, come down a bit. That's better, two hundred and fifty. I said a hundred and fifty. I'll say two hundred. You'll have to pay the other fifty out of your own pocket, will you? Well *do*, please. I shall be delighted. Two hundred then? No? Very good. (*We run downstairs and out of the door.*) Goodbye. What? I didn't hear. Two hundred? I thought so."
>
> "And now a whisky and soda. What do you charge for that? Fifty piastres indeed. Who do you think we are? Anyhow you always give too much whisky. I'll pay *fifteen* piastres, not fifty. Don't laugh. Don't go away either. I want exactly this much whisky, no more, no less; that's only half a full portion. Thirty, you say? Is thirty half fifty? Can you do arithmetic? Soda water indeed. Twenty now. No *not* twenty-five. Twenty. There is all the difference, if you could only realize it. Bring the bottle at once, and for heaven's sake don't argue."

Techniques like this Byron early had opportunities to practice. His first trip abroad, in the spring of 1923 when he was 18, took him to Italy for five weeks. Thirteen years later, the memories of this first journey were still vivid. "I might have been a dentist, or a public man," he writes, "but for that first sight of a larger world." He explored Hungary in 1924, and in autumn of 1925 took an extensive motor tour with two friends through Europe to Athens, a tour, Waugh notices, that "was to set light to the great bonfire of his later enthusiasm for the Byzantine world." At the moment the yield of the motor tour was his first travel book, *Europe in the Looking-Glass*

(1926), a work whose obligatory boyishness—the car must be named "Diana"—cannot entirely conceal Byron's wit, scholarship, sensitivity, courage, and good-humor. The announced serious purpose of the trip is to measure on the spot the intensity of "European consciousness" as a needed counterweight to American influence. But Byron soon abandons this highminded intention and loses himself in amateur and pedantic critical description of architecture and in comic narrative of ironic highjinks involving Diana—her stoppages, punctures, awkward loadings onto ships, and frustration in the face of non-existent Greek roads. (The literary tradition is in large part that of the motoring romance, the sort of picaresque comic fiction about young people with cars exemplified by Sinclair Lewis's *Free Air* [1919] and "Dornford Yates's" [Cecil William Mercer's] *Jonah and Co.* [1927]. The farcical car episode with Fitzgerald in Hemingway's *A Moveable Feast* [1964], while offered as factual, owes much to this tradition.)

Already Byron is manifesting impressive powers of satiric mimicry, especially when American voices and views are audible. In Perugia, he records, "I was writing some letters one morning before breakfast, when a voice from out of an elaborately coiffured head . . . broke on my peace with the words: 'Say, young man, you look about the right age to inform me whether it was right here in Perugia that Shakespeare staged "The Taming of the Shrew." ' " In Perugia also "we were buttonholed . . . by an animated professor, who was anxious to inform us that he had been given a year's holiday, with traveling expenses paid, to go wherever he liked, and that though only four months of it were over, he wished he was nowhere so much as 'back in Chicago, setting down to a good meal of buckwheat fritters and clams.' We seconded his desire." But for all his power of contempt, Byron, like Waugh, surprises us by his fluxes of sympathy with the simple and the unlearned, evidence of the high humanity which moves him to adjust the blanket around the shoulders of the thoroughly undeserving Persian guide and later to hate Nazism almost to madness. He is such a good critic of architecture because he understands human beings. Witness his palliation of the people—mostly British—who over the years have defaced the temple at Cape Sounian with their vulgar names and initials. "One may laugh—one may deplore them," he writes. Yet, despite the appearance of mere vandalism, there's something else here: "There is often something strangely touching about the names that are to be found on ancient monuments. It is a primitive rather than a vulgar instinct that impels the cutting of them. They imply not self-advertisement but a deep-felt appreciation of the spot itself and an honest pride in having visited it." Byron, a writer, sympathizes with those who are not and thus have no means of understanding or registering their appreciation and their pride. "Untrained to such rare emotions, the mind of the Hull shipping magnate bursts to express them; spontaneously he writes: 'F. A. WILSON, HULL, '75.'" A similar sympathy attaches to Byron's rendering of an idyllic public holiday near Athens, with the whole local populace out in the country and on the beaches. Byron and his friends are out for the day too, swimming and boating nude, wine-drinking, eating, and sunning. The ecstasy that only the Mediterranean (or the Aegean) can arouse in a Briton suffuses Byron as they drive back to Athens at night, totally fulfilled: "At last we drove off back to Athens. The voices seemed to wail farewell, the sea to murmur softly, 'Come again.' Writing now, three months later, with the wind in the branches of the forest and a paraffin lamp illumining the snow-flakes as they fall outside the window pane, it murmurs still, 'Come again. Come back. Come again. Come back. Come. . . .'"

He did return to Greece, twice, once in 1926, when he first visited Mt. Athos (Yeats was writing "Sailing to Byzantium" at the same moment), and again in 1927, when, his expenses paid by the publisher Duckworth, he returned to Mt. Athos with Gerald Reitlinger and his old Eton friends Mark Ogilvie-Grant and David Talbot Rice. Byron was only 22. The object of this trip was to photograph the frescos in the churches and monasteries, and the result was Byron's book of 1930 with Talbot Rice, *The Birth of Western Painting*, one point of which is that Giotto and El Greco constitute the connection between Byzantine and Western art. But a more immediate result was Byron's travel book *The Station*, subtitled *Athos: Treasures and Men*, published in 1928. Despite some self-conscious post-adolescent over-writing, *The Station* is an agreeable book, learned and comic at once, testifying to Byron's electric delight in transforming anything he's witnessed into language. The main source of the comedy is the disparity between the monks' proclaimed spirituality and their readiness to cheat their visitors. But "Kyrie Vyron," as he is called, is essentially sympathetic with these simple, devout souls with their beards and black gowns, and the dynamics of *The Station* are established by a contrast between the aimlessness and incoherence of life in England, "a world of arid sequences," and the intensity and purity of focus (despite the terrible food and loathsome sanitation) dominating life on Mt. Athos. And a persistent theme is the superiority of Byzantine art and architecture to the "classical" models oversold to a pugnacious Byron at Eton and Oxford and still hoodwinking a credulous public: "Americans are expending £1,000,000 to convert the most picturesque quarter of old Athens into a pillared playground for cats [he's referring to the restoration of the ancient Agora], that they may unearth yet another shoal of those inert stone bodies which already bar persons of artistic sensibility from entering half the museums in Europe." There is considerable comic dialogue in the vein which Byron is beginning to make his own:

> "A few years ago a man died here [one of the monks tells Byron] who had a number of English medals" (Greeks frequently obtained them in the war).
>
> "Medals?" I replied, not wholly understanding the word.
>
> "Yes, medals," he repeated, drawing imaginary ribbons on his chest. "When you return to England, will you send me some?"
>
> "Send you medals? But how, and for what reason?"
>
> "Why not? Can't you go to the Foreign Office in London, and have them sent to me?"
>
> "But why? You have done nothing."
>
> "No, but I will. I will do great things. I love England."
>
> "You must do them first. Besides, the Foreign Office does not distribute medals."
>
> "The Foreign Office does not distribute medals? Who does?"
>
> "The King."
>
> "Have you visited the King?"
>
> "No."
>
> "I visited our Kings three times." Pause. "But when you get back, you will send me those medals?"
>
> "No."
>
> Silence. Each gazes at the sea, breathing hard.
>
> "What can I do to be famous? I do want to be famous."

Regaled with that sort of thing, Lawrence pronounced *The Station* "charming" when he reviewed it for *Vogue*. He was impressed by

Byron and his friends' determination to "*do something*," to hurl themselves into an intense purpose despite their air of levity. If Byron's
obsession exhausts Lawrence a bit ("Byzantine is to Mr. Byron what
Baroque is to the Sitwells"), and if "the unfailing humoresque of the
style becomes a little tiring," making one crave some "honest-to-God
simplicity" now and then as a relief, the book Lawrence finds infinitely
preferable to the sort about Mt. Athos that might have been written
by some earnest academic.

The trip to Mt. Athos was followed by a year of study at home.
From this emerged Byron's remarkable work of history, *The Byzantine
Achievement* (1929), published in his twenty-fourth year. At first, he
planned to write a history and analysis of the modern Greek political
situation, from 1919 to 1923, including the sack of Smyrna in 1922.
But he found that he had to supply background first, and the background gradually became the book. He never did write the book on
modern Greece, but, says Sykes, "when I last heard him speak about
it, some two years before his death, he had enlarged his original intention to writing a history of the First Great War." Considering the
author's youth, *The Byzantine Achievement* is an extraordinary book.
It is an elaborate history from antiquity through the Middle Ages and
Renaissance of Byzantium in the largest sense and an enthusiastic
celebration of Byzantine arts, dress, customs, and styles. Both narrative
and argument reveal the author to be a fully professional, if largely
self-taught, historian of art and architecture, as well as a telling polem-
icist. The enemy—Byron always had to sense one nearby—is the deni-
grating "classico-rationalist criticism" of Byzantium practiced by the
timidly educated at school and university, when the general view of
Byzantium still derived from Gibbon and such outmoded works as
Lecky's *History of European Morals* (1869). "Even those familiar
with the eternal dotage of our Universities," Byron writes, "will
scarcely believe that at Oxford, until as late as 1924, Gibbon's *Decline
and Fall* was still presented as a set book to candidates about to embark on two years' study, not of literature, but history." The "classicism" which has found Byzantium repugnant, he concludes, is stigmatized by a sentimental fondness for "vacuous perfection" in anatomy
and physiognomy, lack of curiosity, a silly naturalistic aesthetic, and
complacency.

His vigorous, contentious spirit touches everything, even his bibliography, an immensely learned compilation of works in Greek, French, and German as well as English. At the head of his bibliographical section for Chapter VIII, on the General History of the Orthodox Church, he says: "Those wishing to study this subject and its particular aspects are warned against the numerous works of English Roman and Anglo-Catholics. Under cover of spurious erudition and pretended impartiality, they exhibit a feminine spite, which makes the reader realize, after perhaps hours of attention, that he has been wasting his time." Altogether Byron mounts a fully committed, elegant argument, secure in its positions, brave in its assaults on the timid, the conventional, and the facile. And the reader is not allowed to forget the origin of the book in the travel experience, nor the way it reposes its generalizations on the hard foundations of empirical data. Thus he is careful to retain the travel atmosphere in his note on the illustration showing the mosaic of the Christ Pantocrator at Daphni, "the most absolutely spectacular example of Byzantine representational art extant." "Even today, in a ruined church," he writes, "with the motor ticking outside, it terrifies. The effect of its majesty, during an Orthodox service, upon those who lived in ultimate expectation of the actuality [i.e., the Second Coming], can scarcely be imagined." To the historian G. M. Young *The Byzantine Achievement* seemed "a brilliant and forcible statement," and Rebecca West pronounced it "a remarkable effort, . . . a wholesome corrective to the nonsense that used to be talked about the decadence of Byzantium."

The book was no sooner finished than Byron's restlessly curious intellect began to twitch again. This time the target was Tibet, but to get there, he had to get to India. He got there by writing articles about the new England-to-India airmail service for Lord Beaverbrook's *Daily Express*. He got to Tibet too, but before he could write about that he had to discharge his troubled mind of its Indian impressions. "My sojourn in India," he writes in *An Essay on India* (1931), "was a period of acute intellectual strain. The strain began as I stepped from an aeroplane at Karachi on August 4th, 1929; and it by no means ended when I boarded a P & O at Bombay on April 4th, 1930. I went to India, primarily in order to reach Tibet, secondarily because Lord Beaverbrook gave me a ticket. I had never felt, nor wished to feel, any interest in India. Now, having returned from India, I am burdened with thoughts that give me no peace and have destroyed the harmony

Christ Pantocrator, mosaic, dome of convent church, Daphni, Greece. (J. Powell)

of my former way of life." What he witnessed in India while traveling sixteen thousand miles by rail was an appalling spectacle of British snobbery, race prejudice, complacency, and imperiousness. Forster's *A Passage to India* had appeared five years before Byron set down at Karachi, and his *Essay on India* can be said to constitute a redaction, in the form of an expository polemic, of Forster's novel. Indeed, Byron writes, "I purposed, at one period of my Indian sojourn, to write a novel of the Indian scene, whose theme, like Mr. E. M. Forster's, must inevitably have been the tragi-comedy of an Englishman lacking in color prejudice and impervious . . . to the conventions of the English community in which he found himself. This theme I discussed with certain Indian friends, [but] . . . to them it seemed unreal and impracticable. . . . Nothing could convince them that such an Englishman existed." Unlike Forster's Fielding, the standard Englishman in India has not had his values humanized by experience of any other non-British place. He arrives in India young, says Byron, and "he has probably traveled little, if at all. He has never therefore learned that most difficult of all lessons for the Englishman, the tolerance and understanding of the customs and mentality of foreigners." The humanistic failure of British colonialism Byron thus virtually imputes to insufficient, or insufficiently imaginative, travel. The results

are visible all over the British establishment in India, especially, perhaps, in the British clubs, with one of which each station is equipped:
"It is reasonable that the English, if they so desire, should confine
the membership of their clubs to themselves. But to apply the color
distinction to guests, as is universally done, seems to me nothing more
than an affront to each individual member, implying that his Indian
friends, should there be any, are drawn from the gutter." But Byron
knows that he's implicated himself, for all his ability to stand off and
survey the sad situation as a critic. "Look at them," says one of his
English friends, pointing to the Indian masses. "It makes you realize
what we're up against here in India." Byron comments: "It did. It
made me realize that the thing we are up against existed in myself."

Byron was now 26. His next trip was to the U.S.S.R., or, as he
insists on calling it, Russia. He was there with Sykes for six weeks in
1931-1932, and his account of it occupies half of *First Russia, Then
Tibet* (1933), which also presents for the first time his earlier Tibetan
tour. For Anglo-Saxons the U.S.S.R. was a popular topic in 1933: that
year the U.S.A. extended diplomatic recognition, and at a London
economic conference Litvinov signed important trade agreements with
Britain. In New York E. E. Cummings published *Eimi*, while in
London Malcolm Muggeridge published *Winter in Moscow*. Russia
and Tibet have little in common, and Byron's book is really two, simply bound together. For all that, it contains his richest consideration
of the travel experience and its meaning. In a Preface, "The Traveler's
Confession," he explains that he has taken the measure of both Russia
and Tibet, the one constituting the "grim apotheosis" of the Industrial Revolution, the other as yet untouched by it, to ascertain by
contrast the vigor or weakness of pre-industrial Western humanistic
values. The question was lurking at the periphery of everyone's awareness, having been posed by Spengler's *Decline of the West*, the two
volumes of which first appeared in English translation in 1926 and
1928. (Waugh carried Spengler along on the Mediterranean cruise
that resulted in his first travel book, *Labels*.) "As member of a community and heir to a culture," Byron writes, "whose joint worth is now
in dispute, I would discover what ideas, if those of the West be inade-
quate, can with greater advantage be found to guide the world." And
now he goes on to justify travel as a form of knowledge, and to do so
by recourse to traditional British assumptions about the primacy of

sense experience. Among men of all types, "the traveling species," he says, is distinguished from others by a quest for "an organic harmony between all matter and all activity, whose discovery is the purpose of their lives." When this impulse intensifies until it resembles "a spiritual necessity,"

> then travel must rank with the more serious forms of endeavor. Admittedly there are other ways of making the world's acquaintance. But the traveler is a slave to his senses; his grasp of a fact can only be complete when reinforced by sensory evidence; he can know the world, in fact, only when he sees, hears, and smells it.

Hence the traveler's "craving for personal reconnaisance." The traveler can be defined as a hypertrophied freak of British empiricism.

The epigraph with which Byron begins the Russian half of the book implies his response to the Soviet experiment, as it was then called. It is from Chapter VIII of Norman Douglas's *South Wind*, Count Caloveglia's reprehension of the life of utilitarian materialism, and it serves as a distinctly "Mediterranean" rebuke to the U.S.S.R., whose conception of life omits everything—original thought, wit, paradox, irony, elegance, nuance—treasured by a Westerner raised on "European humanism." The Northerner, says the Count, who spends all his time feeding himself and keeping warm and materially comfortable, "has not touched the fringe of a reasonable life. He has performed certain social and political duties—he knows nothing of duties towards himself." But for all Byron's disapproval of the Soviet Union—its "banal ideology," its obsession with class ("worse than England"), its terror of disinterested thought, its hostility to lyricism, and the malice and suspicion everywhere—despite these things, he is wonderfully ready to value the anomalies of its fantastic architecture, replete with "twisting rooflets" and "immense bulbosities," its sensitive deployment of color, obvious in Leningrad but notable even in Lenin's tomb, with its red, gray, and black stone. But in the Russian portion of the book most readers will feel that the visual yields too often to the merely polemic. After a brilliant opening in Red Square, the proceedings are interrupted by a 43-page series of essays on the Soviet hostility to intellectual freedom. And later, Byron tosses in an inert 23-page "paper" on early Russian painting and its relation to

Byzantine tradition, a paper he actually delivered before a group of academics in Moscow. It is a little too much like book-making. But there are sufficient glimpses of colorful rural monasteries and kremlins and enough comic moments to keep the book from wilting, and throughout, the elegance and irony of Byron's style function as their own implicit critique of the new utilitarian paradise.

The Tibet portion of the book is more like the bright young man's comic adventure of the sort Fleming was making popular with his *Brazilian Adventure,* published the same year. Another popular book in 1933 was James Hilton's *Lost Horizon,* exploiting a "Tibetan" locale. On this trip Byron's companions were two young peers, Lords Rosse and Faringdon, one of whom finally bursts out, "Why have you brought us to this horrible place?" It is true that the Tibet journey was more like exploring than traveling: moving on foot, and on ponies, horses, and mules with bearers, the party encountered cold and wet, snow and ice, winds and avalanches. The thin air at over fourteen thousand feet gave Byron intense headaches, bringing him sometimes "to the borders of insanity." Sunburn blistered his face, the scabs of which ran with pus. Even so indefatigable a traveler as he was reduced to despondency: "Immediately I sat down the blood in my head began to pound with a violence unknown to the previous days, and I relieved the monotony by picking my face." But the experience of the flagrant anomaly of the Tibetan scene made the quest worthwhile. In none of Byron's other travel books do words like *strange, odd, uncanny, outlandish, astonishing,* and *unnatural* occur so often.

"To travel in Europe," he writes, "is to assume a foreseen inheritance; in Islam, to inspect that of a close and familiar cousin. But to travel in farther Asia is to discover a novelty previously unsuspected and unimaginable. It is not a question of probing this novelty, of analyzing its sociological, artistic, or religious origins, but of learning, simply, that it exists. Suddenly, as it were in the opening of an eye, the potential world—the field of man and his environment—is doubly extended. The stimulus is inconceivable to those who have not experienced it." Since Byron generally writes like a man dressed in a three-piece suit, not the least of the entertainments this book provides is the image of his stoutish figure encased in coat and jodhpurs "of a carpet-like material, blackish green in color," a wind-proof vest, and "water-proof gloves without fingers," the whole topped by "a Tibetan hat of black felt, heavily embroidered with gold, and possessing four fur flaps." Byron's encounter with oddities will remind us of Gulliver's: "The hats of the men-servants [at Gyantse] were . . . astonishing. There were two kinds: one a circular plate, a foot and a half across, balanced on top of a close-fitting cap, which was hidden by a thick red fringe descending from the rim of the plate; the other a butter-cup yellow hot-cross-bun, nine inches in diameter, whose connection with the head was maintained by no visible means. . . ." And sometimes not Swift but Lewis Carroll seems to be presiding. Invited to luncheon at one o'clock by a local dignitary, Byron and his friends enter ceremoniously to find their host "all in purple silk" and manifesting some distress:

> A cheap kitchen clock hung in one corner. On a chest stood another of a late Empire design, mahogany and ormulu. From his pocket the Kenchung produced a fat silver watch, to whose chain was attached a gold toothpick, later to be freely used. In addition to these, a servant came in bearing an alarm-clock still wrapped in cotton-wool and cardboard. By dint of consulting all four timepieces, our host informed us that we were late. We admitted to five minutes, but he said half an hour. We saw in this stricture no discourtesy, but rather a desire to convince us of a life regulated on business lines.

But Byron grows serious whenever he can speak of architecture, and he grows rhapsodic descanting on two un-European characteristics of Tibetan building: its unparalleled use of color, and its "universal convention of the batter, which makes every wall of every building . . . slope inwards in a straight line from the ground-level." (The same effect had charmed him about the exteriors of the monasteries on Mt. Athos.)

Colored architecture: that's what obsesses Byron as he enters his late twenties. He had occasion to explore its implications on his eleven-month tour of Persia, Afghanistan, and India in 1933-1934, with Sykes, a tour refracted in their joint comic novel of 1935, *Innocence and Design.* The vogue of "travel" and the familiar image of the brash young traveler are suggested by the title-page name Byron and Sykes devised for themselves: "Richard Waughburton." The *Richard . . . burton* points toward Richard Halliburton, the American whose boyish account of a trip round the world, *The Royal Road to Romance*, had been one of the hits of 1925. And the *Waugh* acknowledges the fame of both Alec and Evelyn as travel writers. *Innocence and Design* is a "novel" barely disguising its real identity as both a travel book—it includes maps of Persia, called "Media"—and a collection of architectural and topographical essays. The hero is Sir Constantine Bruce, an eccentric Scot, who journeys to the Middle East in search of the Moslem principles of "chromatic architecture"—he plans to re-do Riggs, his Scottish estate, in color, but with greater subtlety than we might imagine, for he hopes to "employ color only so as to accentuate the general form, instead of swamping it in theatricality." Comedy arises from the conflict between Sir Constantine's innocence, architectural, aesthetic, and political, and mid-Eastern intrigue: he constantly blunders into plots hatched by the Foreign Office and Military Intelligence, plots reflecting the struggle between British and Russian interests in Persia. Sykes and Byron drafted the book while actually there, "sitting amid saddlebags in the courtyards of caravanserais," and we can infer the division of work: Sykes contrived the horseplay narrative, while Byron contributed the inset essays—overwritten, most of them— on Persian national character, colored architecture, Islamic building, and the sad state of Persian thought and feeling under the dictatorship of Byron's bête noire, Reza Shah. The alternation of narrative and exposition here characterizes most travel books generically, and can be seen to resemble the essential mechanism of conversation seriously pursued, which, as Waugh once perceived, consists of narrative alternating with "comment."

Oxiana means the country of the Oxus, the ancient name for Amu Darya, the river in northeast Afghanistan serving as part of the border with the U.S.S.R. From the desert a thousand miles away, in adjoining Persia, rise a number of odd and beautiful medieval brick tomb-towers of startling height and purity, pre-eminently "masculine," even phallic. Byron had seen photographs of some in a book while he was in India, and Sykes remembers Byron's wondering whether they weren't somehow the source of much that was admirably un-dainty in early Islamic architecture. One of the brick towers had impressed him especially. It was the Gumbad-i-Kabus, the tower of Qabus: 167 feet high, made of hard-fired brick that looked tan, bronze, or gold in different lights. Where a classical column would have flutes, this tower had ten extruded, sharply-angled flanges rising to its conical roof. Kufic inscriptions running in two bands around the top and bottom of the tower indicate that the ruler of Gurgan, King Qabus, built it as his mausoleum in 1006 and 1007. Tradition says that his body was raised to the top of the tower and suspended from the ceiling in a glass casket. It was a photograph of the Gumbad-i-Kabus alone, Byron says, that drew him to Persia. He had to see it with his own eyes.

The Persian mosques in Isfahan and elsewhere were first opened to Western inspection only in 1931. Up to that time, says Sykes, "They had been seen by so few Europeans that no reliable record of them existed; not one single photograph had been taken of them." The opening of the mosques stimulated widespread and rather undiscriminating interest in Islamic art: an analog would be the Tutmania of the 70's. The extravagant and often sentimental praise of seventeenth- and eighteenth-century Islamic architecture provided Byron with an opportunity to do what he did best, namely, oppose a prevailing opinion. What he wanted to do was locate and define the preceding masculine, vigorous tradition later largely effaced by the pretty, dreamy, and in his view epicene and decadent art of Isfahan and Shiraz. The opposition he constructed here was another version of his favorite collision, the one between the beautiful of the Byzantine and the pretty of the Classical, only now the enemy was not the sentimental schoolmasters of Eton and Oxford: it was "the Omar Khayyám fiends," as he called them.

If one product of Byron and Sykes's Persian tour of 1933-1934 was the immature and hastily run-up *Innocence and Design*, another was Byron's thoughtfully matured *The Road to Oxiana* (1937). Its distinction tempts one to overpraise, but perhaps it may not be going too far to say that what *Ulysses* is to the novel between the wars and what *The Waste Land* is to poetry, *The Road to Oxiana* is to the travel book. It is virtually unknown in the United States, a fact I take to imply serious cultural impoverishment. (The only available edition is a paperback issued by Jonathan Cape, London.) Such is the current generic snobbery that scholars and critics ashamed to own ignorance of the jottings of Wyndham Lewis or William Burroughs are satisfied never to have heard of it, for it seems not to be a fiction.

But it is. It is an artfully constructed quest myth in the form of

an apparently spontaneous travel diary. Sykes observes: "So conscien-
tiously is it disguised as a book of hurried entries into a diary that a
reader may easily and pardonably read it too quickly, mistaking it for
an amusing record of an amusing trip, and no more." In aid of the
"diary" fiction, Byron has titled his table of contents "Entries." But
the book is fully written: after returning from Persia and Afghanistan
Byron devoted three years to the task, and labored hard, Acton reports, "to obtain an effect of spontaneity." Byron wrote some of it in
Peking in 1935, and we hear of his writing ten hours a day at Savernake, planted before his typewriter, cigarette in mouth, Beethoven
turned up loud on the gramophone. Byron's choice of the travel-diary
convention enabled him to overcome what had been his defect as an
artist, stylistic affectation and a leaning toward "fine writing" and arch
pedantry. His early quarrel with Gibbon had required him to attend
closely to Gibbon's text, and in the process soak himself in Gibbon's
Latinate sentences and humanistic metaphors (where personification
comes naturally, things constantly *betraying* or *proclaiming* something;
cf. *First Russia, Then Tibet*: "A few wisps of smoke proclaimed the
town"). For years Byron's style aspired to the Gibbonian high-horsed.
But now he shook himself free of that influence. The pretended pressure of the daily and the material and the "low," as well as the assumed ignorance of the future enjoined by the diary form, pointed
him toward both a new stylistic directness and a new structural subtlety. Before, he had been committed to the convention of the "essay";
now, he was able to invest his prose with the air of the unknowing
ad hoc. He had now mastered the secret of the travel book. He had
now learned to make essayistic points seem to emerge empirically from
material data intimately experienced.

As they do at the very beginning of *The Road to Oxiana*, where
he begins his journey into anomaly from a by-now familiar Europe:
"*Venice, August 20th, 1933.*—Here as a joy-hog. . . . We went to the
Lido this morning, and the Doge's Palace looked more beautiful from
a speed-boat than it ever did from a gondola. The bathing, on a calm
day, must be the worst in Europe: water like hot saliva, cigar-ends
floating into one's mouth. . . ." If this, and Harry's Bar, help define
contemporary Europe, inspection of works by Tiepolo and Tintoretto
and explorations of the nearby Palladian villas help recall "the triumphant affirmation of the European intellect" during the Renaissance.

Robert Byron at work
on *The Road to Oxiana* (Lucy Butler)

Both experiences, the reader will realize, are there right at the beginning of the book to serve as a backboard for what is going to come, a criterion enabling us to sense the uniqueness of Islamic artifacts, the distance from our expectation of Near-Eastern habits of mind and emotion. We are already embarked on the quest for the Tower of Qabus thousands of miles and many cultures away, but we aren't told that yet.

After five days in Venice, Byron proceeds to Cyprus for a week. Sykes joins him there, arriving on the S.S. *Martha Washington*, to begin their long passage. Byron says only, "I found Christopher on the pier, adorned with a kempt but reluctant beard five days old." Sykes's account of their meeting gives the other side:

[I] spent a day scouring the island in vain for a trace of him. I grew anxious. Twilight was falling rapidly and the boat due to sail in a few minutes, when to my relief I saw a round figure dressed in jodhpurs and a tweed jacket, and with a cigarette dangling from his lower lip, fairly charging along the jetty to a sound of clattering cameras, pencil-cases and folios which hung about him. . . . I watched from the deck. Arrived at the boat.

he showed his ticket, returned it to his pocket, and then made a sort of dive at the officials, as it were, swam through them on a breast-stroke, and mounted the gangway. "Hallo, I'm late," he said. . . .

Their initial target is Beirut, where they hope to join a group of young people in two charcoal-burning Rolls-Royces who have agreed to convey them to Persia. But having learned that this motoring party has been delayed a week by an accident in France, they decide to stop over in Jerusalem. A vignette of a moment on the ship reminds us of what Byron is escaping from, as well as establishing early in the book a gauge of his intelligence and disdain for cant:

> At dinner, finding myself next to an Englishman, I opened conversation by hoping he had had a fine passage.
> He replied: "Indeed we have. Goodness and mercy have followed us throughout."
> A tired woman struggled by, leading an unruly child. I said: "I always feel so sorry for women traveling with children."
> "I can't agree with you. To me, little children are as glints of sunshine."
> I saw this creature later, reading a Bible in a deckchair. This is what Protestants call a missionary.

Arriving at Jerusalem, Byron undergoes further unpleasantness at the hands of the British port authorities, who prove to be motivated largely by a very home-like lower-middle-class envy. One of them discovers that Byron has traveled in the Soviet Union:

> When? and why? O, for pleasure was it? Was it pleasurable? And where was I going now? To Afghanistan? Why? Pleasure again, indeed. I was on a pleasure-trip round the world, he supposed.

In the Church of the Holy Sepulchre Byron runs into an Orthodox priest whose brother he has met on Mt. Athos, and he uses him as the mouthpiece for some remarks disdainful of Roman Catholics that are said to have helped open the unhealable breach between Byron and Waugh.

After a week in Palestine, Byron and Sykes move on to Damascus and Baalbek, and then to Baghdad, where we are reminded that a searcher on a quest has numerous impediments to overcome and multifold trials to undergo. Baghdad's mud is an example. Mesopotamia, Byron writes, is a

> land of mud deprived of mud's only possible advantage, vegetable fertility. It is a mud plain. . . . From this plain rise villages of mud and cities of mud. The rivers flow with liquid mud. The air is composed of mud refined into a gas. The people are mud-colored; they wear mud-colored clothes, and their national hat is nothing more than a formalized mud-pie. Baghdad . . . lurks in a mud fog; when the temperature drops below 110, the residents complain of the chill and get out their furs. For only one thing is it now justly famous: a kind of boil which takes nine months to heal, and leaves a scar.
>
> Christopher, who dislikes the place more than I do, calls it a paradise compared with Teheran.

The charcoal-burners having failed them entirely, they get a car to continue eastward, and on September 29th cross into Persia from Iraq at the border town of Khanikin. Here Byron begins to notate his contempt for Reza Shah's absurd, tyrannical attempt to Westernize his country. One of his ukases requires citizens to wear the "Pahlevi hat," resembling a gendarme's *képi*. It makes the typical Persian look like "a decayed railway porter." Since spies are everywhere, Byron and Sykes agree that "Marjoribanks" will be their code-word for the Shah, "Mr. Smith" being already in use for Mussolini when they are in Italy and "Mr. Brown" for Stalin in Russia. By October they've arrived in Teheran, where they archeologize while maturing their plans to move east. A two-week journey toward the eastern border by car and horse is halted when Sykes's legs swell and blister with infected flea bites. Disconsolately, they return to Teheran to start all over again. It will take Sykes months to recover. Their plans, they perceive, are going to meet constant frustration: they are assumed to be spies, and they meet bureaucratic obstruction everywhere. It is clear that no one wants them to see the Tower of Qabus.

While Sykes mends, Byron grows impatient and decides to explore alone. He buys a Morris car and gets as far east as Ayn Varzan.

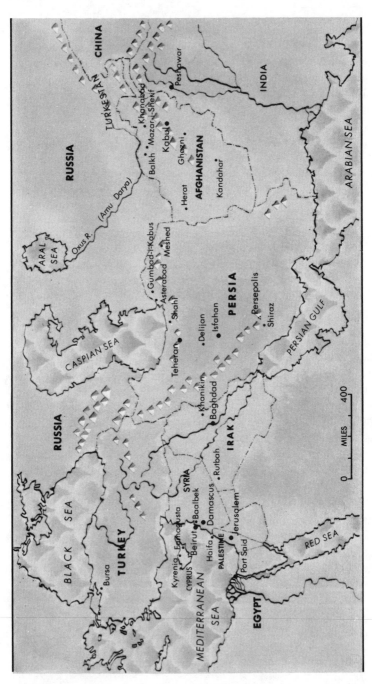

ROBERT BYRON'S NEAR EAST

There the back axle breaks. He continues obstinately by buses and trucks, and on November 21st manages to drag himself across the Afghan border to Herat. After a pause, he proceeds, but ten days of horrible food bring on diarrhoea, which finally turns to dysentery. "I must go back," he concludes, back to Meshed and ultimately to Teheran in January to wait for spring and a new chance. Even though Meshed offends him because Omar Khayyám was born there, the town poses a challenge which begins to intrigue him. It contains the sacred shrine of Imam Reza, reputed to be the finest example of the use of color in all Islamic architecture. But the shrine is rigorously closed to infidels. From distant rooftops Byron studies it with field-glasses and determines somehow to get in: "I must and will penetrate this mosque before I leave Persia." And he will do it, we know.

The atmosphere in Teheran is viler than usual. Marjoribanks fears a coup, as well he might, and all foreigners, the British especially, are suspected and ill treated. Christopher has now recovered, and there is time for some easier touring while waiting for spring. They aim for Isfahan, but twice are prevented by snow. The dysentery hits Byron again, and he spends two days back in the hospital. Finally started for Isfahan, he is detained by unprecedented flooding at Delijan, and the details of his attempt to sketch a courtyard there speak eloquently of the current state of his whole enterprise: "In the afternoon I drew the courtyard: one pollarded tree-stump, an empty pond, and a line of washing all dripping with rain, give a new idea of a Persian Garden. At the end stood a vaulted summer-house, but just as I put pencil to it, the whole thing collapsed in a heap." He arrives in Isfahan three weeks late. There, on the magnificent bridge of Ali Verdi Khan, he begins to recover from his depression. As usual his happiness begins with architecture and spreads out from there:

> The bridge encloses the road by arched walls on the outside of which runs a miniature arcade for foot passengers. This was crowded with people, and all the town was hurrying to join them; there was never such a flood in living memory. The lights came out. A little breeze stirred, and for the first time in four months I felt a wind that had no chill in it. I smelt the spring, and the rising sap. One of those rare moments of absolute peace, when the body is loose, the mind asks no questions, and the world is a triumph, was mine. So much it meant to have escaped from Teheran.

Next, south to Shiraz and Persepolis. Byron sustains his delight in Shiraz and environs: the warmth and flowers and wine remind him of the Mediterranean, and although Sykes is now "detained" on suspicion of being a spy ("Mr. Sykes talks with peasants," is the official reason), Byron persuades himself that Persia can't be all bad and determines to enjoy the south alone. Persepolis especially excites him. He wants to photograph architectural details there, but discovers that the German Professor Ernst Herzfeld, in charge of the excavations, "has turned Persepolis into his private domain" and forbids all picture-taking. It is a situation ready-made for Byron: it promises a bitter confrontation with a stubborn scientist governed by "a code of academic malice controlled from Chicago," who can be depicted in all his anti-humanistic authoritarian pomposity, and depicted in dialogue with stage directions:

> R.B.: . . . You may think you have the legal right to prevent my taking photographs at all. But you must admit it would be morally indefensible. It would be as if the Parthenon had suddenly become a private villa and the rest of the world been excluded from it.
>
> Herzfeld (bridling): Not at all. In Europe there have always been these rules. When I was a young man, making excavations, we were never allowed to photograph anything.
>
> R.B.: But that is no reason why you should follow a bad example now you are older.
>
> Herzfeld (puffing furiously at his cigarette): I think it is perfectly rrrright!

The next day Byron brought this letter to Persepolis:

> Dear Dr. Herzfeld,
>
> Since both the Governor of Fars and Dr. Mostafavi [the Persian observer at the excavations] have stated categorically that you have no right to prevent my photographing the portions of arches and columns which have always been above ground, the only means of stopping my photographing them are either
>
> (1) to show me the wording of your concession proving that you are right, or
>
> (2) force.
>
> Please choose your means.

It is one of Byron's finest moments. "While I was photographing," he continues, "a small round figure twinkled across the platform. 'I have never,' it said, 'met with a way of acting as illoyal as yours,' pirouetted, and twinkled away again. Illoyal to whom, I wondered. It was a question of principle. I got my pictures, and did a service to travelers in calling Herzfeld's bluff."

Byron's description of Persepolis prepares for his ultimate reaction to the Tower of Qabus the way his recall of cigar-butts floating into his mouth on the Lido prepares for his response to the perpetually lovely bridge at Isfahan. "The columns," he finds, "have no bearing on the general course of architecture, and hold no precepts for it." The bas-reliefs are "as slick as an aluminium saucepan." They are hard and witless and clean, and "this cleanness reacts on the carving like sunlight on a fake old master; it reveals, instead of the genius one expected, a disconcerting void." When Byron looks at one of the grand staircases, his first thoughts are, "How much did this cost? Was it made in a factory? No, it wasn't. Then how many workmen for how many years chiselled and polished these endless figures?"

In March, Byron returns north by car and truck through Isfahan, and finds the beauty of that place growing on him. As usual, he honestly registers his waverings of mind. It's the use of color in the mosques and madressahs that finally wins him over. In April he's back in Teheran again, where Christopher has been temporarily released from confinement "to collect his things"—a splendid opportunity for the two to slip off at once if they can get away without being noticed. On April 22nd they manage to escape by car, and head for Shahi and Asterabad and the Tower of Qabus. As they finally near the country where the Tower is said to be, they arrive suddenly at a steppe whose abundant vegetation contrasts dramatically with the snow-covered sand and rock they've known before: "a scent of sweet grass," "a dazzling open sea of green," "pure essence of green, indissoluble, the color of life itself"—this is the setting as they approach the object of their quest. "The sun was warm, the larks were singing up above. . . . In front, the glowing verdure stretched out to the rim of the earth." It is all soft and green, and "we shouted for joy, stopping the car lest the minutes that were robbing us of the unrepeatable first vision should go faster." In the midst of this virtual heaven, something appears in the distance: "A small cream needle stood up against the blue

The tower of Qabus. (Christopher Sykes)

of the mountains, which we knew was the Tower of Kabus." An hour later they are at its foot, where they have wanted to be, and Byron registers what he sees: a fixed, inert object rendered so kinetic by its art that it can be described only in the language of movement:

> A tapering cylinder of café-au-lait brick springs from a round plinth to a pointed grey-green roof, which swallows it up like a candle extinguisher. . . . Up the cylinder, between plinth and roof, rush ten triangular buttresses, which cut across two narrow garters of Kufic text, one at the top underneath the cornice, one at the bottom over the slender black entrance.
>
> The bricks are long and thin, and as sharp as when they left the kiln, thus dividing the shadow from the sunshine of each buttress with knife-like precision. As the buttresses recede from the direction of the sun, the shadows extend on to the curving wall of the cylinder between them, so that the stripes of light and shade, varying in width, attain an extraordinary momentum. It is the opposition of this vertical momentum to the lateral embrace of the Kufic rings that gives the building its character unlike anything else in architecture.

What a moment, and what superb prose: precise, clear, and magical the way its own devices of motion recognize the life of its subject. Thus Byron's initial reaction, from his assumed diary: he sustains the verisimilitude of that convention by adding in brackets, as if on an entirely different occasion,

> [Superlatives applied by travelers to objects which they have seen, but most people have not, are generally suspect; I know it, having been guilty of them. But re-reading this diary two years later, in as different an environment as possible (Pekin), I still hold the opinion I formed before going to Persia, and confirmed that evening on the steppe: that the Gumbad-i-Kabus ranks with the great buildings of the world.]

After this climax, where is there to go? On to Meshed to watch Byron redeem his promise to enter the forbidden shrine, a promise, we realize, he has planted earlier just to provide a continuing suspense after the Tower has been attained. May 7th is the day. The Byron who has always enjoyed dressing up has entered the precincts the night before for a reconnaissance, his pink, Anglo-Saxon face darkened with burnt cork, accompanied by a Sykes who must keep blowing his nose to cover his beard. The night visit is all right, but Byron must return in the daytime to see the colors, a much more risky operation. Islamic sensibilities were tender. Ten years before, an American Vice-Consul, Major Robert Imbrie, had been murdered by a Shi'ite mob outraged by his appearance with a camera near a Muharram procession. In the daytime Byron makes up again and costumes himself in true Westernized-Persian style, wearing "brown shoes with black trousers four inches too short; grey coat; gold stud instead of a tie; our servant's mackintosh; and a black Pahlevi hat which I aged by kicking it. . . ." He must proceed from the hotel to the shrine on foot because he dare not try to pass as a local before a cab-driver:

> The sun was at my back; I sweated under the mackintosh as I invented a quick Persian-looking trot of short high steps . . . , but no one looked at me. Everything depended on my pace. . . . If it faltered, I was exposed. So I kept to it . . . , found the dome where I turned to the left, and was greeted, on coming out into the court, by such a fanfare of color and light that I stopped a moment, half blinded. It was as if someone had switched on another sun.
> The whole quadrangle was a garden of turquoise, pink, dark red, and dark blue, with touches of purple, green, and yellow. . . .

This vision is a matter of seconds, for feeling that he is about to be discovered, he departs immediately.

On to Afghanistan, and to Herat, where six months before he was defeated by dysentery and had to turn back. Having seen the Tower of Qabus and sneaked into the shrine at Meshed, he is happier now. He and Christopher have actually reached Turkestan, which Byron has been trying to visit for years. And his excitement and pride at being there trigger an excursus on the civilized act of literary traveling, as opposed to mere physical exploring: the one is an affair of the mind, the other of the body. As for explorers,

> their physical health is cared for; they go into training; they obey rules to keep them hard, and are laden with medicines to restore them when, as a result of the hardening process, they break

down. But no one thinks of their mental health, and of its possible importance to a journey of supposed observation. Their . . . equipment contains food for a skyscraper, instruments for a battleship, and weapons for an army. But it mustn't contain a book. I wish I were rich enough to endow a prize for the sensible traveler: £10,000 for the first man to cover Marco Polo's outward route reading three fresh books a week, and another £10,000 if he drinks a bottle of wine a day as well. That man might tell one something about the journey, . . . at least he would use what eyes he had. . . .

The challenge now is to get to the Oxus River, not easy, for both Russians and Afghans fear spies in this border area, and there are frequent inchoate military incursions. Sykes's and Byron's only hope is to request permission in a letter to the Minister of the Interior for Turkestan written in a style so ornate that a friendly local Indian will have to be called in to translate, and thus may take the opportunity to recommend the petition. The texture of this letter may remind us of Boswell requesting his interview with Rousseau:

> In undertaking the journey from England to Afghan Turkestan, whose tedium and exertions have already been thrice repaid by the spectacle of Your Excellency's beneficent administration, our capital object was to behold, with our own eyes, the waters of the Amu Darya, famed in history and romance as the river Oxus, and the theme of a celebrated English poem [*Sohrab and Rustum*] from the sacred pen of Matthew Arnold. We now find ourselves, after seven months' anticipation, within forty miles of its banks.

(The adjective modifying Matthew Arnold's pen was Sykes's contribution, and even as he wrote it he feared he'd gone too far.)

> There are indeed some countries where the Light of Progress has yet to pierce the night of medieval barbarism, and where the foreign visitor must expect to be obstructed by ill-conceived suspicions. But we consoled ourselves, during our stay in Persia [during which, actually, both had been arrested], by the consideration that we should soon be in Afghanistan, and should thus escape from a parcel of vain and hysterical women to an erect and manly people, immune from ridiculous alarms, and happy to

accord that liberty to strangers which they justly demand for themselves.

Were we right? And on returning to our country, shall we say that we were right? The answer lies with Your Excellency. Certainly we shall tell of the hotel in Mazar-i-Sherif equipped with every comfort known to the great capitals of the West; of a city in course of reconstruction on lines that London itself might envy,

etc., etc. But their request is denied: permission to visit the Oxus must come from Kabul, and that would take a month. Nothing for it but to get as close as possible, to Khanabad, where finally politics and nationalism prevent their going further, although they are accompanied everywhere by two military guards to make sure they photograph nothing of consequence. "We were lucky to have got as close as we did," Byron writes, because the canard was widely believed "that we were Secret Service agents engaged in map-making." He goes on: "Next time I do this kind of journey, I shall take lessons in spying beforehand. Since one has to put up with the disadvantages of the profession anyhow, one might as well reap some of its advantages, if there are any." Back home now through the Khyber Pass to Delhi, thence to Bombay and a P & O. Throwing topees ceremoniously into the sea, they proceed to Marseilles and to Savernake, nineteen and a half days after leaving Afghanistan.

I have said that *The Road to Oxiana* is the *Ulysses* or *The Waste Land* of modern travel books. One reason this can be said is that its method is theirs: as if obsessed with frontiers and fragmentations, it juxtaposes into a sort of collage the widest variety of rhetorical materials: news clippings, public signs and notices, letters, bureaucratic documents like *fiches*, diary entries, learned dissertations in art history, essays on current politics, and, most winningly, at least 20 comic dialogues—some of them virtually playlets—of impressive finish and point, which we appreciate the more when we have digested Sykes's later observation that because Byron was not just a poor linguist but a "very poor" one, "all the non-English conversations recorded in his book are invented." That includes a masterpiece like this:

> Christopher . . . was reading in the back of the lorry, where his companions were a Teherani, an Isfahani, two muleteers, and the driver's assistant.

TEHERANI: What's this book?

CHRISTOPHER: A book of history.

TEHERANI: What history?

CHRISTOPHER: The history of Rum and the countries near it, such as Persia, Egypt, Turkey, and Frankistan.

ASSISTANT (*opening the book*): Ya Ali! What characters!

TEHERANI: Can you read it?

CHRISTOPHER: Of course. It's my language.

TEHERANI: Read it to us.

CHRISTOPHER: But you cannot understand the language.

ISFAHANI: No matter. Read a little.

MULETEERS: Go on! Go on!

CHRISTOPHER: "It may occasion some surprise that the Roman pontiff should erect, in the heart of France, the tribunal from whence he hurled his anathemas against the king; but our surprise will vanish so soon as we form a just estimate of a king of France in the eleventh century."

TEHERANI: What's that about?

CHRISTOPHER: About the Pope.

TEHERANI: The Foof? who's that?

CHRISTOPHER: The Caliph of Rum.

MULETEER: It's a history of the Caliph of Rum.

TEHERANI: Shut up! Is it a new book?

ASSISTANT: Is it full of clean thoughts?

CHRISTOPHER: It is without religion. The man who wrote it did not believe in the prophets.

TEHERANI: Did he believe in God?

CHRISTOPHER: Perhaps. But he despised the prophets. He said that Jesus was an ordinary man (*general agreement*) and that Mohammed was an ordinary man (*general depression*) and that Zoroaster was an ordinary man.

MULETEER (*who speaks Turkish and doesn't understand well*): Was he called Zoroaster?

CHRISTOPHER: No, Gibbon.

CHORUS: Ghiboon! Ghiboon!

TEHERANI: Is there any religion which says there is no god?

CHRISTOPHER: I think not. But in Africa they worship idols.

TEHERANI: Are there many idolaters in England?

Probably closer to the originals are Byron's mimicries of an affectedly Anglicized Assyrian patriarch, now a refugee on Cyprus ("They took me away by aeroplane against my will, but what will become of may poor people, raeped, shot down bay machine-guns and soe on and soe forth, Ai doen't knoew"); a school friend of Christopher's who meets him in the hotel bar in Jerusalem and urges him to remove his beard ("I mean to say, Sykes, you know, daffinitely, no I don't like to say it, well, I mean, daffinitely, . . . you see old boy it's like this, I mean daffinitely I should take off that beard of yours if I were you, because people daffinitely think you know . . . I mean people might think you were a bit of a cad you know, daffinitely"); and—his triumph—the horrible American traveler Farquharson, met in Teheran, whom, for one brief moment, Byron thinks he might travel with to Afghanistan while Sykes is laid up:

> FARQUHARSON: There are one or two points I'm vurry anxious to discuss with you. I want to make it clear that if I do go to Afghanistan I shall have to make a vurry hurried trip. Now I want to speak vurry frankly. You don't know me and I don't know you. I think we'll get on. I hope we will. But we must try and get things clear beforehand. . . . I'm prepared to pay a little more than half the car. But you realize I'm pressed for time, I have to make a vurry hurried trip, and it's pahssible I may go right through to India and take a boat from there. Now I understand you're pressed for money, from what you said. I couldn't leave a fellow-traveler stranded in India. So before we start I've gaht to know you've enough money to get back to Persia, and I've gaht to see the notes actually in your hand—
>
> R.B.: What?
>
> FARQUHARSON: I've gaht to see the notes actually in your hand—
>
> R.B.: Goodbye.
>
> FARQUHARSON: . . . before leaving, so's I can be quite sure you can shift for yourself in the event of—
>
> R.B.: GET OUT, if you're not deaf.

There is the traveling Hungarian, encountered in Herat, Afghanistan, beautifully characterized through dialogue which performs an additional function, hinting comically at one of the main themes of the book, the technique of seeing:

"I am not the type, Monsieur, who thinks himself superior to the rest of humanity. Indeed I am no better than others. Perhaps I am worse. But these people, these Afghans, they are not human. They are dogs, brutes. They are lower than the animals."

"But why do you say that?"

"You don't see why, Monsieur? Have you eyes? Look at those men over there. Are they not eating with their hands? With their *hands!* It is frightful. I tell you, Monsieur, in one village I saw a madman, and he was naked . . . naked."

He was silent for a little. Then he asked me in a solemn voice: "You know Stambul, Monsieur?"

"Yes."

"I lived in Stambul a year, and I tell you, Monsieur, it is a hell from which there is no way out."

Equally brilliant are the monologues Byron "scores" with indications of musical dynamics, like one by the Afghan Ambassador to Persia who has visited Buckingham Palace:

"(m) Prince of Wales he talk to me. (p) I tell him, 'Your Royal Highness (ff) you are fool? (*roaring*) You are FOOL!' (m) Prince of Wales he say, (p) 'Why am I fool?' (m) I tell him, 'Sir, because you steeple-jump. It is dangerous, (cr) dangerous. (p) English peoples not pleased if Your Royal Highness die.' (m) King me hear. He tell Queen, 'Mary, His Excellency call our son fool.' He very angree, (cr) very angree. (mf) Queen she ask me why her son fool. I say because he steeple-jump. Queen say to me, (*dim*) 'Your Excellency, Your Excellency, you are right, (cr) you are right.' (m) Queen thank me. King thank me."

But comedy like this Byron found increasingly irrelevant as he finished writing *The Road to Oxiana* while watching the Nazification of Europe. He had time for one more book before the new war started, a pamphlet, really, the sardonic *How We Celebrate the Coronation: A Word to London's Visitors* (1937). We celebrate the Coronation, he says, by tearing down all our most beautiful buildings. The enemy is real-estate developers and "improvers," and Byron urges foreign visitors to "deluge your contempt upon the only nation in Europe that destroys its birthright for the sake of a dividend." (Thank God both he and Waugh, alike detesters of "cad architecture," were spared the later spectacle of the Queen Anne Knightsbridge Barracks replaced by a Fascist monolith.) Byron proceeds to specify where the damage has already been done: Carlton House Terrace; Pembroke House, Whitehall; Wren's All Hallow's Church, Lombard St; Waterloo Bridge. The unique Byron touch is his listing at the end the institutions and people responsible (including the Archbishop of Canterbury and the Bishop of London), with their phone numbers.

He continued to travel, to be sure, to Russia again, and to China and the U.S.A. He worked as a press officer for the Petroleum Information Bureau and lectured for the British Council in Belgium, Holland, and Poland. Appalled by Nazism, he even went across to a Nuremberg rally to see with his own eyes. British appeasement made him purple with fury. Once he scandalized diners at a London club when a man important in the government was praising "extravagantly," Sykes recalls, the Munich settlement and its "architect."

> He paused for breath. Robert leaned across the table and asked him a question. He did not seem to hear. He felt he must have heard wrong. He continued his dissertation and paused again. Robert again leaned across the table and again asked the same question: "Are you in German pay?"
>
> This time it was said very clearly.

"I shall have warmonger put on my passport," he told Sykes. By September, 1939, his violent anti-German views, expressed usually with memorable rudeness, and his contempt for those who didn't see that no conciliation with German wickedness was possible, had given such offense in London that when the war broke out the best job he could get was as a sub-editor in the BBC Overseas News Department.

In 1941, Sykes, in Cairo, was delighted to hear that Robert was on his way "as a Special Correspondent for a group of English newspapers." Later he heard that "various departments were anxious to enlist his services. . . . I could not resist a smile. His destination, secret as such matters always were in the war, was so blatantly obvious. His name was Byron and the battle of Greece was drawing near." Fifteen years before he had heard the sea murmur, "Come again. Come back."

L'AMOUR DE VOYAGE

EVERYONE who has traveled knows what the young Australian Kenneth Minogue is getting at when he recalls the pleasure of his first trip to London: "Like everyone else, I . . . gave myself over to the traditional hobbies of the traveler: lust and sightseeing." For an Australian, "the erotic capital of the world" must be located abroad, just as for the English it may not be London: now it is Venice, now Paris, now Berlin, now the Greek Islands. Making love in novel environments, free from the censorship and inhibitions of the familiar, is one of the headiest experiences travel promises. The very means of transportation, ships and sleeper trains, seem outright provocatives to lust. Perhaps vibration is the reason: the nerves are set "tingling," and heated imagery follows. (The vibration on a train, said Osbert Sitwell, was as good as two cocktails for improving the tremor in his left arm caused by Parkinson's Disease.) Perhaps on ships it's the rich diet and all the drink and the ready availability of plenty of unguarded bedrooms. Perhaps, before the days of the steam turbine, it was the proximity of all the passengers to the piston-and-cylinder principle, which, when you get to thinking about it—. Whatever the reason, the fact is undeniable and seems universally felt. Hermann Hesse's *Wandering*, says Ralph Freedman, is at pains to delineate "the erotic upsurge that . . . shapes all wanderlust." And the English popularity of the term *wanderlust* conveys its own suggestions.

Travel has always been thought *romantic*, and that word is worth a moment's consideration. Whether it is true that in modern tourist ads *romance* is simply a genteelism for "sexual intercourse" ("Find Romance on a Caribbean Cruise"), it is true that *romance* never takes place at home. Mrs. Aldwinkle understands the principle in Huxley's

Those Barren Leaves (1925). She "went the rounds of the [Roman] sights with [the poet] Chelifer. She had hopes that the Sistine Chapel, the Appian Way at sunset, the Colosseum by moonlight, the garden of the Villa d'Este might arouse in Chelifer's mind emotions which should in their turn predispose him to feel romantically towards herself. . . . More proposals are made . . . in the face of an impressive view, within the labyrinth of a ruined palace, than in the drab parlors or the streets of West Kensington." Actually, Berlin will do as well as Rome, a man as well as a woman. In "the deliciously forbidden world of Berlin in 1928," pants the blurbist for the Avon paperback of Isherwood's *The Memorial* (1932), "a World War I flying ace finds daring romance in the muscular arms of his German lover. . . ."

Isherwood and his characters find a great deal of romance, and they always find it abroad. His novel *The World in the Evening*, although not published until 1954, is a virtual register of the erotic possibilities and complications offered by travel and residence abroad in the early 30's. Although married to the novelist and travel writer Elizabeth Rydal, Stephen Monk is susceptible to male charm, and it is abroad that the couple meets the traveling Michael Drummond and abroad, in the Canary Islands, that Stephen and Michael go too far together. The novel radiates the travel spirit of its restless moment ("What shall I do now? What shall I do?"—*The Waste Land*). Elizabeth says to Stephen, "The last few days, I've been feeling so terribly restless. Should you mind dreadfully if we went abroad somewhere, quite soon?" He replies, "Of course I shouldn't. I'd love to." And a moment later:

> STEPHEN: "Where are we going to?"
> ELIZABETH: "Let's look at the atlas, shall we? Oh, isn't this exciting?"

The deviser of dialogue like this is one of the most restive travelers of the period. His infantine instinct for abroad was stimulated by visits to his grandmother's London flat, where, he testifies, "The watercolors and etchings on her sitting-room walls—of Venice, Granada, Avignon, and the Panama Canal—quickened my earliest longings to travel and made me see London as a gateway to the world." He became extraordinarily sensitive to exotic place-names like Tierra del Fuego, the Seychelles, Tristan da Cunha, Quito, Tahiti. "As a youth," he says, speaking of his ultimate residence abroad in Southern California, "I had literally dreamed of palm trees." And later, the South Pacific attracted him because of its literary associations, Western Samoa because of Stevenson, New Zealand because of Katherine Mansfield, Australia because Lawrence wrote *Kangaroo* there. "The mere idea of travel excited [Christopher] so much," he says, "that he loved to enjoy it in the abstract, as an embarrassment of possibilities." Sometimes he imagined traveling as an avenue to total disappearance abroad, like Browning's archetypal English traveler or like Ambrose Bierce, who simply vanished into Mexico. To Isherwood, "home" represented normality and erotic inhibition; "the longing to get away from it" kept him constantly imagining "the other place." Like Norman Douglas's, Isherwood's sojourns abroad were inseparable from his erotic requirements and predicaments. Humphrey Spender observed of one of Isherwood's boyfriends, Heinz, that he is "the decisive factor in his life—the reason for all his wanderings from country to country." The German court which finally catches Heinz in 1938 and convicts him of draft-dodging and perverse sexuality recognizes the wide geographical theater of his and Isherwood's activities, specifying that Isherwood, who was not available for trial, "was accused of having committed reciprocal onanism with the prisoner in fourteen foreign countries," as well as in the German Reich.

Because of the risks of enjoying them in London, boys became for Isherwood an emblem of abroad. One such was Bubi, whom he became infatuated with during his first stay in Berlin. "By embracing Bubi," he writes, "Christopher could hold in his arms the whole mystery-magic of foreignness." Indeed, "Berlin meant boys." Later, there was "Vernon," met in New York in 1938, whom he associated with the fantasies of homoerotic traveling proposed by Whitman, as in

> We two boys together clinging,
> One the other never leaving,
> Up and down the roads going, North and South
>   excursions making.

And another Berlin lover, "Otto," Isherwood recalls by means of images of an exotic abroad not unlike those Pound invokes in "Mauberley": "His body became a tropical island on which they were snugly marooned in the midst of snowbound Berlin." (On the other side of the world Hart Crane was writing, "Permit me voyage, love, into your hands.")

In his reading, Isherwood was quick to respond to works associating love with travel, especially love on ships plying within exotic venues. Like Maugham's South Seas novel *The Narrow Corner* (1932), all about Fred Blake, the beautiful boy from Sydney, whose good looks keep getting him into (heterosexual) trouble, occasioning several suicides, a murder, and finally his own death. "Very glamorous," says Isherwood; "I adore that book." Forster's short story "The Other Boat," about a homosexual affair on shipboard, he finds "a tremendous melodrama of passion and fury," and notes that "it takes place on a liner coming back from India." Forster's writings recommended themselves to Isherwood because they are so full of journeys and because, as John Sayre Martin observes, most often in Forster "the journey . . . takes the traveler from a world of middle-class values and expectations to a new order of experience," much of it arising from involvements "in tabooed relationships." The tradition that "travel" constitutes a special incitement to useful lust is honored by Forster in his story of 1939, "The Obelisk." Here the travel undertaken by a dingy schoolmaster and his wife is not abroad but merely to a nearby seaside resort out of season, but it leads to a significant chance encounter with two sailors, the chance encounter eventuates in tabooed sex, and the sex leads to unprecedented perception, the kind that would never have occurred if the couple had not "traveled." Love with a stranger at the seacoast is something close to a convention of the period. In his autobiography, Tom Driberg tells of an impromptu encounter in a lighthouse near Rapallo with the amiable young lighthouse-keeper, while his innocent mother waits below to continue their genteel stroll.

$=$ SEE IT WITH SOMEONE $=$
YOU LIKE

HE who travels fastest travels alone, to be sure, but he who travels best travels with a companion, if not always a lover. Peter Fleming's ambition of solitariness during his journey to China was extraordinary enough to provide the catching title for his travel book *One's Company* (1934), as well as to generate his final chapter, an over-elaborate justification of traveling alone:

It is easy enough for one man to adapt himself to living under strange and constantly changing conditions. It is much harder for two. Leave A or B alone in a distant country, and each will evolve a congenial *modus vivendi*. Throw them together, and the comforts of companionship are as likely as not offset by the strain of reconciling their divergent methods. A likes to start early and halt for a siesta; B does not feel the heat and insists on sleeping late. A instinctively complies with regulations, B instinctively defies them. A finds it impossible to pass a temple, B finds it impossible to pass a bar. A is cautious, B is rash. A is indefatigable, B tires easily. A needs a lot of food, B very little. A snores, B smokes a pipe in bed. . . .

Each would get on splendidly by himself. Alone together, they build up gradually between them a kind of unacknowledged rivalry. . . . Each, while submitting readily to the exotic customs of the country, endures with a very bad grace the trifling idiosyncrasies of the other. The complex structure of their relationship . . . bulks larger and larger, obtruding itself between them and the country they are visiting, blotting it out.

"Occasionally," he admits, "you find the ideal companion." But this time he's not been able to get Roger Pettiward, who went to Brazil with him two years before, to join him in China, and instead he's made the mistake of picking up the non-stop talker Gerald Yorke to accompany him part of the way. From this experience he has learned abundantly what Hemingway learned from his French auto-trip with Fitzgerald: "Never go on trips with anyone you do not love."

Fleming did love—*like* is a better word—Roger, and in *Brazilian Adventure* thanked him for being one "who always saw the joke." In that book, Peter and Roger are a pair of comical critics set down in the midst of absurdity. They take their place as one of the most notable traveling couples of the age, those teams of "We" who multiply reactions by refracting them from one to the other or by pooling their respective talents for noticing. Travel-writers in the preceding tradition, before the war, had tended to go alone, like Stevenson in Spain, Doughty and T. E. Lawrence in Arabia, Rupert Brooke in Tahiti. And so do travel-writers in the post-modern tradition, like Paul Theroux. It is between the wars that we find these teams, either social or erotic, like Byron and Sykes, Auden and MacNeice (*Letters from Iceland*, 1937), Auden and Isherwood, Isherwood and Heinz, Osbert Sitwell and David Horner (*Winters of Content*, 1932), Graham Greene and his cousin Barbara, D. H. Lawrence and Frieda (called Q.B., for Queen Bee, in *Sea and Sardinia*, a usage adopted 14 years later by Hemingway for *Green Hills of Africa*, where Mrs. Hemingway becomes P.O.M., or Poor Old Mama). Further teams are Lawrence and Earl Brewster, Alan Pryce-Jones and Robert Pratt-Barlow (*The Spring Journey*, 1931), Peter Quennell and his first wife (*A Superficial Journey through Tokyo and Peking*, 1932), Geoffrey Gorer and Feral Benga (*Africa Dances*, 1935), Maugham and Gerald Haxton, Alec Waugh and Eldred Curwen, Evelyn Waugh and Patrick Balfour, Beverley Nichols and Cyril Butcher, Forster and Syed Ross Masood, Connolly and Logan Pearsall Smith ("he talks too much"), Connolly and Noël Blakiston.

Blakiston was a "romantic" friend of the young Connolly's in the late 20's, and on their travels he serves as a backboard or litmus paper for thrills and sensations occasioned by viaducts, peasants, whiteness against greenness, noble architecture, and amusing hotels. Seeing anything together makes it doubly exciting: "I am keeping the Sistine for us," Connolly announces. And after a springtime trip to Sicily in 1927, Connolly writes Blakiston a highly-charged thank-you note:

> Thank you for coming to Sicily and for contributing to the most sustained ecstasy of my life. . . . I shall never be able to travel with anyone else again. (Of course I shall travel with them probably but I mean that there will be a reservation in every moment and a condescension in every enthusiasm)—for I on honey dew have fed and drunk the milk of paradise. . . . O Noël!

The ecstasy of companionship implied in "O Noël!" Connolly annotates 36 years later, boyhood long past. He writes Blakiston: "The Sicilian expedition ends the age of romantic friendship because it was so perfect that it could not go forward unless we lived together . . . and we weren't homosexual." Maugham's stammer made social encounters a torment, but as he says, "I was fortunate enough to have on my journeys a companion who had an inestimable social gift. He had an amiability of disposition that enabled him in a very short time to make friends with people in ships, clubs, bar-rooms and hotels, so that through him I was able to get into easy contact with an immense number of persons whom otherwise I should have known only from a distance." Without a companion like Haxton, Maugham probably wouldn't have traveled at all.

NORMAN DOUGLAS'S
TEMPORARY ATTACHMENTS

THE titles of the two travel books Douglas published in the 20's, *Alone* (1921) and *Together* (1923), will suggest the alliance in his mind between companionship and the impulse to record perceptions of abroad. According to Acton, "He told me that each of his books had ripened under the warm rays of some temporary attachment: unless he was in love he had little or no impulse to write. Each of his books, therefore, was mingled with the happiest associations of a lifetime." Or to put it another way, each of his books becomes a way of talking about pederastic satisfactions—not all of them sexual—with boys like Eric and René in an atmosphere where such things are not discussed, or if discussed, discussed in such terms as those of George V's reputed assertion, "I won't knight buggers."

Douglas's is a pre-modern sensibility. He was born in 1868, and although he lived until 1952, nothing in his emotional outlook or literary posture prompted him to any interest in Joyce, Yeats, Eliot, or Pound. Darwin and Herbert Spencer were his thinkers, Conrad his writer. He was a Scottish late-Victorian, a sort of Field Marshal Sir Douglas Haig turned inside out. Such a formulation at least would recognize the importance of his Germano-Scottish origins while doing justice to the Puritan determination of his atheism and hedonism, the stubborn assiduity of his pederasty, and the strongmindedness of his performance as a British eccentric abroad. His Nietzschean brand of naughtiness is of the 90's: like Shaw's or Samuel Butler's, his subversiveness does not threaten the *status quo*, it teases it and requires it. His reputation for shadiness is like Frank Harris's (born 1856), as is his conviction that the Mediterranean is the natural locale for the seduction of very young persons. His Italy is the Italy of Pater, Symonds, and Baron Corvo. His improper limericks (with of course their perverse geography) suggest an Edward Lear who has cast off all restraints except verse-form, just as his pleasure in little boys resembles Dodgson's in little girls. If rough-trade homosexuality of the Genet stamp is one sign of the self-consciously modern or post-modern, pederasty— Douglas seems to have been fondest of children ten to twelve—is premodern. Maurice Richardson remembers lunching with Douglas in 1943: "By the end of the lunch Norman was enthusing about the smell of children's armpits and I got faintly embarrassed."

The pattern of his life was a series of flights abroad. So often was he obliged to decamp across frontiers, or, as he says, "put a slice of sea" between himself and outraged parents, that he became learned in the details of European extradition treaties. "Burn your boats," he advised. "This has ever been my system in times of stress." His first precipitate departure was in 1896, from St. Petersburg, where, having impregnated a lady, he abandoned his post as Third Secretary in the Embassy and took off for Naples. In those days he was fond of ladies, marrying one in 1898 and fathering two boys. But his tastes had changed probably by 1908, when he lived with a peasant boy in Italy while writing *Siren Land* (1911), and certainly by 1916, when he was arrested in the South Kensington tube station for paying a boy too much attention and fled to Italy to escape trial. In the 30's there were two more similar flights, one from Austria, one from Florence. He finally came to rest, much passion spent, in southern France, only to be forced by the Second World War to Portugal and then back to London, which he hated. (In London under the bombings of 1943, with little drink and terrible food, and in appalling cold, he and Nancy Cunard would sit on a sofa and solace themselves by pretending it was the seat of a wagon-lit speeding across Italy to France in the old days of sun and freedom.) Despite poverty and age, his halcyon period began in 1946. He was now an Honorary Citizen of Capri (the only other one was Benedetto Croce) and one of the local sights, and he lived there in a handsome villa provided by his friend Kenneth Macpherson. He was attended by the ten-year-old Neapolitan Ettore, tenderly beloved by Douglas although denominated "a little tart" by some. His happiness was only slightly tarnished by the badgerings of somewhat faded American fans of *South Wind*. Near the end he had a few regrets but no apologies: "If I had stuck in the Dipl. Service," he wrote, "I should certainly have become an Ambassador and be now living on a pension of £5,000 a year." Instead he was raggedy, although he managed to maintain, Acton recalls, "the elegance of a Scottish Jacobite in exile." His constitution was rugged—another Scotticism. After a lifetime of excesses—confronted by temptation, he always followed his own favorite suggestion, "Why not, my dear?"—he apparently couldn't die, even at the age of 84, and finally had to put himself down with an overdose of pills.

He had a remarkable mind and vast learning, the result in part, as he liked to notice, of his having escaped a university education. His school was the Karlsruhe Gymnasium, and he was there in the 80's, when a German education meant languages (Russian, French, Italian), music (piano), and science. It did not include absorption in the self. The objectivity and curiosity Douglas learned at Karlsruhe made him an ideal traveler, and he started early. At the age of 19, he wrote his grandmother before his first trip to Naples: "I have been studying my Baedeker very diligently, and already *seem* to know my way about Naples quite well." Grown up and preparing for a trip to Greece, he writes: "I read one book on Greece every day, and will soon know the country and the language so intimately that it will be sheer waste of time and money going there." He grew up a scholarly, meticulous young mineralogist, taxidermist, and scrutinizer of lizards, author of the treatise *On the Herpetology of the Grand Duchy of Baden* (1891) and later scholar of the geology, archeology, and history of Capri, the Sorrentine Peninsula, and Calabria. "Externalize yourself!" enjoins the Count in *South Wind*. Douglas's curiosity about "out there" is Aristotelian, like his empiricism about sex, drink, food, and study. He was a scientist, a dissector. "Finding everything wonderful," as Mark Holloway says, "but nothing miraculous," he was that rare creature, "a happy man, who has got his values right for himself and knows it." In this he's like the other literary travelers of this period: all superbly know what they're doing, an achievement some will find refreshing.

If Douglas resembles any other twentieth-century writer it is Nabokov. The two share a similar erudition and devotion to natural history (Nabokov's lepidoptery is Douglas's herpetology), a similar secure individuality and contempt for the modern world, a similar commitment to the value of the aristocratic intellect, and a similar playfulness and waggery. Douglas's sense of security when he commends something resembles Robert Byron's, but he is a little like Lawrence too in his instinct to make literature out of his sense of being embattled and his tendency to visit verbal violence upon the English. As in this Lawrentian moment from *How About Europe?* (1939):

> Ribald persons used to say: Wake up, Britain! Easier said then done. The Anglo-Saxon is hard to wake up, being phlegmatic and self-righteous to such a degree that the only thing which will really wake him up is brute force. Sad, but true.

His literary and historical admirations offer a key to his own character and talent. One of his favorites was the nineteenth-century German historian of Rome, Ferdinand Gregorovius, some of whose chapters Douglas translated into Italian while a student at Karlsruhe. "I liked Gregorovius even then," he wrote 40 years later, "and in later years learned to appreciate more fully his humanism, his alloy of learning and descriptive power." Likewise he never forgot the model of Count Campo Alegre, whom he had known at the Spanish Embassy in St. Petersburg, "scholar and man of the world, [who] impressed his character on all he possessed and all he said. . . . He belonged to an almost forgotten race, the humanist; the man of boundless curiosity and boundless tolerance—of that tolerance which derives from satisfied curiosity, and can derive from nothing else." What he liked about the translations of Petrarch by another of his idols, Frederick Wharton Mann, is that they had nothing touristic about them: "His work was meticulous and refined, exclusive, anti-vulgarian."

It was in the spirit of these admirations that he traveled, not just in Russia and Italy, but to Africa (with Nancy Cunard), Greece, Turkey (he loved the beautiful, studious town of Bursa), India, Ceylon, Syria, and Kenya. He was accompanied everywhere by "Alfred" (sometimes "Alfredino")—the small hard pillow necessary to his sleep. But he spent more than half his life in Italy, and it is as an interpreter of the Italian mode of abroad to a grey, hangdog Anglo-Saxonry that he finds his career. He began before the war with *Siren Land,* a consideration of the ancient Siren myth in relation to the topographical and archeological features of the Bay of Naples. Here he achieves what will be his lifelong method of grasping "a place": he moves eye and mind rapidly over the whole, like someone "reading" a painting, in order to possess all the elements at once and unite them, no matter how contradictory the details or how puzzling the result. In aid of this method, his prose attains a wonderful dynamics. It is full of exclamations, assertions, and queries as he moves back and forth from present datum to past association. And in *Siren Land* he develops his personal structure for the travel book: narrative and description interrupted by frequent interlarded essays—on the ethics derivable from ruins, the local winds and their folklore, the character of Tiberius, local spooks and saints, caves and their traditional narratives, leisure, local wines. The method is a form of geographical gossip. Underlying the whole busy performance is the theme that he will develop a hundred different ways, the nastiness of positing "the antagonism of flesh and spirit, the most pernicious piece of crooked thinking which has ever oozed out of our poor deluded brain." That's a way of talking about his delight in the company of the peasant boy he took up with at Nerano while writing *Siren Land,* whose conversation gave Douglas most of what he needed of local folklore for the book. (This boy later cooked for Douglas on Capri while he was writing *South Wind.*) His next travel book, *Fountains in the Sand* (1912), follows the same method in its treatment of Tunisia. Here his companion was a German schoolmaster, "tall, young, and attractive." Despite Douglas's technique of associative impressionism, the book is topographically precise, and he was pleased to be told by an army Colonel in 1943 that his book had been more useful to the planners of the North African campaign than any official materials.

His companion while touring southern Italy for *Old Calabria* (1915) was the twelve-year-old Eric (Ernest Frederick Eric Wolton), a Cockney he picked up (his words) at the Crystal Palace. The grown-up Eric continued as Douglas's friend and ended as a police official in East Africa, retiring finally as Chief Superintendent of the Tanganyikan police. Eric kept his own diary of the trip ("Salami is a kind of sousage it is very beastly"), and seems to have enjoyed everything but the food and the malaria. "His curly hair dropped out," Douglas notes, "till he was nearly bald."

Douglas once said, speaking of the Great War: "A continent which can make such an exhibition of itself is not to be taken seriously." *South Wind* (1917) was designed in part as an uncontaminated island's rebuke to northern Europe, a plea for youth and sun and tolerance addressed to nations at suicidal war apparently contemptuous of these things. The novel is sometimes taken as a satyr's mere naughty recommendation of pleasure as the end of life, but seeing it in the context of the war makes it appear a more thoughtful critique. And a more subtle one than sometimes imagined. For example, its implicit celebration of the institution of conversation, especially conversation about ideas liberally conceived, makes its own comment on the nationalistic rigidities presiding up north, exposing the incivility of the noisy, wordless confrontation occurring in Belgium and France (as Count Caloveglia says, "Northern people, whether from climatic or other causes, are prone to extremes"). *South Wind* appears to be "a novel," but its earliest readers, like Arthur Eckersley writing in the *English Review,* sensed its proximity to the travel book: "One knew already that Mr. Norman Douglas was the ideal writer of travel volumes; the setting of *South Wind* enables him to give some vivid pictures of Italian scenes, so vividly realized that the book may be regarded as a kind of holiday substitute." There is a plot, a boyishly subversive one, but it's there less for its own sake than as a justification for the "travel" essays, which treat Nepenthe like an actual island visited by an actual curious traveler. Thus we are told about its topography, geology, and mineralogy, its customs, antiquities, and floraculture, sometimes almost in guidebook idiom. We encounter essays on aesthetics, fanaticism, comparative theology, folk-medicine, and cookery; as well as numerous character-sketches and even a mock saint's-life. But *South Wind* is most like a travel book in its wonder about the magic of place, its curiosity about the intercourse between place and character. It is the anomalous sirocco, inseparable from Nepenthe, that tempts foreigners there to "strange actions," just as in *A Passage to India*, the work of another traveler and one of Douglas's admirers, it is the echo in a strange "place," the Marabar Caves, that changes everything.

In 1919, arriving in Menton by train, Douglas met a sweet-tempered boy of fourteen, René Mari, who helped him carry his suitcase. One thing led to another, and it was René (his parents approving) who accompanied Douglas on most of the walking tours in Italy recalled in *Alone*, published in 1921. Since he's toured with a companion, Douglas, in a footnote at the end, acknowledges that his title is "rather an inapt one." But, he concludes, "Let it stand!" It has the merit of some ironic concealment, as well as implying the author's aloneness as the last remaining honest man with aristocratic tastes and scorn for the modern world. The Introduction (first published as "The Tribulations of a Patriot") helps explain what this odd, strongminded Briton is doing in Italy. It details with rich sarcasm and anger his frustrations trying to get some kind of war work at home in the autumn of 1914. Rejected everywhere, he naturally packs his bags and takes off, alone. From Menton he proceeds to Levanto, Siena, Pisa, the resort town Viareggio, dead in February but awakening in May, and thence to Rome, "the most engaging capital in Europe." Off again to Olevano, Valmontone, Sorrento, and back to Rome again. Then finally to Soriano and Alatri. Douglas's method is to invite the places visited to convey their associations of earlier trips and earlier visitants, with the result that the book blends, as Holloway observes, "fact, fiction, and semi-fiction in a completely satisfying whole." As usual,

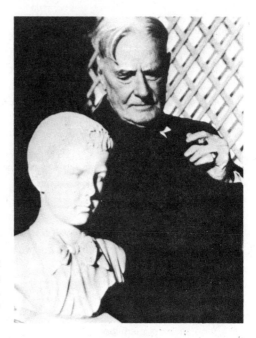

Norman Douglas at eighty, contemplating a bust of himself at ten. (Martin Secker & Warburg)

Douglas throws in what interests him and ties it to a place. We meet characters, mostly rascals or nice children. We get natural-history notes on snakes, lizards, and birds; exotic speculations about human motives or institutions, examined historically; accounts of flirtations with young girls; renderings of walks and conversations with intelligent and unschooled—and therefore sensitive—young boys; hedonistic notes on local wine and food; quasi-dirty jokes, set forth so shrewdly they could pass for clean; anti-Puritan diatribes, focussing on "over-legislation" everywhere; an attack on gross-feeders (most of them British), who betray coarseness of soul by not caring what they eat; an excursus on the delusions of the mob and the orthodoxies and public pieties threatening the first-rate man; and observations on the corruption of rural life by cities and machinery. There is an essay on whether youth should drink wine at all or should leave it to age, which needs it more and knows how to manage it better. There are half-whimsical anthropological inquiries: why do the French develop noses that make them resemble rats? whence their devotion to scent? There are invectives against telephones, trams, noise, "progress"; and plans for outré literary projects, like an anti-fly anthology. All these excursions are realizations of curiosity in action, showing the reader what it's like to be interested in something for its own sake. They are exercises in a "liberal" kind of noticing, which misses no nuance and treasures associations because experience is blank without them. He once knew a lady in California whose fondness for the large, lurid wild flowers there prompted her to contemn the European varieties. If flowers were mere objects, Douglas says, she'd be right. He tried to explain to her that European flowers bear about them seven millenia of literary, mythological, and historical associations, which constitute their meaning: "a nimbus of lore had gathered around the humblest of them; they were hallowed; they had a past, an ancestry. There was nothing, I insisted, at the back of California flowers; no memories, no associations. . . . What poet had ever sung their praises? What legend had twined about them? She was deaf to this argument. . . ."

In *Alone* Douglas exploits virtually all literary methods, producing even mock-proverbs: "Consider well your neighbor, what an imbecile he is. Then ask yourself whether it be worth while paying any attention to what he thinks of you." Douglas divided up and scattered through the text of *Alone* essays already prepared, and the reader encountering the sentence, "Whoever suffers from insomnia will find himself puzzling at night over questions which have no particular concern for him at other times," might think himself embarked on an essay by Hazlitt or Lamb or Stevenson. Douglas has just described the disappointing Arno at Pisa, and is making one of his "transitions" to what he thought last night about heredity. With *Alone* Douglas begins his practice of making his own vigorous comic indexes:

Acqua santa, mineral fountain, its appalling effects
Alpenglühen, an abomination
Bacon, *misquoted*
Beds in England, neolithic features of
Cement floors, a detestable invention
Ghosts, mankind surrounded by, 111; away with them, 137
Imagination, needful to travel literature
Shelley, . . . recommends caverns to his readers, but lives comfortably himself

Viareggio, an objectionable place
Whistling, denotes mental vacuity,

and finally, with deep irony,

Zürich, its attractions.

He returned to the technique of the comic index in *Together*, and the
index to *Some Limericks* (1928) provided ample opportunity for associating the outrageous with abroad:

Australia, floral design by a native of
Coblenz, a lucky kitchen-maid of
Horn, Cape, hypochondria among its aborigenes, 86; imports
    French goods, *ibid*.
Madras, indelicate behavior of local cobra
Stamboul, case of varicose veins at.

(It's like Nabokov, we notice, in his comic index to *Pale Fire*, where
fanciful geography joins mock-scholarship and wry mock-*Sehnsucht*:

Kalixhaven, a colorful seaport on the Western coast, a few miles
    north of Blawick (q.v.), 171; many pleasant memories.
Kobaltana, a once fashionable mountain resort near the ruins of
    some old barracks, now a cold and desolate spot of difficult
    access and no importance but still remembered in military
    families and forest castles, not in the text.)

If *Alone* is about intellectual curiosity satisfied in proximity to a
beloved person, *Together*, while affecting to be about a walking tour
in the Austrian Vorarlberg, is a tour in time back to Douglas's childhood in that area. His companion is again René (here, "Mr. R."),
whose young fondness for milk and eggs at inns is disclosed in the
third paragraph. "I am past his stage," writes Douglas, "though still
young enough to revel in that delicious raspberry jelly." Thus the
theme of the book, the sweet conflict between youth and age, is set in
motion. Douglas dedicated *Together* to his two sons, and it is full of
memories and anecdotes about fathers and sons, families and heredity,
and always the affectionate abrasion between young and old. To Douglas, Mr. R. appears pig-headed; to Mr. R., Douglas's problem is, as he

puts it, "*troppo vino.* You comprehend?" The odd thing is that Douglas used to be Mr. R. "How one changes!" Now, in every one of his perceptions, Douglas is conscious of the perceptions of the boy beside him. Maybe it was this feature that appealed so strongly to Lytton Strachey and Forster, both fervent admirers of *Together.* "The thrill that only you can give," Strachey wrote him, "goes down my back."

Every literary traveler has an habitual practice. Douglas's is climbing up to an eminence whose height allows him to see something special in the prospect before him or to learn something inaccessible to ground-dwellers. In both *Alone* and *Together,* he performs this action numerous times; in *South Wind* the Count avails himself of it as a figure for arguing the loss of a former extensiveness of thought. The disappearance of Latin and of European commonality, he says, has led to narrowness and provincialism, to everyone's retreat behind the frontiers of his own vernacular. Modern commerce "has demarcated our frontiers with a bitterness hitherto unknown. The world of thought has not expanded; it has contracted and grown provincial. Men have lost sight of distant horizons. Nobody writes for humanity . . . they write for their country, their sect; to amuse their friends or annoy their enemies." On the other hand, "Pliny or Linnaeus or Humboldt—they sat on mountain-tops; they surveyed the landscape at their feet, and if some little valley lay shrouded in mist, the main outlines of the land yet lay clearly distanced before them." Over and over Douglas ascends to mountain- or hill-tops, and thence, like the speaker in an eighteenth-century prospect poem, surveys the land below, inviting it to serve now as matter for metaphor, now as data for historical speculation, now as a trigger of associative recall. His travel essay *One Day* (1929) is the record of trying to pack into a final twelve hours an indelible image of Greece. His method is to climb up: "Why not scramble in earliest morning, before breakfast, up the stony steps of the Lykabettus . . . for the sake of the view, and to watch the town at one's feet beginning to throb with life once more?" Why not, indeed. At the top, his felicity is complete, for in addition to the view he is vouchsafed the company of two schoolboys, typical of the Greek variety: "If you . . . care for their society, they will take you for walks singly, or in couples, or by the dozen, and ask sensible questions and impart useful and even edifying information. . . ."

These were his friends and his lovers, the temporary attachments he traveled for. "He could endure the society of fewer and fewer people over the age of fourteen," Acton reports of him in the 30's, by which time his main work was finished. Brigit Patmore asked him why he wasn't writing anything now. "I can only write if I have *this*," he said, gripping her arm tightly. "I knew he didn't mean *my* arm or me," she says, "but the confiding closeness, that ardent heightening of mind and senses through love or passion." In *Aaron's Rod* Lawrence delivered a portrait of Douglas as "James Argyle." Some of it is caricature, but some is not. Argyle says to the Marchese:

> "A man is drawn—or driven. Driven, I've found it. Ah, my dear fellow, what is life but a search for a friend? A search for a friend—that sums it up."
> "Or a lover," said the Marchese, grinning.
> "Same thing. Same thing. . . ."

═══ THAT SPLENDID ENCLOSURE ═══

BY issuing *South Wind*, Douglas was reminding the British of the Mediterranean. They had always known it, but after the war they reclaimed it with frenetic and often self-destructive enthusiasm. To sketch the history of the British imaginative intercourse with the Mediterranean in modern times is virtually to present a survey of modern British literature. It was a magical place, like the island in *The Tempest*, capable of generating God knows what lubriciousness and of virtually unmanning the intellect. No adult could write a novel as silly as Connolly's *The Rock Pool* about the irresistible "influence" of any other place. Put an Englishman there and he goes all to water. Or drowns himself in Ricard and Pernod, like Connolly's Edgar Naylor, who, like James's Strether visiting Paris in *The Ambassadors*, visits Trou-sur-Mer to "study" its exiles and delinquents and ends by joining them. Since Lord Byron and Shelley the Mediterranean has had the power to hustle Englishmen into hyperbole, to make even so phlegmatic and civil-servantlike a soul as R. H. Bruce Lockhart suddenly come alight and blurt out that the Mediterranean Sea has "more history in one of its waves than the Atlantic has in the whole expanse of its 24,000,000 square miles." Waugh's highly autobiographical Gilbert Pinfold, normally stuffy and inhibited, is moved to similar hyperbole when in the 50's he looks at the Mediterranean and recalls his life there in the 20's and 30's: "The sea might have been any sea by the look of it, but he knew it was the Mediterranean, that splendid enclosure which held all the world's history and half the happiest memories of his own life; of work and rest and battle, of aesthetic adventure and of young love." It's a rare, vulnerable lyric moment for Waugh, and it's the Mediterranean that seduces him into it.

The Mediterranean is the model for the concept *south*, and it is a rare Briton whose pulses do not race at mention of that compass direction. The magic works even outside Europe proper, as it does when Robert Byron arrives in Shiraz, after a dreary winter in Teheran: "The South, the blessed South!" he sings. "It gives me the same exhiliration as a first morning by the Mediterranean." Asked once what makes life worth living, Connolly thought carefully and then answered, "There are only three things which make life worth living: to be writing a tolerably good book, to be in a dinner party for six, and to be traveling south with someone whom your conscience permits you to love." The south ("the South of France, Italy") is to be the venue of the lover Connie Chatterley fantasizes in the midst of "these filthy Midlands" who will give her a child. In the south, resistance to lust was thought so difficult that Geoffrey Gorer believed the Protestant missionaries in West Africa when they asserted that their Catholic counterparts "do not take the vow of chastity" when assigned there.

Another treasured possession of the British imagination between the wars is the belief that people of the south are less hypocritical than northerners. As a respite from the rigors of "London," Louis MacNeice sets off for the Continent in 1938, persuaded (as he says in *Autumn Journal*) that

The Land of Cockayne begins across the Channel.

But he soon finds that Paris lacks what he needs, and that

> *. . . I must go further south.*

He does so, driving into Spain, where he is gratified to find that

> *these people contain truth, whatever*
> *Their nominal facade.*

To Auden, poetry, conceived as the truest way of saying, is a river, and
in his poem "In Memory of W. B. Yeats," it flows south:

> *[Poetry] survives*
> *In the valley of its saying where executives*
> *Would never want to tamper; it flows south. . . .*

One doesn't want to be frivolous about a serious subject, but it does
seem notable that the "Civil War" of the 30's that attracted so many
British, a war full of emotion and passion and suffering and hope, was
the Spanish—i.e., a "Mediterranean"—civil war, and not, say, one
taking place in Sweden or Switzerland. The thing is perfectly con-
sonant with British expectations about the hotter, "more passionate,"
more sincere, and thus more interesting "south." It is from there, not
the north, that Douglas's "wind" originates. In 1929 Lawrence found
Paris too far north for him, and wrote the Huxleys: "I don't want to
go north, don't want to *be* North, shan't have any peace till I see the
Mediterranean again, all the rest hell! . . . the North has all gone
evil—I can't help feeling it morally and ethically. I mean anti-life."

The way you got to the south was to go first to Victoria Station,
an unlikely gateway to faërie, with its dirty brick and nasty prole food.
But as Anthony Carson says, the station "meant, ultimately, the Mediterranean, the blueness, the whiteness, the chaos of our strident, civilized mother" because the famous Blue Train started there and took
you all the way to the Riviera. The Blue Train. There is excitement in
just writing the words. The Blue Train connoted escape ("Sleep your
way from the City's fogs to the Riviera sunshine"), exotic food (an
eel-tank was part of the dining-car), and, since the passage to Calais,

Paris, and Monte Carlo was made at night, lust. The rapid contrast between London and the Riviera was a treasured experience the train promised: one departed "on a cold grey day," says Patrick Howarth, and woke the next morning "to the sight of mimosa and orange trees," with "the red rocks of the Esterel on one side of the line and the blue waters of the Mediterranean on the other." On his way to Mt. Athos, Byron took the Blue Train: "Happiness untrammelled," he noted. Waugh's William Boot, in *Scoop*, took it to Marseilles on his way to Ishmaelia. It was the preferred way to get to the popular French ports like Toulon, where Anthony Powell was to be found, working on *Afternoon Men*. It is by the Blue Train that Henry Green's holiday-makers in *Party Going* plan to get to the south of France until stopped by the London fog. The train was so splendid, so luxurious and grand with its blue and gold cars (manufactured in Leeds, actually), blue velvet upholstery, barbershop, and comfortable berths, that arriving could be a disappointment. Connolly found that "Nice is never worthy of the Blue Train."

The Blue Train entered so deeply into the needy British imagination that we find outcrops everywhere in the 20's and 30's. One of the hits of 1924 was Diaghilev's ballet *Le Train Bleu*, with scenario by Cocteau, music by Milhaud, costumes by Coco Chanel, and curtain by Picasso, and three years later, a London musical, *The Blue Train*, displayed the magical theme before a more plebeian audience. Agatha Christie jumped aboard with *The Mystery of the Blue Train*, and in the early 30's one could dine at The Blue Train, a popular London restaurant. It is out the window of the Blue Train that Jeanette MacDonald warbles in Ernst Lubitsch's film *Monte Carlo* (1930), her melodies taken up by the pretty farm- and vineyard-workers along the right-of-way. At the same time one of the social fixtures of upper London was Barbara Cartland's "Train Ball," where one came costumed as various exotic conveyances like the Golden Arrow, the Southern Belle, and the Blue Train.

The kind of felicity to which the Blue Train conveyed you as it let you off at Marseilles or Toulon or Cannes or Nice or Monte Carlo, whence you could go on to the Italian Riviera, to Rapallo and all the way down to the Amalfi Coast, seemed novel in the 20's. It seems novel no longer because those places have provided the model for the décor and atmosphere of successful international tourism ever since.

THE EUROPEAN SOUTH

Wherever exported and transplanted out of Europe—to Turkey, Mexico, even the U.S.S.R.—the style is the same, involving beach and sun, bright colored aperitifs at little tables outdoors, copious fish and shellfish to eat, folk- or popular music played on string instruments, cheap drinkable local wine, much use of oil (olive for cooking, suntan for browning), all in a setting of colored architecture and "colorful" street markets. A maximum exposure of flesh guarantees a constant erotic undertone, and a certain amount of noise (Vespas, children shouting on the beach) provides a reassurance of life and gaiety. There must be colorful fishermen and boat-people, playing *boules* or something like it. There must be love on top of the sheets after the large wine lunch, with occasional hints of Roman Catholicism (processions, the locals attending early mass, the public blessing of fishing vessels) just sufficient to lend the whole frivolous operation a slight air of wickedness. This scene, constituting one of the main presiding myths of the desirable for the modern urban and suburban middle proletariat, has become our version of pastoral, and in the 20's and 30's it was gradually displacing, or at least powerfully opposing, the earlier British image of the hankered-after, the traditional pastoral scene of quiet inland waters, wildflowers, sheep-filled meadows, and silence broken only by birdsong and softly lowing cattle. These two images of the ideal divide not just generations (Aldous Huxley *vs.* George Meredith and William Morris), but whole worlds: on the one hand, the world of traditional England, satisfied with its usages; on the other, the new international world spawned by the Great War and explored by literary travelers too young, most of them, to have fought.

But one did not need to embrace this gaudy holiday image in its entirety to propose the Mediterranean as a model or norm. One could point to the Mediterranean as "Rome" in the largest sense, the place where the writings construed at school originated, the place associated with the combined skepticism and sensuality and insistence upon clarity resulting from the British version of "a classical education." Complaining in *Enemies of Promise* (1948) that Eton has taught him nothing useful, Connolly listens while Eton answers:

> You imply our education is of no use to you in after life.
> We are not an employment agency; all we can do is to give you
> a grounding in the art of mixing with your fellow men, to tell
> you what to expect from life and give you an outward manner

and inward poise, an old prescription from the eighteenth century which we call a classical education, an education which confers the infrequent virtues of good sense and good taste, and the benefit of dual nationality, English and Mediterranean. . . .

In Forster's *Passage to India* Cyril Fielding is unique in exhibiting "good sense and good taste." Among the British in Chandrapore he's the only one trained to resist the vulgar appeals of jingoism and color prejudice and self-righteousness, and his training-ground has been (no surprise for the reader of Forster's earlier novels) Italy. He has known it from his youth, and even the shape of his house in India reminds him of a bit of Florentine architecture, the Loggia de' Lanzi. After the mess and scandals at Chandrapore, Fielding returns to England for a vacation, and on the way he pauses in Venice, which offers an aesthetic and thus a moral norm for gauging India. "The buildings of Venice," he finds again, "stood in the right place, whereas in poor India everything was placed wrong. . . . In the old undergraduate days he had wrapped himself up in the many-colored blanket of St. Mark's, but something more precious than mosaics and marbles was offered to him now: the harmony between the works of man and the earth that upholds them, the civilization that has escaped muddle, the spirit in a reasonable form, with flesh and blood subsisting." In short, Fielding realizes, "The Mediterranean is the human norm. When men leave that exquisite lake, . . . they approach the monstrous and extraordinary." And that's what's the matter with India: it's too far from the olive trees and the grapes, too far from the great continuous opposition between Christianity and "Rome" in the old sense that so superbly enacts the perpetually interesting quarrel between spirit and flesh in mankind.

THE NEW HELIOPHILY

FOR the Mediterranean to be re-appropriated after the war, its most ubiquitous natural asset, the sun, had to be redeemed from the social stigma it had borne in the nineteenth century. Then, the better sort of people had tended not to sit in it, believing that if its effects were indispensable to the welfare of flora, they were of very dubious value to persons. Before the war the white-skinned, in India and other colonies, adhered to the socially-comforting myth that whatever might be its effects on darker races, the sun was a menace to them, so fine of weave were they. To omit one's solar topee for only a few minutes was to invite madness, "brain fever," or death. When one young man, Rupert Mayne, went out to India, his parents told him that "the three most dangerous things that I had to watch out for in the East were wine, women and the sun." (It's ironic that these are roughly the three things that in the 20's one went to the Mediterranean specifically to embrace.) In India, an Other Rank of H. M. Forces who failed to wear his topee outdoors was punished instantly with a sentence of fourteen days confined to barracks. And back home as well as abroad, women and girls of the upper orders protected their faces with parasols and wide-brimmed hats and their hands with gloves. Heliophobia like this was an indispensable accessory of the class system, at home distinguishing the fine from the less fine, in the colonies demarcating administrators from underdogs.

But subversive influences were at work. As early as 1902 André Gide, in *L'Immoraliste*, depicted the tubercular Michel deriving magic benefit from nude sunbathing (in Italy, of course), and later one of Gide's faithful readers, Hermann Hesse, imitated Michel, sunbathing in Italy to cure his headaches and gout. The German nudist movement, often thought a manifestation of Weimar, actually dates from the 1890's (Whitman can be considered a precursor), and as early as 1903 the Swiss physician Auguste Rollier (later the author of the influential treatise *Heliotherapy* [1923]) was moving his tubercular patients into the sun. The tubercular Lawrence was later going to assert, "My inmost need is the sun." After the war, sunbathing was found the readiest remedy for children's vitamin-deficiency ailments occasioned by the British blockade of Germany, and the sun was likewise recommended for those recovering from the 'flu epidemic of 1918 and 1919, which killed 21 million people worldwide. In England alone 200,000 died of it. "Sunshine is Life," proclaimed a British railway poster of the 20's, soliciting the traveler to "Come to the Riviera."

John Weightman has called the whole movement the Solar Revolution, and it is one of the most startling reversals in modern intellectual and emotional history. In the nineteenth century the "poetic" heavenly body was, by common consent, the moon—as in Tennyson and Poe. In the twentieth century it was conventionally the sun which sent forth mystical emanations, and by the 30's the motif of the sun was everywhere. Art Deco would be impoverished without it. "It turned up all over the place," says Sarah Howell, "on suburban garden gates, shoes and cigarette cases, and the stepped shapes of the temples where the ancient Aztecs had worshipped their sun gods inspired the design of millions of fireplaces and wireless sets; . . . cactuses, transplanted from the desert, seemed suddenly the most desirable of house plants." The whole craze helped sustain the property booms in Florida and California as well as the vogue of "Spanish" architecture in such places. And even in the 70's, if the movement has grown automatic and intellectually unselfconscious, it has by no means spent itself: witness the rush of the French to acquire real-estate on the Côte d'Azur, polluted though its waters may be; witness the popularity of the American "sun belt" and the continuing vigor of the seaside industry. But in the early 20's the sun fixation was so novel that at Oxford Connolly created a sensation by announcing that the time for the Riviera was not, as had been customary among valetudinarians, the winter, but during the very hottest summer months; and to advertise this heresy, Peter Quennell remembers, he formed a self-conscious "Cicada Club" of five undergraduates, devoted to broiling themselves on the beaches between Marseilles and Menton.

The power of the sun idea to take over entirely a malleable mind can be studied in the case of Harry Crosby, the ultimately mad American who settled in France, naming his residence Le Moulin du Soleil. He established the Black Sun Press and devised a homemade ritual of sun worship in which onanism played some part. On his back he had tattooed a sun (to testify to his fidelity to "the Sun God"), and he solicited from Lawrence the short story "Sun" for his press to publish, paying him in "sunny" twenty-dollar gold pieces. He seemed to grow madder and madder until he finally murdered his mistress and killed himself. But he is only an extreme example, just as Mr. Norris is an extreme example of the frontier fixation. The sun obsession was visible everywhere. In 1922 Katherine Mansfield, deciding to subject herself to the discipline of Gurdjieff's eccentric colony at Fontainebleau ("The Institute for the Harmonious Development of Man"), rationalized thus: "That's enough. To be a child of the sun." (For his study of "the imaginative life of English culture after 1918," Martin Green has invoked the traditional designation of the Italians and come up with the perfect title: *Children of the Sun* [1976].) When Lawrence arrived at Bandol in 1929, it was the Villa Beau Soleil he selected to rent, despite its ugliness and tininess. From there he wrote Huxley: "This place is nothing much in itself—but I seem to be happy here, sitting on the tiny port and watching the 'life'—chiefly dogs—or wandering out on the jetty. I find I can be very happy quite by myself just wandering or sitting on a stone—if the sun shines. Yes, one needs the sun. If anything, one needs to go farther south than here. . . . But it is *wonderful* how sunny it is here. . . ." In 1935 Lawrence Durrell was celebrating Corfu and "the incandescence of the sun" that drew him there. A year later it was in the hot sun of the eastern Mediterranean that Edward VIII stripped down to demonstrate his restlessness and his longings for "freedom" on the yacht *Nahlin* with Mrs. Simpson. (On that notorious yacht trip, Lady Diana Cooper took along Fleming's *News From Tartary* to read.) Looking for a title for his novel of 1926, with its final scenes set at the port and on the beach of San Sebastian, Hemingway goes to *Ecclesiastes* and comes up with his title, *The Sun Also Rises*. It is one of a plethora of "sun" titles during the period, like Alain Gerbault's *In Quest of the Sun* and *The Gospel of the Sun*, and Alfred Noyes's *The Sun Cure*. As early as 1920 Ezra Pound's antennae had sensed the direction things were moving when he imagined Mauberley's reveries of "Thick foliage / Placid beneath warm suns." And it is from the period between the wars that we can date most of the Hotels or Gästhäuser *Sonne* that cropped up in Germany, Austria, and Switzerland.

The Germanic world was the center for hedonistic nude sunbathing, and Stephen Spender was attracted there partly for that reason. (In England nudism was still attended by Fabian highmindedness and a Puritan sense of therapeutic duty, reflected in the term *naturism* and registered in books like Dr. Maurice Parmelee's *The New Gymnosophy* [1926].) Spender's account of Germanic sun worship in *World Within World* (1951) is classic. For the good-looking young Germans who befriended him, "the life of the senses was a sunlit garden from which sin was excluded":

> The sun . . . was a primary social force in this Germany. Thousands of people went to the open-air swimming baths or lay down on the shores of the rivers and lakes, almost nude, and sometimes quite nude, and the boys who had turned the deepest mahogany walked amongst those people with paler skins, like kings among their courtiers.
>
> The sun healed their bodies of the years of war, and made them conscious of the quivering, fluttering life of blood and muscles covering their exhausted spirits like the pelt of an animal: and their minds were filled with an abstraction of the sun, a huge circle of fire, an intense whiteness blotting out the sharp outlines of all other forms of consciousness, burning out even the sense of time. . . .

(At about the same time, Lawrence, imagining Mellors' relation with Connie Chatterley, sees him "Burning out the shames, the deepest, oldest shames, in the most secret places," and he explains to Harry Crosby that *Lady Chatterley's Lover* is "a phallic novel, but good and sun-wards, truly sun-wards. . . .") Under the all-powerful influence of the sun, Spender goes on, "I went to the bathing places, and I went to parties which ended at dawn with the young people lying in one another's arms. This life appeared to be innocuous, being led by people who seemed naked in body and soul, in the desert of white bones which was post-war Germany."

Not everyone, it is true, responded with Spender's enthusiasm. In

1930 Evelyn Waugh wrote a skeptical piece, "This Sun-bathing Business," for the *Daily Mail*, where he deposed: "I hate the whole business. . . . All this is supposed to be good for you. Doctors say so. Nowadays people believe anything they are told by 'scientists,' just as they used to believe anything they were told by clergymen." Another who refused to play was Auden, who carefully kept his skin its original ghastly blue-white. But Waugh and Auden generally distrust the wilder romanticisms of their countrymen. More customary was the notion that the sun both causes and betokens a rare and precious "sincerity," and that one reason the British display a special talent for hypocrisy is that the sun is rare in their climate. "The weather," says Henry Green, "lies at the root of the way women and men behave," with the result that "the English in their relations with each other are less frank than other nationalities to the extent to which their skies are less clear and so by the less amount of sun they have." Forster would agree (although he'd write it better), and so would Durrell, who argued that only under the sun could "the essential male and female relationship" flourish "uncomplicated by mirages and falsities. . . ."

$\equiv$ THE PLACES OF D. H. LAWRENCE $\equiv$

MIRAGES and falsities, we gather, have characterized the relation between the New York lady Juliet and her husband Maurice in Lawrence's "Sun" (1926). "Take her away into the sun," is her physician's injunction, and she sails from New York with her child John, her mother, and a nurse, leaving a world of grey to arrive abroad at a place like the Sicilian coast. There she takes "a house above the bluest of seas, with a vast garden, or vineyard, all vines and olives. . . ."

Mother having departed, Juliet awakens to an awareness that a relation can be posited between the sun's "coming up" and a male erection. This happens on "a morning when the sun lifted himself naked and molten, sparkling over the sea's rim. . . . Juliet lay in her bed and watched him rise. It was as if she had never seen the sun rise before. She had never seen the naked sun stand up pure upon the sea-line, shaking the night off himself." If here the rising sun is an erection, in Lawrence's later *The Man Who Died* (1929) (also published by the Harry Crosby who couldn't help associating the sun with the rites attaching to his own phallus) the erection experienced by Jesus in the presence of the Priestess of Isis is the rising sun:

> He crouched to her, and he felt the blaze of his manhood
> and his power rise up in his loins, magnificent.
> "I am risen!"
> Magnificent, blazing, indomitable in the depths of his loins,
> his own sun dawned, and sent its fire running along his limbs. . . .

Juliet is similarly astonished, and immediately "the desire sprang secretly in her to go naked in the sun." On her rented property, she finds a spot hidden by cypresses, and there she strips and invites the sun's rays, "half stunned with wonder at the thing that was happening to her." What was happening was that she was "mating" with the sun. It *"knew"* her, in the cosmic carnal sense of the word"; and what results is a deepened Lawrentian contempt for other people who are not abroad, "so unelemental, so unsunned, . . . so like graveyard worms." She soon inducts her infant boy into therapeutic sun-bathing, rolling the orange, a toy sun, across the patio tiles to him. "Now, most of the day, she and the child were naked in the sun, and it was all she wanted." A surprise visit from her husband, who climbs down to her sun-bathing place "in his grey felt hat and his dark grey suit," makes it clear that "he was utterly out of the picture," hopelessly representative of the other place, the place Lawrence is constantly trying to flee. Juliet and Maurice agree that she cannot return to New York after what she's found here; she will stay and he will visit. But while this agreement is being reached she sees something he does not: a neighboring "hot, shy" peasant whose child she wants to bear. He is like the sun: "She had seen the flushed blood in the burnt face, and the flame in the southern blue eyes, and the answer in her had been a gush of fire. He would have been a procreative sun-bath to her, and she wanted it." But the situation aborts in the final sentence of the story: "Nevertheless, her next child would be Maurice's. The fatal chain of continuity would cause it." The mirages and falsities, we know, will resume, because regardless of Juliet's effort to re-identify herself, "the middle classes," as Lawrence insists in the poem of that title,

> are sunless.
> They have only two measures:
> mankind and money,
> they have utterly no reference to the sun.

Juliet exemplifies Mark Schorer's axiom that "Lawrence's people discover their identities through their response to place." Of course all characters in fiction respond to place, but Lawrence's more than most because he is so extraordinarily sensitive to physical context and physical cause. "A delicate sensorium," H. M. Tomlinson calls him, "quivering and vociferating to every physical fact." The place where he writes becomes a part of what he writes. He is notable among poets, for example, for frequently appending to a poem an indication of the place where he's written it: *San Gervasio, Icking, Beuerberg, Gargnano, Florence, Baden-Baden, Taormina, Kandy*. And his place-sense is so intimately a part of his character that his poetry comes close to being a prepositional poetry, pivoting on his sensual awareness of locations like *behind, before, in, on, beyond, out of, between*. His best-known poems are those in which prepositional location is an often surprising feature, like "Piano," popularized partly by I. A. Richards's use of it in his *Practical Criticism* (1929): here the child sits *under* the piano, to the bafflement, it may be noticed, of many of Richards's students, whose imagination for locations is, compared with Lawrence's, undeveloped and visually inhibited: "I have experimented on one or two friends," writes one, "and each has started to grin when we have arrived at the phrase 'a child sitting *under* a piano. . . .' Allowing that it may possibly have been a grand and not an upright piano that the child was sitting under . . . ," etc. Again: "I don't see how a child could sit under the piano. He could sit under the keyboard but not under the piano." But Lawrence assumes an audience willing to imagine everything spatially, everything in a place:

GIORNO DEI MORTI

Along the avenue of cypresses,
All in their scarlet cloaks and surplices
Of linen, go the chanting choristers,
The priests in gold and black, the villagers. . . .

And all along the path to the cemetery
The round dark heads of men crowd silently,
And black-scarved faces of womenfolk, wistfully
Watch at the banner of death, and the mystery.

And at the foot of a grave a father stands
With sunken head; and forgotten, folded hands;
And at the foot of a grave a mother kneels
With pale shut face, nor either hears nor feels

The coming of the chanting choristers
Between the avenue of cypresses,
The silence of the many villagers,
The candle-flames beside the surplices.

Hardy does this too in his poems, but not with the insistence of Lawrence:

Between her breasts is my home, between her breasts.

Some of his most memorable titles are insistently prepositional in this way: "The Song of a Man Who Has Come Through," for example, or "Stand Up!" beginning

Stand up, but not for Jesus!
It's a little late for that.

One recalls such "locational" titles as "Climbing Up," "Up He Goes," "Sun in Me," "Man Reaches a Point—," "There Is No Way Out," "Underneath—," "There Is Rain in Me," "Desire Goes Down into the Sea," "Paradise Re-Entered," "Tommies in the Train," "Under the Oak," "School on the Outskirts," "From a College Window," "In the Spanish Tram-Car," "At the Bank in Spain," and "We Have Gone Too Far." The prepositional sense is behind the dynamics propelling a poem like "Snake":

A snake came to my water-trough
On a hot, hot day . . .
To drink there.

And the poem continues as the speaker recalls going *down* to the trough to watch the snake extending itself "*down* from a fissure" to trail "*over* the edge of the stone trough" and "rest his throat *upon* the stone bottom." The snake flicks away and disappears when the speaker throws a log "*at* the water trough with a clatter." Similarly, the sense of location dominates "Bavarian Gentians," from the opening in the clear bourgeois day,

Not every man has gentians in his house,

to the close in the underworld, reached by a passage

down the darker and darker stairs . . .
to the sightless realm. . . .

The crucial difference between place and placelessness is never far from his focus, even in his most apparently facile satires. In "Bathing Resort," one of a whole series of poems ridiculing the mechanical dullness of beach tourism, he gives us this little snapshot of a swimmer reclining on the sand with

Great thighs that lead nowhere.

Nowhere to Lawrence is simply death, and it has its corollaries in sexlessness and automatism.

Lawrence's signature is his acute, almost neurotic, sense of place. It is more this, perhaps, than his well-known didacticism when he's peddling his "creed" that gives him his uniqueness. His sense of place makes him like no other writer, from his earliest boyish postcards depicting Nottingham Castle ("I guess you know this place") to his equally monosyllabic comment on the sanitorium Ad Astra, Vence, written a few days before his death: "This place no good." (And speaking of prepositions, *Ad Astra* is almost too good to be true.) Some places think they are places, but they are mistaken because they are really "*without . . . place*." This proves to be what in the long run ruins Bandol for him. As he writes the Huxleys, "What a mess the French make of their places—perfect slums of villadom, appallingly without order, or form, or *place*" (Lawrence's emphasis). Like a more intense Norman Douglas, Lawrence always knows precisely where he is, and his readers do too, even his correspondents. Harry T. Moore specifies this notation of place as a special feature of Lawrence's letters, a virtually inviolable convention: "Lawrence frequently sets the scene at the beginning," says Moore, "though sometimes his evocation of place may occur in the middle or at the end . . . , as if he suddenly looked up from his writing and felt the impact of the landscape." Thus he writes A. W. McLeod from Germany: "I write on top of the Drachenfels, in the café under the trees. One can see miles and miles of Rhine—it twists and seems to climb upwards till some of it swims in the sky." That is "description," but Lawrence's presiding sense is not exactly the familiar auctorial talent that issues in description: the performance is more palpable than that, more a matter of touch and feel and presence, the sort of response to physical phenomena that prompted Huxley to call him "a kind of mystical materialist." He wrote Blanche Jennings in 1908: "Somehow I think we come into knowledge (unconscious) of the most vital parts of the cosmos through touching things," and his curious idiom of *coming into* knowledge suggests the attainment of knowledge not by "collecting it," as in the standard figure, but by almost traveling into it, moving toward, arriving at, and finally occupying it as if it were a place. Sex is knowledge, and sometimes Lawrence images it in terms very close to travel terms. "The greatest living experience for every man," he tells Bertrand Russell, "is his adventure into the woman."

His actual travels, says Huxley, were a search, a fruitless search. Yet "in a kind of despair he plunged yet deeper into the surrounding mystery," and "in *Lady Chatterley's Lover* . . . wrote the epilogue to his travels. . . ." It was finally his acute instinct for the spirit of place that cured him of earlier hopes for "cosmic unity, or world unison": to know that such dreams will not come to pass you have to know intensely the different permanent spirit of different places and sense the all-powerful distinctions between people which their places determine. As he writes Rolf Gardiner from New Mexico in 1924: "The spirit of place ultimately always triumphs." And thank God: "To me it is life to feel the white ideas [i.e., of world uniformity] and the 'oneness' crumbling into a thousand pieces [cf. "places"], and all sorts of wonder coming through. . . . I hate 'oneness,' it's a mania." Hence his pursuit of places.

Like Joyce and Robert Graves and Norman Douglas and Isherwood and Pound and Eliot, Lawrence was an exile, and his life was virtually a series of impatient acts of travel, to Germany and Italy, to Sardinia and Switzerland and France, to Ceylon and Australia and Tahiti, to San Francisco and Old and New Mexico, and back to France again. "This place no good," he kept saying as he moved on. In the persisting popular image, Lorenzo was in search of the sun, like most of his contemporaries, even those who were not tubercular or had no interest in what drew him to Taos, the reputation of the local Indians for a cult of sun worship. But unlike many of his contemporaries he was also in search of virtue, of cosmic order, and of perfect harmony between man and his places. Rebecca West perceived that he "traveled to get a certain Apocalyptic vision of mankind that he registered again and again and again, always rising to a pitch of ecstatic agony." Of course he never found what he sought, or, if he thought he had found it, soon discovered that he himself had manufactured the ecstasy and laid it over the actuality of a place. He thus repeatedly took off again, embittered and disillusioned. He is always both escaping and seeking. "One might go away," thinks Ursula in *Women in Love*, as, among the Alps, she dwells on images of "orange trees and cypress." The idea that one might go away, that one might try again, defines a repeated emotional action Lawrence performs, and his elasticity and power of recovery and capacity to rise Phoenix-like from calamity and despair are among the most striking things about him. Like Robert Byron, he has the true traveler's high-metabolic equipment to sustain his boundless curiosity and the boundless energy feeding it.

If he needs the curiosity to propel him abroad, he needs the energy to rebound from disillusion. In August, 1921, he and Frieda are quite happy at Zell-am-See in Austria, as he emphasizes when writing to Catherine Carswell: "The villa is on the edge of the lake, we bathe and boat and go excursions into the mountains. . . . And the Scheibershofens are really very nice to us." Perfect felicity, one would think. "And yet," he goes on, "I feel I can't breathe. . . . Frieda loves it and is quite bitter that I say I want to go away. But there it is—I do."

They move to Taormina, whence two months later Lawrence writes
Carswell again: "Travel is particularly disheartening this year, I find.
Not so much the inconveniences as the kind of slow poison one
breathes in every new atmosphere." And within a week he is exploding
to Earl Brewster, embroidering in several languages to make sure the
point gets across: "It is a world of *canaille*: absolutely. *Canaille,
canaglia, Schweinhunderei*, stink-pots. Pfui!—pish, pshaw, prrr! They
all stink in my nostrils. That's how I feel in Taormina . . . , that's
how I feel. A curse, a murrain, a pox on this crawling, sniffling, spunk-
less brood of humanity." Less than six months later the Lawrences
have moved on, to Ceylon, where things are so disappointing that he
writes Robert Pratt Barlow wondering if his whole forsaking of England hasn't been a mistake. Two months later, having fled Ceylon and
passed through Australia, he determines to try the islands of the South
Seas, but he's not sanguine: "Don't expect to catch on there, either,"
he writes Brewster. "But I love trying things and discovering how I
hate them." Tahiti, once he gets there, is a let-down, "very pretty to
look at," he tells Mary Cannan, "but I don't want to stay, not one
bit. . . . Travel seems to me a splendid lesson in disillusion—chiefly
that." Over the years he gradually learns what he passes on to Brewster in 1927. He's trying to dissuade him from buying a house on
Cyprus, a place Brewster likes to believe close to heavenly, and he
tells him: "*Don't have* ideas about places, just because you're not in
them. All places are tough and terrestrial." "I sort of wish I could go
to the moon," he writes Maria Huxley, in 1929, when Bandol is beginning to disappoint him. There's a tendency, as Clive James has noticed, "to suppose that Lawrence had a firm idea of his spiritual object," to believe that he was rebelling against something so palpable
as "twentieth-century society" or "post-Renaissance Europe," or whatever. "Lawrence was in revolt all right," says James, "but the revolt
encompassed almost everything he knew in the present and nearly all
the past he ever came to know, and this ability to exhaust reality
through intimacy shows up in his travels as in everything else he did."
In short, "Lawrence was in search of, was enraged over the loss of, a
significance this world does not supply and has never supplied." *This
world*: the Christian resonance of James's term is suggestive, implying
as it does the Manichean dualisms Lawrence generates in his travels
and delivers in his travel books.

His first encounter with abroad, in 1912 and 1913, is refracted in *Twilight in Italy*, published in 1916 as a much-revised version of the travel essays he had sent from Italy before the war to the *English Review* and the *Westminster Gazette*. Then he was happy, for he was not merely in his twenties and abroad for the first time; he was enjoying a lovely illicit affair with Frieda. In addition, he was revising "Paul Morel" to turn it into *Sons and Lovers*, a book he knew was a fine one. His cup was running over. "I shall live abroad I think forever," he wrote Edward Garnett. *Twilight in Italy* effuses something of Lawrence's ecstasy and security: If not notable for its order and proportion, it is unforgettable for its lyric richness, visible first in the title. *Twilight in Italy* was a brilliant afterthought. The title Lawrence planned first was *Italian Days*. And he wrote his agent J. B. Pinker: "If Duckworth's hate *Italian Days*—they might like *Italian Hours*—which is detestable, but for some reason, catchy, I believe. At least several women said to me: 'I should *want* to buy a book called *Italian Hours*.' My God, what objectionable things people are!" (The women liked *Italian Hours* because it was familiar, Henry James having used it for his volume of travel sketches in 1909.) But with *Twilight in Italy* Lawrence came up with a title which bears an appropriate burden of meaning. The twilight is evocative of the retreat of the old agrarian Italy as it foolishly but understandably reaches for the industrial future, and its prospects ironically darken. But even more central to Lawrence's total meaning, twilight is also evocative of that condition when the dualisms of light and dark, mind and flesh, time and eternity, achieve reconciliation, the kind of reconciliation Lawrence has become excited about during this first stay abroad. The possibility of reconciling these things will seem more and more difficult as he grows in experience, but now, when he is in love, reconciliation seems imaginable. Before his inner eye he sees joined such tempestuous opposites as himself and Frieda, and in that urgent ecstatic conjunction he finds an analogy and a figure for larger fusions. "I believe in marriage," he asserts as he begins his nine-month encounter with the unfamiliar which will end as *Twilight in Italy*.

He starts his first chapter, "The Crucifix Across the Mountains," by projecting a contrast visible on the road from Munich to northern

Frieda and D. H. Lawrence with Giuseppi (Pino) Orioli in Florence, about 1926. (Harry T. Moore)

Italy, a contrast between Germany and "rosy Italy." The mountain crucifixes are unselfconscious peasant work, but "turning the ridge on the great road to the south, the imperial road to Rome, a decisive change takes place." Now the crucifixes turn elegant, foppish, pretty. "One might imagine the young man had taken up this striking and original position to create a delightful sensation among the ladies." Where the Bavarian peasant crucifixes signify "the true spirit, the desire to convey a religious truth, not a sensational experience," those south of the Brenner overdo "the pathetic turn," presenting the "dead Hyacinth . . . in all his beautiful, dead youth." The fault of the "art" crucifixes is traceable to something like what Eliot will designate five years later as the "dissociation of sensibility." It has been avoided in the Bavarian highlands, "for learning there is a sensuous experience," says Lawrence; there, "the mind is a suffusion of physical heat. . . ." The terms are very near those in which Eliot will celebrate Donne.

Reading *Twilight in Italy* now, after "modernism" has achieved definition through an immense body of work by authors as different as Yeats is from Hemingway, or Hemingway from Eliot, one perceives that regardless of Lawrence's immediately recognizable personal stamp, this travel book is very much of its historical moment. "Authenticity," in the Hemingway sense, is one of the themes: Lawrence's opposing "the true spirit" to a mere "sensational experience" will remind us of Hemingway's distinctions between honest and showy styles of bull-fighting in *Death in the Afternoon* (1932). One large intellectual and emotional atmosphere enfolds writers as different as Yeats, Eliot, Hemingway, and Lawrence, and from this distance what the four are doing seems to look more and more like the same thing. They are mounting a rhetorical critique of industrialism; they are prosecuting a perhaps more richly dramatized and lyricized continuation of the complaints of Ruskin, Arnold, and Morris.

Lawrence's next chapter, "The Spinner and the Monks," is a Yeatsian demonstration inferring from the character of a place that things that should cohere are instead falling apart. The place is Gargnano, on the western shore of Lake Garda, which will be the Lawrences' home from August, 1912, to April, 1913. Lawrence establishes the dualisms necessary to his point: first, two kinds of churches, the churches of the Eagle and the churches of the Dove. The first kind are conspicuous and proud, with lots of visibility and ostentation and ringing of bells; the second kind are "shy and hidden, . . . gathered into a silence of their own." Gargnano offers an example of each. Setting out to visit the Church of San Tomasso, an "eagle church," he finds himself on a terrace at the summit of the town, and as he looks out into the distance, even the mountain across the lake offers itself as an emblem of division: "Across, the heavy mountain crouched along the side of the lake, the upper half brilliantly white, belonging to the sky, the lower half darkened and grim. So, then," he concludes, "that is where heaven and earth are divided." Then he notices a peasant woman spinning on the terrace. "Her world was clear and absolute," he reports after an attempt to converse with her; she was "without consciousness of self." The movement of her fingers is "spontaneous," and her eyes are "candid and open." Once Lawrence has positioned her in the picture, we sense he is going to locate an opposite. "Then, just below me, I saw two monks walking in their garden," heads bent together in "the eagerness of their conversation" just as twilight is falling. They are representative less of spirit or mind than of the neutral dividing line between the poles Lawrence is establishing, mind and busyness on the one hand, primeval gesture and benign vacancy on the other. "It is all so strange and varied," he says,

> the dark-skinned Italians ecstatic in the night and the moon, the blue-eyed old [spinning] woman ecstatic in the busy sunshine, the monks in the garden below, who are supposed to unite both, passing only in the neutrality of the average. Where, then, is the meeting-point: where in mankind is the ecstasy of light and dark together, the supreme transcendence of the afterglow, day hovering in the embrace of the coming night like two angels embracing in the heavens . . . ?

And as he concludes the vision on this Yeatsian note, he projects his own sexual triumph with Frieda as a model for more public metaphysical unions:

> Where is the transcendent knowledge in our hearts, uniting sun and darkness, day and night, spirit and senses? Why do we not know that the two in consummation are one; that each is only part; partial and alone for ever; but that the two in consummation are perfect, beyond the range of loneliness or solitude?

That moment is perhaps the apotheosis of the conception that one travels best with a beloved companion.

So far Lawrence has dramatized the desirability of the unified sensibility. He does this too in the next chapter, "The Lemon Gardens," but here he begins developing the second implication of "twilight," the threat of industrialism to Italy's selfhood. An absurd but likeable aristocrat of Gargnano, who speaks French there because he thinks it grand, solicits Lawrence's help in installing a patent screen-door closer, which, because he is an Italian, he has applied reversed, with the result that his door flies open mechanically instead of properly closing. Lawrence helps him, and then is given a tour of the lemon gardens on the property. Lemon culture, we learn, used to be an important enterprise in Gargnano, but now it is all but defunct. Economics and rational agriculture further south are making it clear that Lake Garda "cannot afford to grow its lemons much longer. The gardens are already many of them in ruins. . . ." The aristocrat wants Italy to use machines, and Lawrence thinks of the ruination machines have wrought in England. It is they which have dissociated people from themselves and from each other, leaving them "teeming swarms of disintegrated human beings seething and perishing rapidly away. . . ."

Division is an inescapable image also in Lawrence's account of the local theater, formerly a church. In "The Theater," he observes that the women all sit on the left, the men on the right, an emblem of the deep dissociation of the sexes that makes courtship and lovemaking acts of hostility. Among the plays Lawrence sees is a ridiculous local *Hamlet*, and as he speculates why he can't stand Hamlet as a character he emphasizes Hamlet's "self-dislike and . . . spirit of disintegration." Indeed, "the whole drama is the tragedy of the convulsed reaction of the mind from the flesh, of the spirit from the self." Lawrence's sense that there is something wrong with the play, that it doesn't work the way it's supposed to, comes close to anticipating Eliot's essay "Hamlet and His Problems," published three years later. In Lawrence's empirical terms: "The close fell flat. The peasants had applauded the whole graveyard scene wildly. But at the end of all they got up and crowded to the doors, as if to hurry away. . . . It was the end of *Amleto*, and I was glad."

After Easter the Lawrences move even higher up the mountain to a house managed by Paolo and Maria Fiori. He is from the mountain, she from the plain, and their difference constitutes a further figure of division. "Paolo and she were the opposite sides of the universe, the light and the dark. . . . She was the flint and he the steel. But in continual striking together they only destroyed each other. The fire was a third thing, belonging to neither of them." Maria's rapacity toward money, which opposes Paolo's "aristocratic" inattention to it, Lawrence makes representative of the gradual transformation of Italy from a natural to an unnatural place, like England: "The earth is annulled," he says, "and money takes its place. The landowner . . . he, too, is annulled. There is now the order of the rich, which supersedes the order of the Signoria. It is passing away from Italy as it has passed from England. The peasant is passing away, the workman is taking his place. . . . And the new order means sorrow for the Italian more even than it has meant for us. But he will have the new order." Both money and the new order are conceived by the northern Italians to be

available in America, and it is there they travel to earn, returning disillusioned. Or they go to Switzerland to work unnaturally in factories,
like the group of anarchists Lawrence meets there.

Of course the author of the poem "How Beastly the Bourgeois Is"
despises Switzerland, and his final chapter, "The Return Journey,"
registers some of the emotional complications of walking from there
south into Italy again. Clive James has said that *Twilight in Italy* is
about "north and south, hill and dale—it is the tentative prototype
for a great sequence of increasingly confident polarities" Lawrence was
to project, "by which Lawrence the traveler was to go on splitting the
world in two until there was nothing left of it but powder." Thus the
opening of Lawrence's last chapter:

> When one walks, one must travel west or south. . . . It is
> a sad and gloomy thing to travel even from Italy into France. But
> it is a joyful thing to walk south to Italy, south and west. . . .
> So whilst I walk through Switzerland, though it is a valley of
> gloom and depression, a light seems to flash out from under every
> footstep. . . .

As he proceeds through Switzerland there are Hemingway moments:
"I went to bed in the silent, wooden house. I had a small bedroom,
clean and wooden and very cold. Outside the stream was rushing.
. . . In the morning I washed in the ice-cold water, and was glad to
set out. . . . I had breakfast and paid my bill. . . ." And there are
Eliot moments, as Lawrence continues to complicate the theme of
time and eternity, locating his meditations at places where the water
rushes "like the sound of Time itself," places where he is aware, like
the author of "The Dry Salvages" thirty years later, of "the rushing of
Time that continues throughout eternity." And there are *Waste Land*
moments too as Lawrence paces the dead mechanical new roads built
by Mussolini's workmen, formerly peasants:

> It is as if the whole social form were breaking down, and the
> human element swarmed within the disintegration, like maggots
> in cheese. The roads, the railways are built, the mines and quar-
> ries are excavated, but the whole organism of life, the social or-
> ganism, is slowly crumbling and caving in, in a kind of process of
> dry rot, most terrifying to see. So that it seems as though we

should be left at last with a great system of roads and railways and industries, and a world of utter chaos seething upon these fabrications: as if we had created a steel framework, and the whole body of society were crumbling and rotting in between. It is most terrifying to realize; and I have always felt this terror upon a new Italian high-road—more there than anywhere.

Lake Como with its miles of villas exemplifies the totally dead result of "mechanical money-pleasure," and Milan, where he finally arrives, is in the grip of the same mechanism. But the situation there is more complicated, and it is on a note of masterful complexity that Lawrence concludes *Twilight in Italy*. It is "place" and its people—here, Milan, swarming with businessmen and "operators"—that persuade him that given sufficient vitality and personal coherence, even the process of disintegration can be "vivid" and "vigorous," devoted, to be sure, to "a multiplicity of mechanical activities," but almost redeemed because these activities "engage the human mind as well as the body." But after this brief ascent to something like hope, Lawrence drops in the final sentence—a *But* is his transition—to the polar view: "But always there was the same purpose stinking in it all, the mechanizing, the perfect mechanizing of human life." And even there, *perfect*, where we might expect a word like *total*, complicates the vision, resolves it to a lifelike twilight.

"Did you see the idiotic and *false* review [of *Twilight in Italy*] in the last *Times Lit. Supplement?*" Lawrence asks Catherine Carswell. "Really, I do object to being treated like that." The reviewer, secure in his non-traveler's naïve epistemology, has assumed a simple fixed reality securely "out there" which it is the literary traveler's business to "describe." Lawrence, he writes, "might have written a good book about Italy if he had been content to take things simply, and to see no more than he really saw. But he preferred the easier course of discovering the Infinite." But what Lawrence really saw in things and places was the Infinite. Like all literary travelers worth reading, he played a spume of imagination upon empirical phenomena, generating subtle emotional states and devising unique psychological forms and structures to contain them. He "felt the urgency to describe the unseen so keenly," says Rebecca West, "that he has rifled the seen of its vocabulary and diverted it to that purpose." To perceive that is to notice that there is no way, ultimately, to distinguish his travel writing from his fiction except by its insistence that it is a "true" account of real, verifiable places.

If *Twilight in Italy* satisfies its curiosity by proceeding south no further than Milan, *Sea and Sardinia* (1921) plunges into the full south of a Mediterranean newly revived in the British consciousness. And in this book we meet a more flexible, even comical, Lawrence, happy to satirize his own outbursts of anger and Frieda's pride and violence. The image of himself Lawrence now projects is that of a small, perky, idealistic, quarrelsome British eccentric abroad, the kind who at home might take to sandals, home-ground flour, spelling reform, and earnest naturism. On this tour he causes tongues to wag by carrying a knapsack instead of the expected suitcase, while Frieda carries the "kitchenino," a sack holding food, drink, and a spirit-stove for eccentric British tea-making in bedrooms and train-compartments. The two went to Sardinia in early January, 1921, spending only twelve days there. If we credit the tradition that Lawrence wrote *Sea and Sardinia* in six weeks without a single note, we can only wonder at the joyous power of a creative memory which, back in Taormina, recalls a vegetable market thus:

> Never have I seen a lovelier show. The intense deep green of spinach seemed to predominate, and out of that came the monuments of curd-white and black-purple cauliflowers: but marvelous cauliflowers, like a flower show, the purple ones intense as great bunches of violets. From this green, white, and purple massing struck out the vivid rose-scarlet and blue-crimson of radishes, large radishes like little turnips in piles. Then the long, slim, grey-purple buds of artichokes, and dangling clusters of dates, and piles of sugar-dusty white figs and sombre looking black figs, and bright burnt figs: basketfuls and basketfuls of figs. A few baskets of almonds, and many huge walnuts. Basket-pans of native raisins. Scarlet peppers like trumpets: magnificent fennels, so white and big and succulent: baskets of new potatoes: scaly kohlrabi: wild asparagus in bunches, yellow-budding sparacelli: big, clean-fleshed carrots: feathery salads with white hearts: long, brown-purple onions, and then of course, pyramids of big oranges, pyramids of pale apples, and baskets of brilliant shiny mandarini, the little tangerine oranges with their green-black

leaves. The green and vivid-colored world of fruit-gleams I have never seen in such splendor as under the market-roof at Cagliari: so raw and gorgeous.

And he remembers even the prices:

And all quite cheap . . . , except potatoes. Potatoes of any sort are 1.40 or 1.50 the kilo.

The *Sea* of the title has largely an alliterative office, and indeed Lawrence's first idea for the title was *Diary of a Trip to Sardinia*. He and Frieda stayed inland, traveling up the center of the island from south to north by train and bus, eating terrible food and noting numerous anomalies like a children's elegant eighteenth-century fancy-dress ball in "strange, stony" Cagliari. In Nuoro they arrive at the moment an immense carnival *passeggio* is in progress, the street filled with women and girls who, on closer inspection, prove to be the young men of the town. Lawrence's prose is attractively loose in *Sea and Sardinia*, alive with comic apostrophe and interjection, and he does not scruple to register simple wonder in language like *it was marvelous, it was curious, it was extraordinary*. He aspires to no consistency of vision. On the boat from Palermo to Cagliari, he first delights in, then execrates the movement of the ship, just as he told his American literary agent that he didn't care what cuts American periodicals made in these materials, and then was distressed when *The Dial* cut freely. In Lawrence's travels, each moment effaces past moments as each place fills his whole awareness, displacing others. In his travel writings, as Clive James says, Lawrence "clearly shows his untroubled ability to uproot all the attributes he has just so triumphantly detected in a place, move them on to the next place, and then condemn the first place for not having them in sufficient strength or never having had them."

Why Sardinia? Lawrence's answer would echo Douglas's, "Why not?" His first sentence—and he never wrote one more typical—implies the theme of the book: "Comes over one an absolute necessity to move." It is moving and freedom and the delight of feeling your own feet in contact with the road that the book is about, not Sardinia, although Lawrence now and then asserts his formal interest in "creative spontaneity" and related primitivistic themes as he celebrates the peasants and their charmingly colored costumes. Early in the morning in the town of Mandas, he wanders outside:

> Wonderful to go out on a frozen road. . . . Wonderful the bluish, cold air, and things standing up in cold distance. . . . I am so glad, on this lonely naked road, I don't know what to do with myself. . . . It is all so familiar to my feet, my very feet in contact, that I am wild as if I had made a discovery.

Limestone is no good to walk on, he says. It is dead, offering "no thrills for the feet." Granite is the thing to make you glad. "It is so live under the feet, it has a deep sparkle of its own." The road may feel familiar to his feet, but something else, something he's read as a boy in the Midlands, is still familiar to his mind: Stevenson's *Travels with a Donkey* (1879). "For my part," Stevenson writes, "I travel not to go anywhere, but to go." Pure Lawrence. And Stevenson goes on in a way that persuades us we're listening to Lawrence: "The great affair is to move; to feel the needs and hitches of our life more clearly; to come down off this feather-bed of civilization, and find the globe granite underfoot and strewn with cutting flints."

Andiamo: let's go. That's what the sword-flourishing heroes shout in the epic marionette theater at Palermo at the end of *Sea and Sardinia.* "What does one care?" Lawrence concludes. "What does one care for precept and mental dictation? Is there not the massive, brilliant outflinging recklessness in the male soul, summed up in the sudden word: *Andiamo!* Andiamo! Let us go on. Andiamo!—let us go hell knows where, but let us go on." *Sea and Sardinia* could be said to celebrate sheer kinesis, and to that degree it is at the center of Lawrence's whole enterprise.

More so, I think, than the unconvincing *Mornings in Mexico,* (1927), which displays a more conventional leaning toward primitivism and the Dark Gods in the insistent programmatic mode that makes *The Plumed Serpent* so unwittingly comic, with its portentous free verse and the "sperm-like water" of the lake. Mexico somehow makes Anglo-Saxon authors go all to pieces, as Jeremy Treglown notices: "Somehow the nearer a writer gets to Mexico the more likely he is to be affected by the literary-perception scrambler which Malcolm Lowry helped to engineer and was ruined by. . . ." Hart Crane would seem to be another case in point. When the writer has installed himself in Mexico, "programs" tend to take over, rhetoric grows flamboy-ant, the Mediterranean spirit vanishes. Anger and frustration mount, and things grow forced and simplified, as in Waugh's *Robbery Under Law* (1939) and Greene's *The Lawless Roads* (1939). Huxley's *Beyond the Mexique Bay* (1934) also seems to betray the difficulty experienced by the civilized mind in coming to grips with Mexico. "A Black Country town," says Huxley, "is a fearful sin of commission." Mexican towns, on the other hand, "are sins of omission. Omission of the mental and the spiritual, of all that is not day-to-day animal living." So uninteresting is this spectacle of *nada* to contemplate and render that Huxley prefers not to. Instead, he turns his eyes from the squalor and emptiness and devotes himself to analyzing ideas about Mexico set forth in prior literary works, ideas about art and the primitive, about literacy, industrialism, and economics. The essay element takes over the book, and we are given prose as unelectric as this:

> Man's biological success was due to the fact that he never specialized. Unfitted by his physique to do any one thing to perfection, he was forced to develop the means for doing everything reasonably well. Civilization reverses the evolutionary process. . . .

Or as preachy as this:

> The general improvement of technical processes has helped to bring about the general deterioration of taste. . . . One fact emerges clearly from the history of art: that whenever men have had the means to be vulgar, they have generally succumbed to the temptation and made use of them.

Paul Theroux's recent *The Old Patagonian Express* (1979) is merely the latest in a long series of failures to make literary travel sense of Mexico. The problem would seem to be the absence there of sufficient resonance and allusion and nuance. In their absence, the writer is left to descant on a hot sun which seems ignorant of Apollo, or to describe the bright colors which have no reference to Tyrian purple or the red of the flowers associated with traditional European elegy. The writer is left to survey the empty desert and, according to his emotional and ideological bias, to emphasize either the beatitude or the horrors of poverty and illiteracy.

Mornings in Mexico is Lawrence's briefest travel book, half the length of *Sea and Sardinia*. In the absence of human interest, he begins with an arch chapter assigning Disney lines to dogs and monkeys and snakes and parrots. Taking a hot walk to a nearby town, he locates the essential character of the place: he finds that it belittles life because it is too large and empty and, cactuslike, malign:

> Nowhere more than in Mexico does human life become isolated, external to its surroundings, and cut off tinily from the environment. Even as you come across the plain to a big city like Guadalajara, and see the twin towers of the cathedral peering around in loneliness like two lost birds side by side on a moor, lifting their white heads to look around in the wilderness, your heart gives a clutch, feeling the pathos, the isolated tininess of human effort. As for building the church with one tower only, it is unthinkable. There must be two towers, to keep each other company in this wilderness world.

The Mexican vagueness, the mañana tendency, is the fruit of this open, characterless environment. Distances are felt only vaguely, orientation is lost, the sense of time has no exactitude, and even the coinage is unreal: "The natives insist on reckoning in invisible coins, coins that don't exist here, like *reales* or *pesetas*. If you buy two eggs for a *real*, you have to pay twelve and a half *centavos*. Since also half a *centavo* doesn't exist, you or the vendor forfeit the non-existent."

Indian market-day in Huayapa, with strenuous bargaining visible everywhere ("A threading together of different wills. It is life") leads Lawrence to a consideration of Indian dance, the heart of the book and an illustration of the principle of inevitable racial and national distinctions at which he finally arrived:

> The Indian way of consciousness is different from and fatal to our way of consciousness. Our way of consciousness is different from and fatal to the Indian. The two ways, the two streams are never to be united. They are not even to be reconciled. There is no bridge, no canal of connection.

(Thus far he has come from his honeymoon hopes for reconciliation in *Twilight in Italy*.) The Indian absence of self-consciousness means that their dance is not "theatrical" in the European way. "They are not representing something, not even playing. It is a soft, subtle *being* something." In the chapter "The Hopi Snake Dance," written earlier in New Mexico, Lawrence reverts to the feeling for exact place that Mexico itself·seems to deaden, and his prose revives, propelled by emphatic prepositions. At the end of the snake dance, "two young priests" gather up armloads of snakes and "run *out of*" the plaza:

> We followed slowly, wondering, towards the western, or north-western edge of the mesa. There the mesa dropped steeply, and a broad trail wound down to the vast hollow of desert brimmed up with strong evening light, up out of which jutted a perspective of sharp rock and further mesas and distant sharp mountains. . . .
>
> Away down the trail, small, dark, naked, rapid figures with arms held close, went the two young men, running swiftly down to the hollow level, and diminishing, running across the hollow towards more stark rocks of the other side.

And so it goes on, with *behind, down, before, into, from, upon, back to,* and *out of,* bringing us to this prepositional perception supporting itself by a metaphor of traveling: "Awareness, wariness, is the first virtue in primitive man's morality. And his awareness must *travel back and forth, back and forth, from* the darkest origins *out to* the brightest edifices of creation."

The final inconclusive chapter contemplates the primitive American experience from the northern Italian shore of the Mediterranean, where, on St. Catherine's Day, Lawrence sips vermouth, back in the world of exact time and significant place. And clarity too: he imagines going to bed back at the ranch in New Mexico after "the dangerous light" has gone out. Where he is now, even "the night is very bright and still." It virtually has "place." The "dark" of the New World Mexicos is a function of their paradoxical antiquity, which the traveler can sense uniquely from the vantage place of the Mediterranean,

> so eternally young, the very symbol of youth! And Italy, so reputedly old, yet for ever so child-like and naïve! Never, never for a moment able to comprehend the wonderful, hoary age of America, the continent of the afterwards.

Lawrence was now growing old himself. Even if he was only 42, his poor "bronchials" warned him that he hadn't long to live. As his time grew short he thought much about his end, although he said nothing directly. In the "grotesque and monumental art of the Aztecs in Mexico," he had seen, as David Cavitch says, "the Indian awe of death." But he knew there were other attitudes and other styles, and in pursuit of them he turned to the tombs and funerary urns of ancient Etruria (northwest of Rome), finding in "the Etruscan preparations for a continuing existence the images, the mood and the strength to express his own passage." In contrast to "the great pyramid places in Mexico," what he chose to discover in an Etruscan necropolis was, he said, "a kind of homeliness and happiness." That, after all his wandering, was what he needed now.

With his American friend Earl Brewster he visited the Etruscan sites for only about a week, in the cold early April of 1927. In June he began the essays that make up *Etruscan Places*, published in 1932 after he had been dead two years. He had originally planned a book of eighty thousand words and twelve essays, but he was too sick to finish more than six. But in the six he managed to lodge and develop his theme, the delicacy, subtlety, and modesty of Etruscan funerary art, and thus the superiority of the Etruscans to the merely powerful Romans who conquered them. (Out of the corner of his eye he is attending to the dynamics of contemporary Italian fascism.) The Etruscans built wooden temples, now vanished except for a few frail terra-cotta pediments; the Romans, stone temples. "Lawrence loved the Etruscans," Huxley reports, "because they built . . . temples which have not survived." Only the painted underground tombs survive, and one reaches them across fields of asphodel, literal asphodel, real flowers. But entering the tombs, one feels none of the creepiness the modern West associates with "the Underworld":

> The tombs seem so easy and friendly, cut out of rock underground. One does not feel oppressed, descending into them. It must be partly owing to the peculiar charm of natural proportion which is in all Etruscan things of the unspoilt, unromanized centuries. There is a simplicity, combined with a most peculiar, freebreasted naturalness and spontaneity, in the shapes and movements of the underworld walls and spaces, that at once reassures the spirit.

The effect of the Etruscan tombs is the opposite of the Western notion of the Inferno, whose imagery adheres to an Eliotic vision Lawrence once experienced of wartime London before he was able to flee. In 1915 he wrote Ottoline Morrell: "London seems to me like some hoary massive underworld, a hoary ponderous inferno. The traffic flows through the rigid grey streets like the rivers of hell through their banks of dry, rocky ash."

The modern archeologist Emeline Richardson has warned against Lawrence's interpretation of the Etruscans: "The reader will believe anything Lawrence says about ancient Etruria and the Etruscans only at his own risk." But the point is that what he says about these remote people and their art which greets death with a quiet joy is less about them than about his own need:

> Death, to the Etruscan, was a pleasant continuance of life, with jewels and wine and flutes playing for the dance. It was neither an ecstasy of bliss, a heaven, nor a purgatory of torment. It was just a natural continuance of the fullness of life.

To enforce his personal identification with the Etruscans, Lawrence depicts himself hassled by a suspicious Fascist "spy-lout," who insists on seeing his passport. Modern "Rome" poses as dangerous a threat to wit and sensitivity as ancient. But the Etruscan spirit is still alive, as in the boy hotel-keeper Albertino in Tarquinia, who, assigning Lawrence and Brewster adjoining rooms, calls attention to the very thin partition between them and feels pleased that "we should not feel lonely nor frightened in the night." No more than the Etruscans felt setting out on "the journey out of life, . . . the death-journey, and the sojourn in the after-life." To Lawrence, educated by the Etruscans, death seems even "the wonder-journey of life," the final travel of man conceived as by nature a traveler. The Etruscan instinct for the imagery of travel surfaces even on their alabaster funerary ash-chests, with their repeated motif of the dead setting off gaily in covered wagons. "This," says Lawrence, "is surely the journey of the soul." He can interpret so boldly because he is writing "a travel book," that is, a book about himself in relation to unfamiliar stimuli. In the process he creates a lively meditation on death fit to be brought next to Sir Thomas Browne's *Urn Burial,* another work which baffles generic classification.

Lawrence's travel books were *ad hoc* and, as we say, "occasional." Yet, because he lived with such intensity of perception and such shrewdness of imagination, his four travel books seem to sketch the stages of his own life. And because the emanations of genius touch on all of human life, his travel books do more than that: they seem to designate and explore the four stages of everyone's life—youth, whose happiness is inseparable from satisfied sensual love; young adulthood, where happiness derives from social awareness and social self-hood; older adulthood, when vacancy and disillusion trouble the spirit; and old age, the moment for elegy and the wish for peace. *Twilight in Italy*, with its fervors about "reconciliation," is about youth; *Sea and Sardinia*, devoted to social comedy, is about young adulthood; *Mornings in Mexico* is about loneliness and disappointment; *Etruscan Places*, about dying happily. For Lawrence to produce in half a normal lifetime, and in a genre sometimes thought literal-minded and trivial, a virtual allegory of a full span of life is an attestation of his self-knowledge and his understanding of life in general. The achievement is no small part of the gift Frieda said "he gave in his writing to his fellow men, . . . the hope of more and more life."

Little pots of excrement for sale

IN modern Mexico, Lawrence reports, "the natives use human excrement for tanning leather. When Bernal Diaz came with Cortés to the great market-place of Mexico City, in Montezuma's day, he saw the little pots of human excrement in rows for sale, and the leather-makers going round sniffing to see which was the best, before they paid for it. It staggered even a fifteenth-century Spaniard." And it staggered and delighted the contemporary readers of Diaz's eyewitness *True History of the Conquest of New Spain* (1632) because they went to books about abroad specifically to encounter wonders like little pots of excrement for sale. The tradition, which is ancient and continuous, flourished in perhaps its purest form in the Middle Ages and the Renaissance. One of its ablest practitioners was "Sir John Mandeville" in the fifteenth century: abroad he reports seeing Amazons, two-headed geese, and a sea with moving waves consisting entirely of sand and gravel, not to mention such anomalous human specimens as people with hounds' heads, people with one central eye, people with horses' hooves, people with feathers, and people whose heads do grow beneath their shoulders. In the seventeenth century the travel book was so commonly regarded as a repository of wonderful lies that in 1630 Captain John Smith felt obliged to modify the word *Travels* with the word *True* when he published *The True Travels, Adventures, and Observations of Captain John Smith*. But anomaly, if not the outright wonderful, remained a constant of geographical imagining. Witness Milton's pleasure in conceiving of the "Chineses" with their remarkable wind-propelled "canie Waggons light," a moment in *Paradise Lost* singled out by Hazlitt as a prime example of *gusto*, or the artistic pleasure of going too far.

With the empirical eighteenth century, a new skepticism began to oppose the old credulity, although the two were still in sufficient tension to supply the requisite atmosphere of comic verisimilitude to Swift's satire on lying travel books in *Gulliver's Travels* (1726). "There is an air of truth about the whole," says "Richard Sympson," the preparer of Gulliver's copy for the press, and shortly after the book appeared Dr. Arbuthnot reported to the Earl of Oxford that "some folks that I know went immediately to their maps to look for Lilliput, and reckoned it a fault in their maps not to have set down." Furthermore, "Lord Scarborough met with a sea captain that knew Gulliver, but he said [Sympson] was mistaken in placing his habitation at Rothereth, for he was sure he lived at Wapping." Despite the rise of "science" in the eighteenth century, the tradition that a travel book retails wonders echoes throughout the age. Thus John Gay's "The Elephant and The Bookseller":

> *The man who with undaunted toils*
> *Sails unknown seas to unknown soils*
> *With various wonders feasts his sight:*
> *What stranger wonders does he write!*

And thus a parodic letter Thomas Gray sent a friend from France. It is a prospectus for a travel book by a typical traveler, and one thing it promises is a description of a French nunnery, "wonderfully adapted to the use of the animals that inhabit it: a short account of them, how they propagate without the help of a male," etc. The anti-clerical comedy operates only because the convention is still vigorous that travel books are identifiable as writings that describe wonders abroad.

Like any genre, the travel book carries about it the marks of its origins, and if the wonders of Antiquity, the Middle Ages, and the Renaissance have, in the full bourgeois age, attenuated to mere anomalies, these anomalies (like the indispensability of human excrement to the manufacture of huaraches) are still a necessary element in travel writing. "The [modern] reader of travelers' tales is a cautious fellow, not easily fooled," says H. M. Tomlinson. "He is never misled by facts which do not assort with his knowledge. But he does love wonders. His faith in dragons, dog-headed men, bearded women, and mermaids is not what it used to be, but he will accept good substitutes." The difference is that the substitutes must now be "scientifically" or "anthropologically" plausible, like the news delivered by Jean Cocteau to the novice traveler Charles Chaplin on a ship bound for the Orient. Cocteau said he had seen in China "a living Buddha, a man about fifty, who had lived his whole life floating in a jar of oil, with just his head exposed from the neck of it. Through years of soaking in oil, his body had remained embryonic and was so soft that one could put a finger through it." This traveler's tale is in the tradition of the comic anomalies retailed to twentieth-century visitors by locals. "A favorite leg-pull of the local experts," Bruce Lockhart reports from the tropics, "was supplying tall stories to travelers, especially if they were writers," and seeing, finally, "their best efforts perpetuated in print." For example, the story of the African chief who, "on seeing the sea for the first time, rushed forward to drink it in the belief that it was crème de menthe." This goes as far as some of the African material suggested by Norman Douglas for Nancy Cunard's anthology Negro. He doesn't know much about Africa, he tells her, but he can supply a few Swiftian travel-book wonders: the one about the "Bimbokulo" cure (comically indecent) for infertility, for example; or the one about the cannibalistic tribe on the shores of "Lake Wyami," whose reputation for cruelty is undeserved, for "they devour only children." This tribe also sponsors singing contests, in which "bad singers are punished by having their fingers cut off, one for each wrong note." By the mid-30's one kind of travel (or "adventure") book, like Halliburton's *The Royal Road to Romance*, was so readily conceived as a vehicle for exaggeration and fake excitement that Peter Fleming sustained a whole lucrative career producing travel books of a debunking tendency, full of passages like this, depicting him as the one honest man in a profession of knaves: "I have—I don't know why, for nobody expects a traveler to tell the truth—some scruples in the matter of veracity. They constitute the gravest possible handicap to a man in my *métier*, but I cannot for the life of me get rid of them."

But the traveler's world is not the ordinary one, for travel itself, even the most commonplace, is an implicit quest for anomaly. Not only literary travelers but mere tourists are drawn by curiosities—if not by the Tower of Qabus, then by the Leaning Tower, or the Watts Towers, or by such abnormalities as Lourdes and Fatima, Venice, the Pyramids, the Taj Mahal, and the mummy (or waxwork—opinions differ) of V. I. Lenin. The widespread understanding that travelers are enticed to a place by its anomalies (or, in modern parlance, its "tourist attractions") is nicely illustrated by Roger J. Welsch's *Tall-Tale Postcards: A Pictorial History* (1976). The high vogue of these comic postcards was from about 1905 to 1915, although some are still being produced, and one was sent me from Los Angeles last year (on verso: "Actual photograph of a California watermelon taken after it was loaded on the wagon"). Their function is to attract tourists by implying the anomalous fecundity of the area, most often California or the American Middle West. To this end, they depict bizarre hypertrophied vegetables or Brobdingnagian fruits reposing on large wagons and railway flat-cars; outsized birds and poultry, often so large as to threaten human life and the balance of nature; immense fish and rabbits large enough to be saddled and ridden; as well as anomalies harder to translate into an invitation to tourists, like monstrous grasshoppers, or chickens with the heads of pretty girls, or the "jackalope," a jack-rabbit equipped with antlers, or fish with fur instead of scales. That these things are "photographed" adds to the comedy, parodying the more sober traveler's assumption that he may not be believed without bringing home photographic evidence. Who otherwise would believe the standard costume of the Jungalis, in Luristan, Persia, who wear jackets

The Jungalis of Luristan, Persia. (Freya Stark)

and capes with fantastic dummy arms causing their coat-sleeves to erect themselves parallel with the horizon, while their real arms are concealed underneath? Lest she not be believed—the whole image suggests the odd usages of the people Gulliver encounters on his third voyage—Freya Stark, in *The Valleys of the Assassins* (1936), provides two photographs of this phenomenon. And that the photographs of the western American anomalies are on postcards designed to be sent home is a way of recognizing that every tourist has it in him to be a travel liar in something of the old way. These postcards, though ostentatiously faked, constitute a modern whimsical "displacement" of the travel wonders of the pre-modern age. They convey something of the same sense that travel should "mean something" by inducting the traveler into experience that is extraordinary.

Did Peter Quennell actually have two extraordinary experiences his first boyish day on the Continent? Or in recalling them many decades later did he assign them to that first day because, as his initial moment of abroad, it was itself "an extraordinarily interesting adventure"? Impossible to tell. But in his memoir *The Marble Foot* (1977) he suggestively allies abroad, anomaly, and memory as he remembers first setting foot in Le Havre:

> There, for the first time, I stepped on to foreign soil, an extraordinarily interesting adventure. I recollect a tall gaunt African, stalking down the quayside wearing long linen robes and a round embroidered cap, while a crowd of ragged street-urchins scurried after him and threw stones. "In his own country," remarked my father, "he is probably a chieftain or prince."

Another anomaly followed closely, this one recalled "more vividly" because it was a "hideous scene":

> A laborer pushing a heavy cart suddenly slipped forward between the shafts he held, and a torrent of bright red blood shot from his open mouth and streamed away across the wet grey cobbles. Looking back, we saw that he had fallen to his knees. I was alarmed and moved, yet not disgusted.

It was soon after this that Quennell decided he must become a writer, producing, in due course, the travel book *A Superficial Journey through Tokyo and Peking*. His analogue here was the cinema: "This book," he writes, "should be regarded as a kind of travel film, a sequence in which image suggests image." And the images, notably, are moments of anomaly. The streets furnish an endless supply of oddities, for "nowhere is the incongruous so little shunned." The dwarf trees and shrubs in his Japanese garden assume the character of pitiful human freaks:

> They banked up in a straggling line along the fence, queer evergreens with five-fingered glossy leaves which throve prodigiously yet always looked dishevelled. . . . More unstable with every inch they gain in height, the weak limbs crack hideously beneath the snow or sag and nod despairingly to the ground. Hapless and disconsolate on stormy days, they are oppressive and close-smelling in the warm weather, when they assume a pose of stringy self-importance and collect dust in the sprawling shadow around their feet.

That has the tone of Huxley and Isherwood and Waugh reacting with horrified fascination to the anomalies of Los Angeles.

There seems something uniquely British here, in this ability to spot anomalies and make a travel book by accumulating a great number of them. There's a supreme confidence that one knows what is "normal" and can gauge an anomaly by its distance from the socially expected. Perhaps, as Hilton Kramer suggests, it's the long British imperialist tradition that supplies the British literary traveler with this confidence. Perhaps it's the homegeneity of British culture, compared, say, with American. Whatever the reason, it is an unquestioned understanding of the norm and an unapologetic loyalty to it that underlies the perceptual and expressive techniques of the British travel book. This confident commitment to a norm can be traced back to the eighteenth-century travel book. Tobias Smollett, in *Travels through France and Italy* (1766), securely possesses a norm which informs him that the French are absurd and that their usages betoken "a general depravity of nature." A favorite anomaly abroad for British travelers in the eighteenth century was the Prince of Palagonia's estate near Palermo, with its 600 grotesque statues. Patrick Brydone, in his *Tour through Sicily and Malta* (1773), undergoes a characteristically British reaction to them. The prince, he says,

> has devoted his whole life to the study of monsters and chimeras, greater and more ridiculous than ever entered into the imagination of the wildest writers of romance or knight-errantry. . . . [Of] all that immense group [of statues], there is not one made to represent any object in nature. It would require a volume to describe the whole, and a sad volume indeed it would make. He has put the heads of men to the bodies of every sort of animal, and the heads of every other animal to the bodies of men. . . . This is a strange species of madness; and it is truly unaccountable that he has not been shut up many years ago.

More even than most anomalies abroad, these sculptures oblige the viewer to consult the idea of the normal in the human figure and physiognomy. Brydone's is a very eighteenth-century work but it resembles many succeeding British travel books in its deployment of anomaly to emphasize by implication the objective existence of a norm. No matter how much one hates it in England, like Douglas and Lawrence, one never shakes off the English sense that abroad is odd, that as an Englishman one knows for certain why it is "unnatural" and therefore interesting to offer little pots of excrement for sale.

EVELYN WAUGH'S MORAL ENTERTAINMENTS

A devotee of the norm is Evelyn Waugh, who once wrote, "The writer's only service to the disintegrated society of today is to create little independent systems of order of his own." Even more than his novels, perhaps, his travel books constitute such independent systems of order. It is there that the anomalies of the actual world, those that can be verified by an empirical observer, are noticed and their comic implications inferred as a way of appreciating what is not anomalous, what is not, as the OED puts it, "irregularity, deviation from the common order." At one moment in 1963, with England, the former homogeneous Anglo-Saxon citadel, sadly changed, the empire lost and the streets swarming with wogs and people calling cakes *gateaux* and shops *boutiques*, he solaced himself by re-reading the unmistakably British travel books of Robert Byron and recalling the pleasure of his own travels between the wars. "It was fun thirty-five years ago," he writes in his diary, "to travel far and in great discomfort to meet people whose entire conception of life and manner of expression was alien. Now one has only to leave one's gates."

It was his divorce from the Hon. Evelyn Gardner, his first wife, in 1930 (followed almost immediately by his reception into the Roman Catholic Church) that turned him into a traveler. He was, we might say, a traveler on the rebound. Before his divorce, he had affected contempt for what at Oxford he called "bloody abroad." Christopher Hollis remembers Waugh's rationalizing his innocence of foreign languages: "He prided himself on his obstinate John Bullishness. . . . He would argue that no one who knew more than one language

could ever memorably express himself in any. . . ." To the Waugh of
the 20's the very idea of the foreign seemed outrageous. Or simply
tiresome. Visiting Athens for a few days in 1927, he writes in his diary:
"The truth is that I do not really like being abroad much. I want to
see as much as I can this holiday and shut myself up for the rest of
my life in the British Isles." (It was a standard attitude among the
upper orders Waugh enjoyed half-ironically imitating. One "senior
survivor from the Edwardian era" was once heard by Jeffrey Amherst
uttering the view that " 'abroad' was a beastly place and all foreigners
buggers"; and Lord Redesdale, Nancy Mitford's father, declared: "I
loathe abroad, nothing could induce me to live there. . . . [As] for
foreigners they are all the same, and they make me sick. . . .") But
seven years after his dispirited moment in Athens, Waugh is making
diary entries like this: "I asked [Hugh Lygon] why he was in London
and he said he was going to Spitzbergen on Saturday. . . . I said I
would go to Spitzbergen too." From 1930 to 1937, when he remarried,
Waugh was largely abroad, and four of his six travel books were written during this period of restlessness and anger at his collapsed marriage. He felt Evelyn Gardner had betrayed him, and his eye for
anomaly abroad operates to imply a scheme of social and personal
order. Such an order betokens a world in which vows are sacred and
promises kept.

But he was still married to "She-Evelyn" in January, 1929, when
his literary agent, A. D. Peters, persuaded a Norwegian shipping line
to include the Waughs on a Mediterranean cruise without charge in
return for a travel book publicizing the experience. In February they
set off on the line's *Stella Polaris*, but by March Waugh's wife had
been stricken with pneumonia and had to be set ashore at Port Said
and placed in the British hospital there while Waugh continued the
cruise alone. By June she was well enough to return to England, and
by July she was well enough to cuckold him with John Heygate, ending the marriage. Waugh's revenge was to write her out of the book
that resulted, *Labels: A Mediterranean Journal* (1930), and to replace
her with a fictional character, "Juliet," married to another fictional
character, "Geoffrey." In the book Juliet is the one taken off the ship
at Port Said. Waugh depicts himself as *A Bachelor Abroad*, which became the title of the American edition.

Such egregious departures from fact invite us to consider for a

Evelyn Waugh with his brother Alec at Villefranche. (Weidenfeld & Nicolson Archives)

moment the relation between travel writing and fiction. For Virginia Woolf, "Truth of fact and truth of fiction are incompatible," and the large university library I use agrees. There, if you are searching out Waugh's works, you will find *Vile Bodies*, with its comic scenes of life on shipboard, in the Literature section, but you will find *Labels*, with its comic scenes of life on shipboard, in the Historical Sciences section, on the stack-floor below, because it is a "travel book." In the same way, *Remote People* is shelved among works on the history of Africa and *Ninety-Two Days* among works of "historical science" focussing on the political and economic actualities of British Guiana and Brazil. The actualities of literature and the behavior of numerous writers of travel books, not to mention the conclusions of Heidegger and Gombrich about the nature of perception and artistic and intellectual representation, oblige us to take a more complicated view of the matter and to notice the unsatisfactoriness of such classifications.

Norman Douglas is one who disagrees both with Woolf and the library classifier. "Truth blends very well with untruth, my dear," he

once told his friend Kenneth Macpherson. His admirable sense of the
illusion all writing is implicated in allows him to perceive how silly it
would be to use the poems of the *Greek Anthology* as "evidence" of
fact, as evidence, say, of the high rate of infant morality in antiquity.
As he says,

> Glancing through these pages, one might infer that [Greek] sur-
> geons were not very skilled as obstetricians. There would seem to
> be an inordinately high percentage of deaths in childhood. I
> think we should be cautious in drawing such deductions,

for elegiac convention determines that the best elegies are likely to be
those lamenting the most regrettable and ironic deaths.

One does not have to go all the way to Anthony Powell's T. T.
Waring, who becomes a renowned travel writer without, actually,
going to the countries he describes—he works up the details by con-
sulting guide-books in libraries—to understand that despite its validat-
ing itself by orientation among public actualities, a travel book is ultimately very difficult to distinguish from a fiction. Sometimes this news
leaks out and pleasantly muddies simple classification. Whoever devised the brief checklist of Orwell's work in the Signet edition of
Animal Farm has designated *Down and Out in Paris and London* a
novel. In a similar way, the melodramatic little structures that determine the action in Greene's *The Lawless Roads* have apparently persuaded the deviser of the cover format of the Penguin edition to
ignore the book's ostensible subject, a literal tour of Mexico, and to
label it fiction. Early readers of William Carlos Williams's novel—as
we would be tempted to call it—*A Voyage to Pagany* (1928), the
result of his first excited, troubled, insecure trip to Europe, considered
it, according to Harry Levin, a travel book. "Is Borrow's *Lavengro*
fiction?" asks Northrop Frye. "Everyman's Library says yes; the
World's Classics put it under 'Travel and Topography.'" Certainly a
suspicion that he is encountering something troublingly adjacent to
fiction will tease a reader who notices that in the most successful travel
books, like Fleming's *Brazilian Adventure* and Byron's *The Road to
Oxiana*, the climax, as in a more-or-less conventional novel, occurs two-
thirds of the way through, after a "rising action" has generated enough
suspense to hold the reader to the book.

One of W. H. Davies's Waring-like moments is instructive. When as a youth he set out for America from Liverpool, he had been told so many vivid things about the U.S.A. and its wonders and oddities— skyscrapers, houses made of wood, the immensity of prairies and deserts, the extremes of weather—that before the ship left the dock he "at once went to the steerage cabin and wrote a full description of the country, that very first evening aboard, telling of my arrival in America, and the difference between the old and the new world." This description, embodied in a letter, almost blew the whole gaff, for the letter was postmarked not New York but Queenstown and bore a British stamp. A more recent deposition is equally instructive, Anthony Burgess's saying, "Probably (as Thomas Pynchon never went to Valletta or Kafka to America) it's best to imagine your own foreign country. I wrote a very good account of Paris before I ever went there. Better than the real thing."

In writing a travel book, "one suppresses much," says Douglas, who had much to suppress; "why not add a little?" Like the character of the Polish count, one of the interesting chance encounters in North Africa Douglas describes in *Fountains in the Sand* (1912). Douglas later admitted he'd simply invented him. Considering the close alliance between travel and lust, it will not astonish us that most suppressions and alterations will be social-sexual, like Alex Waugh's in *Hot Countries,* his book about the South Seas and the Caribbean that appeared the same year as Evelyn's about the Mediterranean. Thirty-two years after the event, he disclosed that the Tahitian love-affair he'd ascribed to someone else, a young British tourist named Ray Girling, was his own. Sometimes suppression dictated by international politics can be suspected. British intelligence was skilled in setting its agents to "traveling" and, by the way, indulging in surreptitious surveying, map-making, photographing, and rumor-planting, especially in the Orient and the Middle East. How many of the between-the-wars travelers were doing intelligence work on the side? One assumes Fleming was, for he was a loyal, philistine, and uncomplicated young man with an impenetrable façade, perfect material for MI-5, as his subsequent success in intelligence work in China and India during World War Two would suggest. And sometimes suppressions, or virtual suppressions, are required less for social or political than for purely artistic reasons. Thus Graham Greene in *Journey Without Maps*: although accompanied by his cousin, he mentions her only three times because

he's decided that her objective presence is irrelevant to his decision
that the journey can be made to serve as a metaphor of *his* early life.
The easy intercourse between fiction and the proclaimed travel book
is visible in Alan Pryce-Jones's *People in the South* (1932). This begins as a clear travel book offering empirical social and political perceptions about South America. But without a hitch it turns into a
collection of three *novellas*, set respectively in Chile, Brazil, and Ecuador, each a palpable fiction with a gripping plot, and each lent verisimilitude, in the Maugham manner, by the author's attestations of
knowing the people concerned. By the end of the book, fact and fiction have become hopelessly and pleasantly confused.

Speaking about historiography, Hayden White has observed that
"The facts do not speak for themselves. . . . [The] historian speaks
for them, speaks on their behalf, and fashions the fragments of the
past into a whole whose integrity is—in its *re*presentation—a purely
discursive one." And he goes on: "We [cannot] relate facts to one another without the aid of some enabling and generically fictional ma-
trix." If here we replace *the historian* with *the travel writer* and *the
past* with *abroad*, we can appreciate the complications facing both
the writers of travel narratives and their readers. Travel writers actually
face the same problem of plausibility that confronts so-called novelists:
the actual must be made to appear believable, or it can't be used. An
anomaly must be credited if it's going to work on the reader. Some
things in real life go too far for either fiction or travel books. An example is the excessively melodramatic "rainless thunderstorm" which,
Sykes reports, actually coincided with his and Byron's long-anticipated
arrival at the shrine in Balkh, Turkestan: "A more dramatic first sight
of a historic monument could hardly be imagined; the bright blue of
the shattered dome lit by flashes and standing out from the deep blue
of the thunderclouds. Yet of this overpowering incident there is no
mention in [*The Road to Oxiana*]." In considering the related problem
of the melodramatizing memory, Isherwood provides an illustration of
Wright Morris's remark that anything processed by memory is fiction.
In 1976 Isherwood recalls a superbly symbolic scene in the lobby of
the Imperial Hotel, Tokyo, 36 years earlier. While waiting for Auden
to show up, he saw, he remembers, "a ceremonious meeting between
two officers in uniform, a Nazi and a Japanese—the Berlin-Tokyo axis
personified. They exchange Nazi salutes, then bow Japanese-style, then

shake hands. They are standing beneath a big chandelier; and, as they greet each other, the chandelier begins to sway." It is an earthquake. Certainly a significant moment. Yet Isherwood's diary for the day makes no mention of an event so useful for a travel writer, and looking back on the memory, he concludes that the episode "is rather too symbolic to be strictly true." What applies to that branch of memoir called the travel book applies as well to another popular prose form, the anti-reactionary school memoir, like Connolly's "A Georgian Boyhood" (1938) or Orwell's "Such, Such Were the Joys" (1952). Of Orwell's account of his misery at St. Cyprian's, Peter Stansky and William Abrahams have this to say: "Written with admirable directness, those straightforward sentences create effortlessly an air of candor and intelligence, and lead one to believe that one is being told everything. In fact, Orwell has written a highly selective and purposive work of art, an 'indictment,' . . . and whatever will lessen the force of the argument has been omitted."

In 1926, when he was 23 years old, still a wretched schoolmaster in Berkshire and not yet a writer, Waugh borrowed from the Times Book Club a curious work by Count Hermann Keyserling, *The Travel Diary of a Philosopher*, published the year before in a translation by J. Holroyd Reece. Reading this "philosophical" account of a trip eastward around the world, from Suez to Ceylon, India, Singapore, China, Hong Kong, and Japan, and then back to Europe through the U.S.A., Waugh would have come upon these words:

> This volume should be read like a novel. Although a certain part consists of elements created in me by the external stimulus of a journey round the world, . . . the book in its entirety represents . . . an inwardly coherent work of fiction, and only those who regard it as such will understand its real meaning. . . . facts as such are never an object to me, but only a means of expressing their significance, which exists independently of them.

When Waugh came to write *Labels* four years later, he behaves as if mindful of the technique implied by Keyserling's warning that "most . . . of my descriptive passages do justice rather to potentialities than to facts." From Keyserling Waugh perhaps derived his first awareness that to be refracted in language fact must be fictionalized. Not totally, of course, and that's what enables us to recognize works belonging to that tributary of fiction narrated in the first person that we call travel books, which validate themselves by public topographical location. Sometimes the common reader's reactions here are a better guide than criticism, whether by Virginia Woolf or others. I am thinking of an annotation in the margin of a university library copy of John Dos Passos's *Journeys Between Wars* (1938). Next to a passage describing the author's wanderings in the desert near Damascus populated by dancing-girls, bandits, and other anomalies from literary romance, a student, "thoughtless" only in the social sense, has written—in ink— "Highly reminiscent of *Vathek*."

Waugh still fancied himself an illustrator when he wrote *Labels*, and the whimsical cartoon he supplied as a frontispiece delivers a twenty-seven-year-old's version of the standard British mythology of the Mediterranean as the Other Place. In the foreground is the rail of the *Stella Polaris*, clearly in the Mediterranean as indicated by the touts and the vendors of beads, carpets, and dirty postcards, from one of which, preferred by a wog, a British woman is recoiling. In the distant background lie the British Isles, just visible through grey and black clouds and a violent rainstorm, flagrantly contrasting with an immense southern sun shining on a bit of Egypt with palm trees. Since Waugh can hardly reveal that the purpose of his Mediterranean trip is to recompense the shipping company by producing a book emphasizing the pleasures of the cruise, he must devise a plausible motive for the journey. This he does by asserting that he wants to see Russia and that the *Stella Polaris* will take him as far as Constantinople. Besides, the London winter has been particularly vile, he says in the conventional I Hate It Here opening: "London was lifeless and numb . . . it was intolerably cold. . . . People shrank . . . from the icy contact of a cocktail glass, like the Duchess of Malfi from the dead hand, and crept stiff as automata from their draughty taxis into the nearest tube railway station, where they stood, pressed together for warmth, coughing and sneezing among the evening papers." A thoroughly nasty scene, we would agree. "So," says Waugh, off he went, first to Paris by plane, then to Monte Carlo by train to join the cruise ship.

Waugh calls his book *Labels*, he says, because "all the places I visited on this trip are already fully labelled." The object is to canvass the entirely familiar Mediterranean to determine "the basis for the reputations these famous places have acquired." His problem is thus to disclose the odd in the familiar, that is, to spot anomalies. The first is his discovery that the "little lavatory" on the plane, into which he drops his air-sickness bag to avoid thoughtlessly projecting it out the window, opens directly over the towns and farms below. Next is his experience at the desk of the Crillon: "I asked for the cheapest bed-room and bathroom they had. There was a very nice little one for 180 francs, said the man at the reception counter. I said I wanted a cheaper one. He said I could have the same room for 140, so I took it." In Paris anomalies of gender are much in evidence, ranging from the "fine, manly girl" in charge of the cloakroom at a Lesbian nightclub, whose skill in "very deftly stealing a silk scarf from an elderly German" he much admires, to the young men at another establishment who sat at the bar "repairing with powderpuff and lipstick the ravages of grenadine and *crême de cacao.*" We recognize that we are entirely within the world of the Waugh comic novel with the following superb anomaly, recounted in Waugh's most solemn, pseudo-objective elegant style; he is arrested by

> the spectacle of a man in the Place Beauveau, who had met with an accident which must, I think, be unique. He was a man of middle age and, to judge by his bowler hat and frock coat, of the official class, and his umbrella had caught alight. I do not know how this can have happened. I passed him in a taxi-cab, and saw him in the center of a small crowd, grasping it still by the handle and holding it at arm's length so that the flames should not scorch him. It was a dry day and the umbrella burnt flamboyantly. I followed the scene as long as I could from the little window in the back of the car, and saw him finally drop the handle and push it, with his foot, into the gutter. It lay there smoking, and the crowd peered at it curiously before moving off. A London crowd would have thought that the best possible joke, but none of the witnesses laughed, and no one to whom I have told this story in England has believed a word of it.

On the train to Monte Carlo Waugh meets "Juliet" and "Geoffrey," she sick with 'flu, he solicitous and frightened about her state. What he registers here is his own one-time emotional investment in his ultimately perfidious wife's pneumonia. Monte Carlo offers an anomaly to correspond with the flaming umbrella in Paris:

There was a heavy [snow]fall every night I was there, sometimes continuing nearly until midday, but always, within an hour of it stopping, every trace had disappeared. The moment that the last flake had fallen there appeared an army of busy little men in blue overalls armed with brooms and hoses and barrows; . . . there was no nonsense about merely tidying the unseemly deposit out of the way; one did not come upon those dirty drifts and banks of snow which survive in odd corners of other places weeks after the thaw. The snow was put into barrows and packed into hampers and taken right away, across the frontier perhaps, or into the sea, but certainly well beyond the imperium of the Casino.

Monaco itself is a notable anomaly, entirely artificial, "just as real as a pavilion at an International Exhibition." But besides its comic uses, it also serves as a port, and next day Waugh boards the *Stella Polaris*.

It is now that he must sing for his supper, and in celebratory tones that will strike most readers as very un-Waugh-like. "She was certainly a very pretty ship," he begins, "almost ostentatiously clean; a magnificent Scandinavian seaman stood at the foot of the gangway. . . ." (That last item recalls Waugh's observing one day, at the Christopher Hollises, "What a pretty gardener you've got!"—which moved Conrad Russell later to comment on Waugh, "I am afraid not quite a gentleman—not quite—not quite.") Waugh notes that earlier, proud of his ambition to resemble a traveler rather than a tourist, he has tended to scorn such things as cruise ships, but how wrong he has been. "As I watched my luggage being lifted on to the *Stella* I knew that it was no use keeping up the pretence any longer." He goes on to rhapsodize over the ship's comfort and civility ("she carried an English doctor and nurse"), and the courtesy and efficiency of the staff, from the noble English-speaking officers to the photographer and hairdresser. He manages even to work in such technical data as the ship's weighing six thousand tons and traveling "smoothly" at fifteen knots. As he proceeds he begins to sound like a company brochure, but one oddly in the past instead of the customary present tense:

There were four [luxurious satinwood-panelled suites] in the ship. . . . The smoking-room, lounge, and writing-rooms were much like those to be found in any modern ship. The decks were exceptionally broad and there was a very comfortable deck bar shel-

tered on three sides from the wind. The dining room . . . could
seat all [200] passengers at once. . . .

And the meals! Waugh descants on their frequency and excellence,
telling us not merely of goulash and steak and onions for breakfast,
but of bouillon on deck almost immediately afterward, followed by the
one o'clock cold buffet "laden with every kind of Scandinavian delica-
tessen, smoked salmon, smoked eels, venison, liver pies, cold game and
meat and fish, sausage, various sorts of salad, eggs in sauces, cold as-
paragus in almost disconcerting profusion." Then there is tea at four,
dinner at seven, and at ten o'clock, with drinks, open-faced sand-
wiches, "caviare and *foie gras* with eggs and anchovies." As if all this
weren't attractive enough, he goes on to emphasize that drinks and
tobacco are sold duty-free. In addition, the purser handles all landing
and shore-excursion arrangements. In short, pure heaven.

Having paid for his passage thus, Waugh is now free to resume
his more normal comic-satiric vision. Naples is funny ("Hullo, yes, you
sir. Good morning. . . . You wanta one nice woman?"). Visiting the
crypt of a church there, he is invited by the little-girl guide to thrust
his face into the abdominal "aperture" of a mummified corpse and
breathe deeply, for his health. Further anomalies succeed as the ship
calls at Messina, Catania, and Haifa, and Waugh hurls himself enthusiastically into the touristic shore excursions. At Port Said he leaves
the ship and spends a month gathering material with the object of
"compiling the first travel book to deal extensively and seriously" with
that sink-hole. His account of the town is like a straight-faced parody
of Forster's *Alexandria: A History and Guide* (1922). He supplies an
absurd "Sketch Map of Port Said" indicating such features as Simon
Arzt's Emporium, the boring canal, and the "Red Lamp District," and
solemnly delivers a complete "guide-book" description of the place as
if its touts and whores were admirable and its sights interesting.
"Juliet" having been released from hospital, she and Geoffrey and
Waugh move on to the Mena House, at Giza, whence they do the
tourist sights of Cairo and environs. Waugh leaves them there—they
go on to Cyprus "in a Khedivial Line ship," he fictionalizes—and returns to Port Said to board a P & O for Malta. His money, he says, has
run low. If he is going to make it home conveniently, he must wangle
free hotel accommodation on Malta. He writes the two leading hotels

there, offering a puff in his eventual travel book for a free room. Embarrassingly, when he arrives he is met at the dock by the touts of both hotels. "Each held in his hand a duplicate letter from me, asking for accommodation." He chooses one of them, and when the representative of the other hotel "fluttered my letter petulantly before my eyes," Waugh explained, "shocked at [his] own duplicity": "A forgery. . . . I am afraid that you have been deluded by a palpable forgery."

Waugh likes Malta, and it is while there that he enacts one of his most engaging exposures—the book is full of them—of his own gullibility and ineptitude. He has bought a small guide-book, *Walks in Malta*, by F. Weston, which he admires

> not only for the variety of information it supplied, but for the amusing Boy-Scout game it made of sight-seeing. "Turning sharply to your left you will notice . . .", Mr. Weston prefaces his comments, and there follows a minute record of detailed observation. On one occasion, when carrying his book, I landed at the Senglea quay, taking it for Vittoriosa, and walked on for some time in the wrong town, hotly following false clues and identifying "windows with fine old mouldings," "partially defaced escutcheons," "interesting iron-work balustrades," etc., for nearly quarter of a mile, until a clearly non-existent cathedral brought me up sharp to the realization of my mistake.

By a remarkable coincidence the *Stella Polaris*, on her next cruise, calls at Malta just as Waugh has had enough of the island, and he achieves a berth and climbs aboard, bound for Crete, Constantinople, Athens, Corfu, Venice, and the Dalmatian Coast. He is outspokenly unimpressed by Santa Sophia, perhaps his way of paying back Robert Byron for his contumelies about the art and usages of the Roman church. He is ravished by Corfu and overwhelmed by the richness of the most anomalous spot in Europe, trafficless Venice (which once, it is said, prompted Robert Benchley to wire home: STREETS FULL OF WATER. ADVISE). The cruise takes him back around Italy, and the spectacle of Etna at sunset provokes this well-known travesty of the "I-do-not-think-I-shall-ever-forget" travel-book turn:

> I do not think I shall ever forget the sight of Etna at sunset;
> the mountain almost invisible in a blur of pastel grey, glowing on

the top and then repeating its shape, as though reflected, in a wisp of grey smoke, with the whole horizon behind radiant with pink light, fading gently into a grey pastel sky. Nothing I have ever seen in Art or Nature was quite so revolting.

(Cf. "I shall never forget the first night's experience, when the cattle were brought to the ship in a train."—W. H. Davies, *The Autobiography of a Super-Tramp*, 1908; "I shall never forget my first voyage."—H. M. Tomlinson, "Hints for Those About to Travel," 1923; "I do not think I shall lightly forget the Taj Mahal."—Stella Benson, *The Little World*, 1925; "I shall never forget my first sight of the Queen of Roumania."—Beverley Nichols, *Twenty-Five*, 1926; and perhaps most apposite, a sentence produced by the man Waugh and his friends called Baldhead: "I shall never forget my first sight of Tahiti."—Alec Waugh, *Hot Countries*, 1930.)

At Monaco Waugh's cruise officially ends, but he stays aboard while the ship, on its way to Norway, conveys him and a new group of tourists to Barcelona. There he gratifies his taste for the fantastic viewed against a norm by contemplating the architecture of Gaudi, the apotheosis of Art Nouveau. Like Byron admiring Persian "colored architecture" or delighting in the Russian "bulbosities," Waugh is moved to deep pleasure by anomalies like a roof "colored peacock-blue and built in undulations," and by eccentricities like the entrance to Güell Park, "a double flight of china-mosaic steps, between curving machiolated walls, decorated in a gay check pattern of colored tiles. . . ." And faced with Gaudi's unfinished Church of the Holy Family, looking like the largest dribble-castle in the world, he is almost equally enthusiastic, saying, "I feel it would be a graceful action on the part of someone who was a little wrong in the head to pay for its completion." On to Mallorca, Algiers, Malaga, and Gibraltar, which, with its shabby pseudo-Englishness, revives Waugh's I Hate It Here mood. Then Seville, "certainly a town for a prolonged visit. . . . This year, or next year, or later, I shall go back there." In Lisbon, the Manueline traceries of the sixteenth-century architecture also excite him with their eccentric comedy.

But the cruise can't last forever, and there comes a night when next morning he must land at Harwich and resume real life. Few can return from prolonged traveling without the urge to perform some

ritual to assist re-entry. Waugh's ritual gesture, because it is enacted
by a young man who doesn't yet know enough of life and death, fulfillment and loss, to understand fully what he's doing, seems oddly
touching. He is marking the end of something that can never be repeated, but he doesn't seem to know that's what he's doing. This last
evening, he says, some of the officers and the few remaining Scandinavian passengers held a small party:

> We drank each other's health and exchanged invitations to visit
> each other in our countries. After a time I went out from the
> brightly lighted cabin on to the dark boat-deck. For the moment
> the night was clear and starry. I was carrying my champagne glass
> in my hand, and for no good reason that I can now think of, I
> threw it out over the side, watched it hover for a moment in the
> air as it lost momentum and was caught by the wind, then saw it
> flutter and tumble into the swirl of water. This gesture, partly, I
> suppose, because it was of its own moment, spontaneous and
> made quite alone, in the dark, has become oddly important to
> me, and bound up with the turgid, indefinite feelings of home-
> coming.

Perfectly staged. "It is Margaret you mourn for."

It is good to be home after all, he finds, for home is the norm,
which one occupies more richly for the experience of anomaly. The
known limits of familiar boundaries are psychologically useful. "There
still remains a certain uncontaminated glory in the fact of race, in the
very limits and circumscription of language and territorial boundary;
so that one does not feel lost and isolated and self-sufficient." Par-
ticipating in this glory of normality is what exiles deprive themselves
of, "those exiles, of infinitely admirable capacities, who . . . have
made their home outside the country of their birth." I think he has
Robert Graves in mind. Earlier, giving an account of the deck games
on the *Stella Polaris*, he has alluded to Graves unsympathetically, saying, "I should really like, in the manner of *Goodbye to All That*, to fill
in some pages at this point with descriptions of my own athletic
prowess." It is Waugh's way of implying an association between a
penchant for un-normal self-praise and an impulse toward angry, self-
gratulatory exile. Exiles seem to confess "a deficiency in that whole
cycle of rich experience which lies outside personal peculiarities and

individual emotion." (That sounds like Eliot again.) Exiles have not considered sufficiently the way anomalies assert a norm.

Anyone who has derived a view of Waugh's character either from his diaries or from biographies like Christopher Sykes's is likely to feel astonishment when confronted by the charming, kind, sympathetic persona he projects in his travel books. A few months before his Mediterranean tour the "real" Waugh makes diary entries like these. Of a London cocktail party: "Alec Waugh was there and other dim hot people." Of guests at a dinner party: "Charles Drage with his wife. She is an albino with a mind like a damp biscuit." Of Huxley's *Point Counter Point*: "Infinitely long. . . . It might have been written by an educated Alec Waugh." Asked once by John Freeman why he lived in the country, he answered, "To get away from people like you." Sykes records Waugh's behavior at a dinner party including "a well-known American theatrical producer and his wife." She said, "Oh Mr. Waugh, I have just been reading your new book *Brideshead Revisited*, and I think it's one of the best books I have ever read." Waugh replied: "I thought it was good myself, but now that I know that a vulgar, common American woman like yourself admires it, I am not so sure." But the Waugh depicted in *Labels* is incapable of that sort of thing. He is notably nice: tolerant and benign, decent to his fellow tourists on the ship, happy to find a redeeming merit in everyone, pleased to observe the happiness of others. Reviewing *Labels* in *The Bystander*, Ralph Straus was surprised to find it so little impertinent, "for I have heard Evelyn Waugh described as the second most impertinent young man in London." (Was Brian Howard the first?)

Peter Quennell, noting that the only evidence of Waugh's benignity on his travels is presented by Waugh himself, thinks his character abroad really the same as his character at home—abrasive, difficult, sometimes cruel. I don't entirely agree. While it is true that any travel book requires generically that the narrator depict himself as likable, it would seem that Waugh did try on a different personality abroad. As he confesses in his diary, "I become slightly hypocritical as soon as I am away from my own background, adopting an unfamiliar manner of speech and code of judgments." Abroad, he permits himself a behavior much less rigidly doctrinaire than at home. For example: at Goa once he meets "Youth with insolent-pansy manner named Hall. I took a great dislike to him." The next day's diary entry goes on:

"Hall . . . invited me to join him after dinner. I did so and found him most engaging." I think we will not be wrong to conclude that one reason Waugh enjoyed traveling was the opportunity it provided for being someone else, for escaping the censorious character he'd contrived for use in London and at country house-parties. He traveled to enjoy an activity he did not much permit himself at home, liking people. It's perhaps significant that the period of his travels and his travel writing coincides with his religious conversion, and we may believe that in preparation for his reception into the Church he and Father D'Arcy had some long talks about charity and Waugh's deficiencies there.

Cruel mockery of tourists—often American—is an important conventional element of the British travel book. The absence of this element is one of the things that makes *Labels* so attractive, in contrast to, say, Huxley's *The Olive Tree* (1936), which, in the essay "In a Tunisian Oasis," registers a supercilious contempt towards a group of "professional tourists" depicted losing their topees to the Tunisian wind. I find this difference between Huxley and Waugh ironic, since it is not Waugh but Huxley, with his blindness, his spiritual claims and ambitions, his pacifism, his martyrdom by the burning of his house and the death of his wife, who is often proposed by his biographers and appreciators as a candidate for sainthood. Actually, he is cruel compared with Waugh, who, in the great tradition of English satire, withholds his public attacks from those whose only deficiency is an inborn weakness of mind. He satirizes only characteristics that people can help.

Waugh depicts himself as charming again in his next travel book, *Remote People* (1931), titled—misleadingly—*They Were Still Dancing* for the American edition the next year. That title is simply the first four words and refers not to the Abyssinians and other Africans of the book, but to a silly European couple who continued dancing on deck after the band had quit as the French ship arrives at Djibouti, French Somaliland. It is 1930 and the coronation of Haile Selassie is about to take place in Addis Ababa. Waugh achieved a commission from *The Graphic* to cover the proceedings, and he perceived that a whole travel book about Africa might do well, exploiting the current interest back home in everything Black. This vogue had developed in the mid-20's and would peak in the mid-30's. It had already generated such works

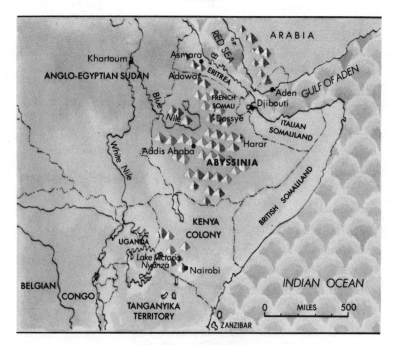

WAUGH'S EAST AFRICA

as Ronald Firbank's *Prancing Nigger* and Carl van Vechten's *Nigger Heaven*, and later would help bring forth Geoffrey Gorer's *Africa Dances*, Nancy Cunard's *Negro: An Anthology*, and Waugh's own *Black Mischief*. (Nancy Cunard's Black lover Henry Crowder was indispensable at any party aiming at style.) London and Paris delighted in the musical entertainers the Blackbirds, in Josephine Baker and ultimately in Paul Robeson. Some people thought the Prince of Wales a bit too intimate with Florence Mills, the delicious star of the Blackbirds. Alec Waugh originally wanted to title his travel book *The Colored* (instead of *Hot*) *Countries* to help it ride the wave. A book by J. G. Williams and H. J. May, *I Am Black: The Story of Shabala*, was once thought central enough to be listed in the Oxford University Press's *Annals of English Literature*. Even Bernard Shaw joined the movement, asserting in *The Adventures of the Black Girl in Her Search for God* that "the next great civilization will be a black one."

The Abyssinian coronation attracted, anomalously, diplomatic delegations from Europe's major powers, hot for commercial concessions, as well as scores of journalists and newsreel men ordered to send back images of Black "color." The grave disparity between the pseudo-event and its journalistic promotion supplies much of Waugh's comedy, and the unconscious Abyssinian parody of the most pretentious European usages in the midst of its own squalor supplies the rest. For Waugh, it was "a preposterous *Alice in Wonderland* fortnight." The coronation itself provided numerous anomalies arising from the behavior of both the royal participants and their guests. In the high ecclesiastical setting of the ceremony, "one lady had stuck an American flag in the top of her sun-helmet," and as the ceremony dragged on, the faces of the diplomats "were set and strained, their attitudes inelegant." Where had Waugh seen that look before? "In crowded railway carriages, at dawn, between Avignon and Marseilles." The coronation itself is followed by six comic days of unveilings, military reviews, and receptions. "There was the opening of a museum . . . , containing examples of native craftsmanship," including "a huge, hollow stone which an Abyssinian saint had worn as a hat." And there are comical cross-purposes and disappointments when Waugh visits a local monastery with Professor Thomas Whittemore from the U.S.A. The library of the monastery is reputed to hold hitherto unseen treasures.

> The Professor . . . asked whether we might visit the library of which the world stood in awe. . . . The Abuna produced a small key from his pocket and directed one of the priests to open the cupboard. They brought out five or six bundles wrapped in silk shawls and, placing them with great care on the table, drew back the door curtain to admit a shaft of white light. The Abuna lifted the corners one after another and revealed two pieces of board clumsily hinged together in the form of a diptych. Professor W. kissed them eagerly; they were then opened, revealing two colored lithographs, apparently cut from a religious almanac printed in Germany some time towards the end of the last century, representing the Crucifixion and the Assumption, pasted on to the inner surfaces of the wood. The Professor was clearly a little taken aback. "Dear, dear, how remarkably ugly they are," he remarked as he bent down to kiss them.

After Abyssinia, Waugh moves on to Aden, and thence to Zanzibar, Nairobi, Kenya, and Uganda. Anomalies aplenty here, not least the rhetoric customary in the Aden troop of Boy Scouts, to a meeting of which the British scoutmaster invites Waugh.

> Tests were in progress for the tenderfoot and other badges. . . . "We generally let them pass after the third or fourth attempt," the scoutmaster explained. "It discourages them to fail too often."

A Somali boy is examined in the Scout Law. "He knew it all by heart perfectly":

> "First scoot law a scoot's honor iss to be trust second scoot law . . ." et cetera, in one breath.
>
> "Very good, Abdul. Now tell me what does 'thrifty' mean?"
> "Trifty min?"
> "Yes, what do you mean, when you say a scout is thrifty?"
> "I min a scoot hass no money."
> "Well, that's more or less right. What does 'clean' mean?"
> "Clin min?"
> "You said just now a scout is clean in thought, word, and deed."
> "Yis, scoot is clin."
> "Well, what do you mean by that?"
> "I min tought, worden deed."
> "Yes, well, what do you mean by clean?"
> Both parties in this dialogue seemed to be losing confidence in the other's intelligence.
> "I min the tenth scoot law."
> A pause during which the boy stood first on one black leg, then on the other, gazing patiently into the sun.
> "All right, Abdul. That'll do."
> "Pass, sahib?"
> "Yes, yes."
> An enormous smile broke across his small face, and away he went capering across the parade ground. . . .
> "Of course it isn't quite like dealing with English boys," said the scoutmaster. . . .

Another useful anomaly is the attempt of the British residents of Kenya to duplicate life at home in every particular. Thus

a baronial hall straight from Queen Victoria's Scottish Highlands
—an open fire of logs and peat with carved-stone chimney-piece,
heads of game, the portraits of prize cattle, guns, golf-clubs, fish-
ing-tackle, and folded newspapers—sherry is brought in, but, instead of a waistcoated British footman, a barefooted Kikuyu boy
in white gown and red jacket. A typical English meadow of deep
grass; model cowsheds in the background; a pedigree Ayrshire
bull scratching his back on the gatepost; but, instead of rabbits,
a company of monkeys scutter away at our approach; and, instead
of a smocked yokel, a Masai herdsman draped in a blanket, his
hair plaited into a dozen dyed pigtails.

Five months later Waugh is back in London, and the final anomaly of
Remote People makes a comic allusion to what he's experienced in
Africa. On his first night back, friends take him to a newly stylish,
awful supper-restaurant. "A Negro in fine evening-clothes was at the
piano, singing. Afterwards, when he went away, people fluttered their
hands at him and tried to catch his eye. He bestowed a few patronizing nods. Someone yelled, 'He's losing his figure.' . . . I paid the bill
in yellow African gold. It seemed just tribute from the weaker races to
their mentors."

As that irony suggests, the "travel" attitude projected in *Remote
People* is, for all the satire, much more affectionate than one might
expect. To compare the account of the journey in Waugh's diary with
the finished product is to appreciate the way the book mitigates asperities, transforming emotions that begin in private annoyance into an
affectionate wonder. And there are the usual suppressions. Very many
things that happened in Addis Abada can never appear in a travel
book, like one incident Waugh records in his diary: "——— arrived
with the [British] Mission, dined with me Thursday, asked me to beat
him." Some outcrops of personal abrasiveness remain in the diary:
"Sacked my servants." "Taxi-driver charged 18 thalers. Wrangle.
Lost." And so do numerous unkind notations inappropriate to the
amiable character of the traveling Waugh: "American cinema men in
green suits"; "odious children"; "odious people called Bethel"; "odious
people at table"; "hideous Miss Guest"; "Got very drunk in the evening"; "Natives savage"; "Dirty little hotel with odious patrons." None
of this appears in the book, where the public attitude is notably un-
snobbish and unpriggish, unlike Waugh's definition there of a *prig* as

"someone who judges people by his own rather than by their standards; criticism only becomes useful when it can show people where
their own principles are in conflict." A reader of the diary might agree
with Alan Pryce-Jones, who reviewed *Remote People* in the *Week-End
Review*, that "Mr. Waugh's principal literary emotion is discontent."
But a reader of the book would more accurately report that Mr.
Waugh's principal literary emotion is wonder. As he transforms diary
into travel book, he develops also a wondering image of himself as a
comic character, a pretend little-Englander and a pretend snob. His
capacity to be both inside himself and outside is remarkable. He is
both actor and critic. Once, crossing the Atlantic first-class, he went
mock-slumming with a friend and found himself outside the second-
class dining saloon. He said: "Can't you just *smell* the poverty?" That
seems to me quintessential Waugh, and any account of him and his
work inattentive to such moments of ironic self-satire is likely to under-
estimate the complexity and difficulty of his achievement.

Comedy results when he installs himself in anomalous contexts.
It was the anomaly of so civilized and sophisticated a creature plung-
ing three hundred miles into the savage bush of British Guiana that
formed the substance of his next journey. Like his fellow convert
Graham Greene's immersion a year later in the wilds of Sierra Leone
and Liberia, Waugh's journey without maps seems all but penitential.
"Heart of lead," he writes in his diary as his ship leaves London. On
board he reads Maritain and, in Guiana, Aquinas. The diary entries
read like the memoirs of a flagellant: "Sat among ants for an hour";
"great heat and suffering from thirst"; "woke at dawn dead tired";
"slung hammock in open and spent cold night with little sleep"; "very
faint with hunger"; "very tired and footsore. Slept in open shelter, very
cold and damp. Badly bitten by fleas and found feet full of jiggers";
"Nail came off toe Sunday." But the narrative of *Ninety-Two Days:
The Account of a Tropical Journey through British Guiana and Part
of Brazil* (1934) is without self-pity, and details like these are largely
subdued by the comic design of the book, which becomes a study of
the dynamics of frustration and disillusion and thus an oblique moral
commentary on the weakness of what Samuel Johnson called "so little
a creature as man."

Peter Fleming was just back from Brazil when Waugh talked
with him in December, 1932, about traveling—or better, exploring—

WAUGH'S BOA VISTA COUNTRY

there. (*Brazilian Adventure* was not published until three months after Waugh returned.) He set off that month, and returned six months later, in May, 1933. His plan was to proceed on foot and horseback from Georgetown, British Guiana, inland to Boa Vista, Brazil, and from there to travel south down the Rio Branco and the Rio Negro to Manaos—a total distance of over seven hundred miles. The plan pivoted crucially on some sort of boat being available at Boa Vista. Guiana was about as rugged then as it is now, re-named Guyana, and even in the capital, Georgetown, Waugh found as few amenities as forty-five years later the reporters found who came to wonder at the mad, murderous proceedings at "Jonestown." (I think Waugh would not have been so surprised.) After ten days of assembling stores and giving and countermanding orders for nonexistent horses, guides, and boats, Waugh set off by train to New Amsterdam, then tramped up-river and through the bush to Kurupukari, covering about 15 miles a day while being tormented by vampire bats, horseflies, ants, and snakes. For this part of the journey he was attended by the non-stop talker "Mr. Bain," an incoherent but insistent authority on all subjects:

> There was one insect which buzzed in a particular manner. "Listen," said Mr. Bain one day, "that is most interesting. It is what we call the 'six o'clock beetle,' because he always makes that noise at exactly six o'clock."
> "But it is now a quarter past four."
> "Yes, that is what is so interesting."

The cuisine consisted of the carbohydrate of the country, *farine*, dried bits of cassava root; and *tasso*, salted dried meat. "I can conceive," says Waugh, "it might be possible for a newcomer to stomach a little *farine* with a rich and aromatic stew; or a little *tasso* with plenty of fresh vegetables and bread. The food of the savannah is *farine* and *tasso* and nothing else."

One of Waugh's stops is at the ranch of the elderly Mr. Christie, crazed by a lifetime of lonely Fundamentalism. "He told me he was at work on a translation of the scriptures into Macushi, 'but I have to change and omit a great deal. There is so much I do not agree with. . . .'" Although it is not quite true to say, even in the face of *Black Mischief*, *A Handful of Dust*, and *Scoop*, that Waugh traveled in order to make novels, it is Mr. Christie whom he transmutes into Mr. Todd in *A Handful of Dust*, the man who makes Tony Last read Dickens aloud for the rest of his life. Throughout his painful and absurd journey Waugh had been sustained by the belief that he is heading for something luscious, the small city of Boa Vista (lovely view, in Portuguese), which lies two hundred miles past Kurupukari. The way there is through virtually impenetrable jungle. Mr. Bain has not been there, but loves to descant on its beauty, sophistication, and importance. "Everyone," says Waugh, "had spoken of it as a town of dazzling attraction."

> Whatever I had looked for in vain at Figuiredo's store was, he told me, procurable at "Boa Vist';" Mr. Daguar had extolled its modernity and luxury—electric light, cafés, fine buildings, women, politics, murders. Mr. Bain had told of the fast motor launches, plying constantly between there and Manaos. In the discomfort

of the journey there, I had looked forward to the soft living of
Boa Vista, feeling that these asperities were, in fact, a suitable
contrast, preparing my sense for a fuller appreciation of the good
things in store.

"So confident" was he that even his first sight of Boa Vista from
across the river—apparently a "ramshackle huddle of buildings on the
further bank"—inspired no emotion but "delight and expectation."

The illusion evaporates instantly. The first locals he meets stare
at him "with an air that I came to recognize as characteristic of Boa
Vista, . . . conveying . . . in equal degrees contempt, suspicion, and
the suggestion that only listlessness kept them from active insult."
Waugh has "heard" that there are two excellent hotels. No more.
"That was in the days of the Company," he is told.

> "Then where do strangers stay?"
> "Strangers do not come to Boa Vist'."

He makes his way to the only place to stay, the decrepit Benedictine
mission, and as he trudges through the town, it is revealed in all its
actuality. The main street

> was very broad, composed of hard, uneven mud, cracked into
> wide fissures in all directions and scored by several dry gullies.
> On either side was a row of single-storied, white-washed mud
> houses with tiled roofs; at each doorstep sat one or more of the
> citizens staring . . . with eyes that were insolent, hostile and
> apathetic; a few naked children rolled about at their feet. The
> remains of an overhead electric cable hung loose from a row of
> crazy posts, or lay in coils and loops about the gutter.

The Benedictines accept Waugh's surprise arrival "with resignation,"
and at first there is some talk of a boat for Manaos.

> "Will it be a question of days or weeks?"
> "A question of weeks or months."

Further exploration of Boa Vista confirms Waugh's first perceptions: it is the Terrible Place of the British traveler's nightmare, in the

tradition of Byron's Phari (Tibet), with its seven-foot-wide streets mere "runnels of filth," or his Baghdad, merging into its world of mud; or Lawrence's Mexican town Ixtlahuacan, in *The Plumed Serpent*, with its "smashed pavements, where every moment you might twist your ankle or break your leg"; or Goyaz and Marabá, in Fleming's *Brazilian Adventure*, or Dzunchia, in *News from Tartary*. The Terrible Place is a staple in between-the-wars British travel writing because it offers an opportunity for the traveler to luxuriate in a precious image of its antithesis, which is always Continental in its fixtures and usually French or at least Mediterranean, and thus part of the I Hate It Here response to England and to modern industrialism. Waugh's Boa Vista is so disheartening because before arrival he has fantasized an image of urban delight, "the city I had had in mind," with

> shady boulevards; kiosks for flowers and cigars and illustrated papers; the hotel terrace and the cafés; the baroque church built by seventeenth-century missionaries; the bastions of the old fort; the bandstand in the square, standing amidst fountains and flowering shrubs; the soft, slightly swaggering citizens, some uniformed and spurred, others with Southern elegance twirling little canes, bowing from the waist and raising bowler hats, flicking with white gloves indiscernible particles of dust from their white linen spats; dark beauties languorous on balconies, or glancing over fans at the café tables.

It resembles the ideal, pre-industrial places of such travelers as Auden, whose "Eden," as he calls it, is a similar retrograde small provincial city, "French" about a century and a half ago, with "no decimal system" and "Roman Catholic in an easygoing Mediterranean sort of way." It has no oil, no airplanes or automobiles; there are frequent religious processions and outdoor band concerts, and the public statues are "confined to famous defunct chefs." The ideal place of J. B. Priestley is similar, though resembling more "the capital of a tiny German dukedom, round about 1830." His "secret dream," he confesses, is

> a place with the dignity and style of a city, but reasonably small and clean, with genuine country only half an hour's walk from its center, its single but superb theater, its opera house, its symphony orchestra, its good restaurant always filled with friends.

> One little civilized place full of persons, with no nameless mob,
> no huge machinery of publicity, no glaring metropolis. . . .
> Everything small but of fine quality, cozily within reach, and
> means and ends in sight of each other. . . .

The ideal place of Lawrence is more fantastic, suggesting Wallace
Stevens at his most rococo, but it equally constitutes a critique of
uniform socialized industrial society. From Switzerland he asks a friend
what it's like in Ireland, where he's never been:

> Do the policemen wear orange trousers and goose-feathers: no,
> orange is Belfast: green: green and pink policemen, and money
> made of glass, and all motor-cars pale pink by law? . . . and the
> pavements with poems let in in little white pebbles . . . and
> ladies at night walking with their white bosoms lit up with a
> necklace of tiny electric lights . . . and nuns in scarlet. . . .

An unbridgeable distance extends between such visions of ideal des-
tinations and the actual Boa Vista, with its half dozen "seedy little
shops," its "open schoolhouse where a fever-stricken teacher could be
observed monotonously haranguing a huge class of listless little boys,"
and its two "cafés," at one of which, the fancier, one could purchase
farine, bananas, fish, and "warm and expensive beer." Clearly a place
to leave as soon as possible. While waiting interminably for the non-
existent boat, Waugh suffers agonies of boredom and horror, bravely
borne. He finally decides simply to return to Guiana, but this requires
horses, which don't seem to exist either. Repeatedly he says goodbye
to the increasingly unfriendly Benedictines and sets out, only to return ignominiously when his arrangements break down. He finally
manages his escape and weeks later arrives back in Georgetown by a
new and terrible route.

Waugh's experience of Boa Vista is the low point, but it is made
the high point of the book. It gave him the opportunity to exercise
himself in the first principle of the successful travel book—never be
boring, no matter how boring the experience. Reviewing Fleming's
News from Tartary three years later, he suggests what he has learned
in Brazil. "The very stuff of travel," he says, is not "the dramatic inci-
dents" but rather "the day to day routine, . . . the delays and uncer-
tainties, the minor vexations—whole drab, uneventful patches of sheer

hard work and discontent." The way to make such experience fascinating for the reader is through sheer style, "letting phrase engender phrase," as he puts it in *Remote People*. Waugh's style—precise, elegant, always controlled, Latinate, "Roman" in the British public-school way—supplies a constant ground-bass or norm implying a measure for outrages and anomalies. As Jonathan Raban has said of this style, it "affords a way of being faithful to an off-key world of wild moral and social disparities without losing authority or poise." (Someone is sure to ask why I've not dealt with the travel books of Freya Stark, and I will have to answer that to write a distinguished travel book you have to be equally interested in (1) the travel and (2) the writing. In Stark's works, admirable as the travel has been, the dimension of delight in language and disposition, in all the literary contrivances, isn't there. Her reward is due not from criticism but from the Royal Geographical Society, which has properly conferred upon her medals and grants. She could never say, as Waugh does, "I regard writing . . . as an exercise in the use of language, and with this I am obsessed." She could never say, as Waugh does, "Style alone can keep [the writer] from being bored with his own work.")

But Waugh's admirable commitment to the art of the travel book begins to attenuate with *Waugh in Abyssinia* (1936), where we are given a foretaste of the gradual corruption of the genre as the 30's begin to gear themselves for war, first in Abyssinia (Waugh disclaimed responsibility for the unpleasant pun of his title, more conspicuous to British than to American readers), then in Spain, and finally in all Europe and in all Asia. As the bourgeois West starts to lose the precarious coherence it has enjoyed between the wars, the travel book begins to take as one of its aims setting people straight about the situation here or there; it abandons subtlety and irony; it grows political, strident, sentimental, and self-righteous; it begins, as Matthew Arnold says of excessively utilitarian criticism, to subserve interests not its own. When, in the summer of 1935, it became clear that Italian pressure on Abyssinia would probably result in war there, Waugh, as an old Abyssinian hand, was commissioned by the *Daily Mail*, "one of the few newspapers in Britain sympathetic to the Fascist cause," as Michael Davie puts it, to go as its correspondent. The "war," beginning in October, 1935, lasted seven months, at the end of which Abyssinia was Italian. Mussolini's designs on Abyssinia prompted the

Hoare-Laval Pact, which signalled the ruin of the League of Nations; the ruin of European security based on the assumptions of the League brought about, ultimately, the ruin of the between-the-wars travel book.

Waugh in Abyssinia is sadly weakened by incoherence and contradictory tones. It consists of a comic center, a delightful, ironic, complex travel-book element, sandwiched between a beginning and ending of a quite different kind. The beginning, a 47-page essay with the unfortunate Shavian title "The Intelligent Woman's Guide to the Ethiopian Question," is an earnest effort to show how awful Abyssinia is politically. With its slavery and thuggery and treaty-violating and contempt for foreigners, it is "an archaic African despotism," and "Signor Mussolini" is in large part justified in forcing upon it some of the benefits of European civilization. The ending of the book is in the same vein, only sillier. It is a 12-page would-be lyrical epilogue, "The Road," celebrating the heroic Italian achievement of supplying the new colony with a modern road system. (One is reminded of Pound's excessive admiration of the self-satisfied statement of the Italian officer after the Abyssinian conquest, "We have all joined in and made roads.") Waugh ends this final section with a mercifully uncharacteristic passage resembling the portentous-sentimental voice-over in some unpersuasive national propaganda film:

> From Dessye new roads will be radiating to all points of the compass, and along the roads will pass the eagles of ancient Rome, . . . bringing some rubbish and some mischief; . . . but above and beyond and entirely predominating, the inestimable gifts of fine workmanship and clear judgment—the two determining qualities of the human spirit, by which alone, under God, man grows and flourishes.

A loathsome passage in every respect, not least in the way it abjures any kind of irony or self-criticism and thus welcomes every possible middlebrow abstraction and cliché. Waugh never wrote worse than that, and if he'd never written better would be entirely contemptible.

But thank God there's a very different center to the book, and thank God it's executed in the old Waugh mode of perceiving empirical particulars with an eye to anomaly. Ironically, the center of the book makes its own comment on the flaccid effusions of ratiocination and sentimentality that enclose it. We might say that Waugh is, unconsciously, his own best critic here. Or perhaps even consciously: the vital center of the book is the only part he chose to retain in *When the Going Was Good* (1946), said on the cover of the Penguin edition to contain "everything the author wishes to preserve from his prewar travel books." The central part of the book begins with a comic vision of London journalism and publishing when Abyssinia suddenly became news in 1935: "Travel books whose first editions had long since been remaindered were being reissued in startling wrappers." Waugh accumulates his tropical traps and soon joins his journalistic competitors on the familiar train from Djibouti to Addis Ababa, "gazing out bleakly upon a landscape of unrelieved desolation." There is an abundance of *Scoop*-like satire of the vanities and cynicisms of industrialized journalism and, once he arrives in the capital, he performs a hilarious critical pseudo-"touristic" survey of the local hotels, all overflowing with a rabble of journalists, newsreel photographers, arms merchants, and assorted adventurers and colonizing concession-seekers. A companion for Waugh is there as well. His old Oxford friend Patrick Balfour is in town, serving as a war correspondent for the *Evening Standard*. A literary traveler like Waugh, he has just published *Grand Tour: Diary of an Eastward Journey*, an account of a trip from London to Sumatra and back. Waugh wrote Laura Herbert, who was to become his second—and permanent—wife:

> I am universally regarded as an Italian spy. In fact my name is mud all round—with the Legation because of a novel I wrote [*Black Mischief*] . . . , with the Ethiopians because of the *Mail's* [pro-Italian] policy, with the other journalists because I am not really a journalist and it is black leg labor. Fortunately an old chum name of Balfour is here and that makes all the difference in the world.

The heart of the book fleshes out the theme of the "bitter disillusion" occasioned by entertaining the reflexes appropriate to a civilized place in a venue so unpromising as Addis Ababa. A closely related theme is the delusion incident to crediting language once it comes detached very far from its empirical referents. An example of Waugh's way with the theme of comic disillusion is his treatment of Mme. Idot's cuisine:

> There were two places of entertainment in the town, *Le Select* and the *Perroquet*, usually known by the names of their proprietors, Moriatis and Idot. Both had a bar and a talking cinema. Mme. Idot had also a kitchen and put it about that her cooking was good. From time to time she would placard the town with news of some special delicacy—*Grand Souper. Tripes a la mode de Caen*—and nostalgic journalists would assemble in large numbers, to be bitterly disillusioned.

Here the problem is that words, like *Grand Souper*, have drifted too far geographically from the place that might give them accurate meaning—Lyon, for example.

Waugh's Fleet Street employers have no idea that there is no news about the war to be had in Addis Ababa, no way of developing any, and no way of getting to a place where there might be any, for the war hasn't started yet. The language of their importunate cables is a language with some meaning in London but no meaning at all in Abyssinia: "*Require comprehensive cable good colorful stuff also news.*" The official Abyssinian press bureau is headed by Dr. Lorenzo Taesas, who gives out nothing and forbids the correspondents to travel to the zone where fighting, if there is any, may be seen, or at least inferred. "Meanwhile there still lingered in our minds the picture we had presented of ourselves to our womenfolk at home, of stricken fields and ourselves crouching in shell holes, typing gallantly amid bursting shrapnel; of runners charging through clouds of gas, bearing our despatches on cleft sticks." That passage uses language the way Waugh had used it ("citizens . . . with Southern elegance twirling little canes") to sustain his delusive image of Boa Vista. He would agree with Johnson that "the use of traveling is to regulate imagination by reality, and instead of thinking how things may be, to see them as they are." Language under the dominion of strong imagination is the thing that cruelly misleads the Italian press officer at Asmara when Waugh arrives by air to call on him. This official knows that Evelyn in English is a woman's name, and he waits for Waugh "in a high state of amorous excitement" with a bouquet of red roses. "The trousered and unshaven figure which finally greeted him must have been a hideous blow, but with true Roman courtesy he betrayed nothing . . . , and it was only some days later, when we had become more intimate, that he admitted his broken hopes."

Finally, after Waugh has been in the country for over a month, general mobilization is ordered, and the Italians attack on October 3. They are said to have bombed the distant town of Adowa, focussing on "the hospital" there in order to destroy women and children. When the rumor reaches London that an American nurse has been blown to pieces, excited cables arrive: *"Require earliest name life story photograph American nurse upblown Adowa."* There is only one way to deal with fantasies couched in such language, and that is to answer in kind, which Waugh does: *"Nurse unupblown,"* he cables back, "and," he says, "after a few days she disappeared from the news." All actions, similarly, are attended by high hopes, which actuality shatters in their turn. For weeks Waugh and Balfour struggle to escape the capital and get to Dessye, 200 miles nearer the presumed "front." Dessye had been "a promised land sometimes glimpsed from afar . . . , always elusive, provocative, desirable. . . . Now that, at length, we found ourselves actually there . . . , we began to wonder what precisely we had gained by the journey." They are still impossibly distant from the action, but all the journalists set to with a will, typing out their picturesque fictions for cable transmission. "Two days later we were cheerfully informed that none of the messages had been sent, that no more could be accepted until further notice, that when the station re-opened there would be a limit of fifty words and a rigid censorship." The *Daily Mail* had not been happy with Waugh's copy—to preserve secrecy, he had sent one cable in Latin, which baffled the London sub-editor—and he and the paper parted company in November. It was impossible to get or send news anyway. As he wrote his wife, "The telephone to the north is cut and the only news we get comes on the wireless from Europe via Eritrea. No one is allowed to leave Addis, so all those adventures I came for will not happen. Sad." But there is a consolation: the whole affair has taken the shape—illusion followed by disappointment—of a Waugh comic episode, and as he perceives, "All this will make a funny novel, so it isn't wasted." The funny novel, *Scoop: A Novel about Journalists*, would appear in 1938, with William Boot and Ishmaelia standing in for Waugh and Abyssinia.

Graham Greene once wrote that "Roman Catholicism in this country has been a great breeder of eccentrics." He was speaking of Eric Gill, but he could have been speaking of Frederick Rolfe (Baron

Corvo) or of Waugh as types of the British eccentric abroad. Recalling Waugh, Dudley Carew says, "There was something inherently thrusting and aggressive about him. It was there in the square, strong body, in the set of the eyes, in the manner of his walk, which somehow suggested that he was always going slightly uphill." The idea of such a creature lapsing into either credulity or uncertainty is unthinkable, and he was thus naturally endowed to produce travel books of the sort described by Jonathan Raban as "fundamentally moral entertainments in the way that novels are moral entertainments." Like Bertrand Russell in a way, Waugh is a hero of British skepticism and empiricism, and although his vision is social and comic, his perception of the norms implied by anomalies must be said to be, at its best, philosophical.

TRAVEL BOOKS AS LITERARY PHENOMENA

AFTER encountering a number of these books, it's time to inquire what they are. Perhaps it is when we cannot satisfactorily designate a kind of work with a single word (*epic, novel, romance, story, novella, memoir, sonnet, sermon, essay*) but must invoke two (*war memoir, Black autobiography, first novel, picture book, travel book*) that we sense we're entering complicated territory, where description, let alone definition, is hazardous, an act closer to exploration than to travel. Criticism has never quite known what to call books like these. Some commentators, perhaps recalling the illustrated travel lectures of their youth or the travel films that used to be shown as "short subjects," call them *travelogues*. Others, more literary, render that term *travel logs*, apparently thinking of literal, responsible daily diaries, like ships' logs. This latter usage is the one preferred by David Lodge, who says of 30's writing that "it tended to model itself on historical kinds of discourse—the autobiography, the eye-witness account, the travel log: *Journey to a War, Letters from Iceland, The Road to Wigan Pier, Journey without Maps, Autumn Journal,* 'Berlin Diary,' are some characteristic titles." Even Forster is uncertain what to call these things. In 1941 he calls them *travelogues,* in 1949 *travel books.*

Let's call them travel books, and distinguish them initially from guide books, which are not autobiographical and are not sustained by a narrative exploiting the devices of fiction. A guide book is addressed to those who plan to follow the traveler, doing what he has done, but more selectively. A travel book, at its purest, is addressed to those who do not plan to follow the traveler at all, but who require the exotic or comic anomalies, wonders, and scandals of the literary form *romance* which their own place or time cannot entirely supply. Travel books are a sub-species of memoir in which the autobiographical narrative arises from the speaker's encounter with distant or unfamiliar data, and in which the narrative—unlike that in a novel or a romance—claims literal validity by constant reference to actuality. The speaker in any travel book exhibits himself as physically more free than the reader, and thus every such book, even when it depicts its speaker trapped in Boa Vista, is an implicit celebration of freedom. It resembles a poetic ode, an Ode to Freedom. The illusion of freedom is a precious thing in the 20's and 30's, when the shades of the modern prison-house are closing in, when the passports and queues and guided tours and social security numbers and customs regulations and currency controls are beginning gradually to constrict life. What makes travel books seem so necessary between the wars is what Fleming pointed to in *One's Company,* "that lamb-like subservience to red tape which is perhaps the most striking characteristic of modern man." Intellectual and moral pusillanimity is another characteristic of modern man. Hence Douglas's emphasis on the exemplary function of the travel writer's internal freedom and philosophic courage:

> It seems to me that the reader of a good travel-book is entitled not only to an exterior voyage, to descriptions of scenery and so forth, but to an interior, a sentimental or temperamental voyage, which takes place side by side with the outer one.

Thus "the ideal book of this kind" invites the reader to undertake three tours simultaneously: "abroad, into the author's brain, and into his own." It follows that "the writer should . . . possess a brain worth exploring; some philosophy of life—not necessarily, though by preference, of his own forging—and the courage to proclaim it and put it to the test; he must be naif and profound, both child and sage." And if the enterprise succeeds, the reader's "brain" will instinctively adjust itself to accord in some degree with the pattern established by the author's travel, both external and internal: that is, it will experience an access of moral freedom. It is thus possible to consider the between-the-wars travel books as a subtle instrument of ethics, replacing such former vehicles as sermons and essays.

A fact of modern publishing history is the virtual disappearance of the essay as a salable commodity (I mean the essay, not the "article"). If you want to raise a laugh in a publisher's office, enter with a manuscript collection of essays on all sorts of subjects. And if you want to raise an even louder laugh, contrive that your essays have a moral tendency, even if they stop short of aspiring to promulgate wisdom. The more we attend to what's going on in the travel book between the wars, the more we perceive that the genre is a device for getting published essays which, without the travel "menstruum" (as Coleridge would say), would appear too old-fashioned for generic credit, too reminiscent of Lamb and Stevenson and Chesterton. Thus the travel books of Aldous Huxley, a way of presenting learned essays which without exotic narrative support would find no audience. Thus also the performances of Douglas and of Osbert Sitwell, who, for all his defects, has thought long and hard about the essayistic element in the travel book and has coined for it the eccentric term *discursion,* as in his titles *Discursions on Travel, Art and Life* (1925) and *Winters of Content and Other Discursions on Mediterranean Art and Travel* (1950). "Discursions," he says, is "a word of my own minting, coined from *discourse* and *discursive,* and designed to epitomize the manner in which a traveler formulates his loose impressions, as, for example, he sits in a train, looking out [the] window, and allows the sights he so rapidly glimpses, one after another, to break in upon the thread of his . . . thoughts." *Discursions,* he goes on, "is an attempt . . . to find a new name for a particular kind of essay, that unites in the stream of travel . . . many very personal random reflections and sentiments. . . ." Thus in Sitwell's "travel books" we find a general essay on cabs,

Norman Douglas and Osbert Sitwell. (Humanities Research Center, University of Texas at Austin)

prompted by the cabs of Lecce, and one on the theory of bourgeois domestic architecture triggered by the sights of southern Germany. Neither essay could achieve a wide audience if detached from the sense data of the place abroad which has justified it. Alan Pryce-Jones's *The Spring Journey* (1931) is a good example of a travel book which functions as a mere framework for essays. The travel is to Egypt, Palestine, Syria, and Greece, but it is only a medium for inset Carlylean essays and discursive flourishes on the follies of modern education, the difference between Imagination and Fancy, the decay of contemporary civilization, and the superiority of music to "the other arts." An American counterpart is Hemingway's *Green Hills of Africa* (1935). Because of the public persona he has chosen, Hemingway can't plausibly write "essays" in the old schoolmasterly sense. He can get away with essays on bullfighting if he connects his learned comments with memories of toreros he has known, and thus validates his remarks as memoir. But for him to discourse professorially about history and literature would seem unnatural—stuffy, pompous, very unoutdoors. He thus lodges his major essay on the character and history of American literature, his version of Lawrence's *Studies in Classic American Literature*, in a travel book, and presents it there as a conversation with a person encountered by chance, the character Kandinsky, an Austrian who is made to ask who the great writers are. "Tell me. Please tell me," he says, not very credibly. Hemingway responds with an essay of 1200 words, presented as dialogue, considering the merits of Poe, Melville, Emerson, Hawthorne, Whittier, James, Crane, and Twain. We easily remember his brilliant remark, one of the most acute critical perceptions any scholar or critic has uttered, that "all modern American literature comes from one book by Mark Twain called *Huckleberry Finn*," but we may forget that it gets uttered at all because on the African veldt "under the dining tent fly" an Austrian has asked him about American writers. It is an open-air remark, a travel, not a library, remark.

Similarly, if one approached a publisher in 1940 with a collection of assorted ethical and historical essays one would have less chance of success than if one arranged them as "A Journey through Yugoslavia" and titled the whole immense work *Black Lamb and Grey Falcon*, as Rebecca West did. We recognize Lawrence's *Aaron's Rod* as akin to a travel book less, perhaps, because it goes to some lengths to describe abroad than because it provides a medium for promulgating essays. Lawrence will suddenly cast away his narrative pretences entirely, face his audience directly, and issue what we perceive is the "topic sentence" of an old-fashioned moral essay. On some of these occasions he sounds like a sort of Hilaire Belloc turned inside out: "The *idée fixe* of today," he will proclaim, "is that every individual shall not only give himself, but shall achieve the last glory of giving himself away." Or: "The David in the Piazza della Signoria, there under the dark great Palace, in the position Michelangelo chose for him, there, standing forward stripped and exposed and eternally half-shrinking, half-wishing to expose himself, he is the genius of Florence."

But to emphasize the presence of the essay element in the travel book is to risk not noticing sufficiently this genre's complex relation to adjacent forms which also require two words to designate them: *war memoir, comic novel, quest romance, picaresque romance, pastoral romance.* The memorable war memoirs of the late 20's and early 30's, by Graves and Blunden and Sassoon, are very like travel books and would doubtless show different characteristics if they'd not been written in the travel context of the period between the wars. They are ironic or parodic or nightmare travels, to France and Belgium, with the Channel ferries and the forty-and-eights replacing the liners and chic trains of real travel, with dugouts standing for hotel-rooms and lobbies and

Other Ranks serving the travel-book function of "native" porters and servants. Curiously, at the end of the Second World War the war book has something of the same "travel" element attached to it, the same obsession with topography and the mystery of place, with even something like Lawrence's adhesions to the prepositional, like *into*. Recalling his first idea for *The Naked and the Dead*, Mailer says: "I wanted to write a short novel about a long patrol. . . . Probably [the idea] was stimulated by a few war books I had read: John Hersey's *Into the Valley*, Harry Brown's *A Walk in the Sun*."

The element of the comic novel is visible not merely in the travel books of Byron and Waugh; it is in *Sea and Sardinia* as well, in much of Douglas, and even, if we can conceive the "seedy" as inherently comic, as a pathetic parody of a civilization not worth imitating, in much of Graham Greene. Anomaly is what unites comic novel and travel experience. A baron "traveling in cosmetics" and shaving in beer because the water in the wagons-lits has run out is an anomaly Anthony Powell met in Yugoslavia once. It fitted perfectly into his comic novel *Venusberg* (1933), where the baron is presented as Count Bobel. The comic novel between the wars would be an impoverished thing without its multitude of anomalous strangers—like Mr. Norris—encountered on actual trains and ships.

If as a form of prose fiction a "romance" is more likely than a novel to be set abroad or in an exotic place, then *romance*, whether "quest," picaresque, or pastoral, will suggest itself as a term to designate an indispensable element of the travel book. One could ask: aren't travel books really romances in the old sense, with the difference that the adventures are located within an actual, often famous, topography to satisfy an audience which demands it both ways—which wants to go adventuring vicariously, as it always has, but which at the same time wants to feel itself within a world declared real by such up-to-date studies as political science, sociology, anthropology, economics, and contemporary history? The proximity of the travel book to the thoroughly empirical picaresque romance, contrived from a multitude of adventures in non-causal series, can perhaps be inferred from Freya Stark's disappointment with Gertrude Bell's *Syria*. She felt the book let her down: "[Bell] did not have enough adventures." (On one of her Persian explorations in 1932 Stark took along *Pilgrim's Progress*, and in Brazil an item in Fleming's travel kit was "1 copy of *Tom*

Jones.") As in a romance, the modern traveler leaves the familiar and predictable to wander, episodically, into the unfamiliar or unknown, encountering strange adventures, and finally, after travail and ordeals, returns safely. Somehow, we feel a travel book isn't wholly satisfying unless the traveler returns to his starting point: the action, as in a quest romance, must be completed. We are gratified—indeed, comforted—by the "sense of an ending," the completion of the circuit, as we are at the end of *Labels* or *The Road to Oxiana* or *Journey without Maps*, where the "hero" invites us to enjoy his success in returning home.

All this is to suggest that the modern travel book is what Northrop Frye would call a myth that has been "displaced"—that is, lowered, brought down to earth, rendered credible "scientifically"—and that the myth resembles the archetypal monomyth of heroic adventure defined by Joseph Campbell. The myth of the hero, Campbell explains, is tripartite: first, the setting out, the disjunction from the familiar; second, the trials of initiation and adventure; and third, the return and the hero's reintegration into society. Even if there is no return, the monomyth still assumes tripartite form, as in *Pilgrim's Progress*, whose title-page declares that the hero's "progress, from this world, to that which is to come" will be conceived in three stages: "The manner of his setting out; His Dangerous Journey; and Safe Arrival at the Desired Country." The first and last stages of the tripartite experience tend to be moments of heightened ritual or magic, even in entirely "secular" travel writings. Eliot understands this, and so does Auden. Witness stanza 4 of Auden's "Dover" (1937):

> The eyes of departing migrants are fixed on the sea,
> Conjuring destinies out of impersonal water:
> "I see an important decision made on a lake,
> An illness, a beard, Arabia found in a bed,
>   Nanny defeated. Money."

Listening to the ship's engine as he sets out from Southampton for Spain, V. S. Pritchett writes in *Marching Spain* (1928), "Every man who heard those sounds must have seemed to himself as great a hero as Ulysses and pitted against as mysterious a destiny, the strange destiny of the outward bound." Starting on his Brazilian adventure, Peter

Fleming notices something odd which he can describe only thus: "We were through the looking-glass." And returning is equally full of portent and mystery. We have seen Waugh throwing his champagne glass overboard, a gesture which, he says, "has become oddly important to me," somehow "bound up with the turgid, indefinite feelings of homecoming." Fleming would suggest that the magical feeling upon returning arises from moving from a form of non-existence back to existence, or recovering one's normal self-consciousness before one's accustomed audience. The traveler "who has for weeks or months seen himself only as a puny and irrelevant alien crawling laboriously over a country in which he has no roots and no background, suddenly [on returning] encounters his other self, a relatively solid and considerable figure, with . . . a place in the minds of certain people." Or, as Auden registers the magical act of reintegration in stanza 5 of "Dover,"

> Red after years of failure or bright with fame,
> The eyes of homecomers thank these historical cliffs:
> "The mirror can no longer lie nor the clock reproach;
> In the shadow under the yew, at the children's party,
>   Everything must be explained."

Indeed, the stages of the classic monomyth of the adventuring hero cannot avoid sketching an allegory of human life itself. As Campbell notes, the "call to adventure" is a figure for the onset of adolescence; adult life is "the travel"; old age, the "return." For the literary imagination, says Auden, "It is impossible to take a train or an airplane without having a fantasy of oneself as a Quest Hero setting off in search of an enchanted princess or the Waters of Life." That's why we enjoy reading travel books, even if we imagine we're enjoying only the curiosities of Liberia, British Guiana, Persia, or Patagonia. Even the souvenirs brought back so religiously by tourists are brought back "religiously." According to the anthropologist Nelson Graburn, tourists bring back souvenirs in unwitting imitation of the Grail Knight returning with his inestimable prize. Even for mass tourists, "the Holy Grail is . . . sought on the journey, and the success of a holiday is proportionate to the degree that the myth is realized."

But travel books are not merely displaced quest romances. They are also displaced pastoral romances. If William Empson is right to define traditional pastoral as a mode of presentation implying "a beautiful relation between rich and poor," then pastoral is a powerful element in most travel books, for, unless he's a *Wandervogel* or similar kind of layabout (few of whom write books), the traveler is almost always richer and freer than those he's among. He is both a plutocrat *pro tem* and the sort of plutocrat the natives don't mind having around. Byron and Waugh and Greene hire drivers and porters and bearers and pay outrageous prices for decrepit horses and cars; Lawrence pays bus and steamer fares; Norman Douglas keeps employed numerous waiters and *sommeliers*. If the cash nexus can be considered "a beautiful relation," the behavior of these characters is like the behavior of the court class in Renaissance pastoral, and there's a closer resemblance between Sidney's *Arcadia* and a modern travel book than is obvious on the surface. Consider the Lawrence of *Twilight in Italy*, attended by his aristocratic consort. Consider the affectionate patronizing of the Persian peasants in Byron's dialogue involving "The Caliph of Rum." And it is with the pastoral strain in travel books that we can associate the implicit elegiac tendency of these works. Pastoral has built into it a natural retrograde emotion. It is instinct with elegy. To the degree that literary travel between the wars constitutes an implicit rejection of industrialism and everything implied by the concept "modern northern Europe," it is a celebration of a Golden Age, and recalling the Ideal Places of Waugh, Auden, and Priestley, we can locate that Golden Age in the middle of the preceding century. One travels to experience the past, and travel is thus an adventure in time as well as distance.

"The King's life is moving peacefully to its close," the BBC announced in January, 1936, invoking for this most solemn, magical moment the root metaphor of human imaginative experience, the figure of time rendered as space. If, as this essential trope persuades us, life is a journey (to the Eliot of the *Quartets*, a never-ending one), then literary accounts of journeys take us very deeply into the center of instinctive imaginative life. Like no other kinds of writing, travel books exercise and exploit the fundamental intellectual and emotional figure of thought, by which the past is conceived as back and the future as forward. They manipulate the whole alliance between temporal and spatial that we use to orient ourselves in time by invoking the dimension of space. That is, travel books make more or less conscious an activity usually unconscious. Travel books are special because the metaphor they imply is so essential. Works we recognize as somehow "classical" derive much of their status and authority from their open exploitation of this metaphor. Housman is an example:

> Into my heart an air that kills
>   From yon far country blows:
> What are those blue remembered hills,
>   What spires, what farms are those?
>
> That is the land of lost content,
>   I see it shining plain,
> The happy highways where I went
>   And cannot come again.

"When I was a young man," says Borges, "I was always hunting for new metaphors. Then I found out that good metaphors are always the same. I mean you compare time to a road, death to sleeping, life to dreaming, and those are the great metaphors in literature because they correspond to something essential." An Italian friend of Norman Douglas's, indicating that his fifteen-year-old son has died of tuberculosis, says, "He has gone into that other country."

And if living and dying are like traveling, so are reading and writing. As Michel Butor points out, the eyes of the reader "travel" along the lines of print as the reader is "guided" by the writer, as his imagination "escapes" his own I Hate It Here world. Thus in reading, of all books, a travel book, the reader becomes doubly a traveler, moving from beginning to end of the book while touring along with the literary traveler.

> "O where are you going?" said reader to rider,

writes Auden in the Epilogue to *The Orators* (1931). His near-rhyme implies the parallelism between reading and riding, a parallelism as suggestive as the one Connolly instinctively falls into when designating the three things his Oxford crowd in the early 20's "had a passion for": "literature, travel, and the visual arts." And writing, as Butor perceives, is like traveling. Figures of travel occupy any writer's imagination as he starts out, makes transitions, digresses, returns, goes for-

ward, divagates, pauses, approaches the subject from a slightly different direction, and observes things from various points of view (like
Norman Douglas on his eminences). Thus, as Osbert Sitwell says, "To
begin a book is . . . to embark on a long and perilous voyage," but to
begin a travel book "doubles the sense of starting on a journey."

Thus to speak of "literary traveling" is almost a tautology, so intimately are literature and travel implicated with each other. Any child
senses this, and any adult recalling his childhood remembers moments
when reading was revealed to be traveling. Peter Quennell's first awareness that he had actually learned to read occurred at the age of four
or five when he was looking through bound volumes of *The Boy's
Own Paper* at home. "The story I scrutinized was . . . the work of
some unknown author who described an African caravan, journeying
to the sound of camel-bells from oasis to oasis. Suddenly, the printed
words I painfully spelt out melted into a continuous narrative, whence
a procession of fascinating images emerged and wound its way across
my mental landscape." Gerald Brenan's mental landscape was formed,
he reports, not just by the romances of William Morris, with their
"descriptions of imaginary travel," but also by Elisée Reclus's *Universal Geography* in nineteen volumes, which he discovered at school.
From Reclus he gathered that "foreign countries alone offered something to the imagination," and he filled notebooks with a plan for a
tour of the world "which would last, with continuous traveling, some
thirty years." As a boy Robin Maugham read all his uncle's short
stories set in the Far East "and then determined," he says, "that one
day I would visit the strange, exotic places about which he wrote. This
I have done." A reading of Maugham also set Alec Waugh on his
traveling career. "Were the South Seas really like that?" he wondered
in the summer of 1926 after reading *The Moon and Sixpence* and *The
Trembling of a Leaf*. "I had to find out for myself. I bought a round
the world ticket that included Tahiti," and "I have been on the move
ever since."

Names like Brenan, Quennell, and the Maughams suggest the
next question: how serious artistically and intellectually can a travel
book be? Is there not perhaps something in the genre that attracts
second-rate talents? Certainly the travel book will have little generic
prestige in today's atmosphere, where if you identify yourself as a
"writer," everyone will instantly assume you're a novelist. The genres

with current prestige are the novel and the lyric poem, although it doesn't seem to matter that very few memorable examples of either ever appear. The status of those two kinds is largely an unearned and unexamined snob increment from late-romantic theories of imaginative art as religion-cum-metaphysics. Other kinds of works—those relegated to simple-minded categories like "the literature of fact" or "the literature of argument"—are in lower esteem artistically because the term *creative* has been widely misunderstood, enabling its votaries to vest it with magical powers. Before that word had been promoted to the highest esteem, that is, before the romantic movement, a masterpiece was conceivable in a "non-fictional" genre like historiography or memoir or the long essay or biography or the travel book. As recently as 1918 things were different. Fiction had not yet attained its current high status. *Ulysses* was waiting in the wings, not to appear until 1922. *À la Recherche du Temps Perdu* had not been translated. *The Magic Mountain* hadn't been written, not to mention *Les Faux-Monnayeurs, The Sound and the Fury,* and *The Sun Also Rises.* In the *Century Magazine* for February, 1918, Henry Seidel Canby felt obliged to plead for the dignity and importance of fiction, which, as an editorial in the *New York Times Review of Books* commented, the reading public was accustomed to treat with "a certain condescension." But now a similar condescension is visited on forms thought to be non-fictional. Martin Green is one who doesn't think travel books are serious. They seem to him the natural métier of the dandy. "In *Work Suspended,*" he says, "Waugh portrayed himself as a writer of detective novels; in *Brideshead Revisited,* as a painter of English country houses; these occupations, and writing travel books, were the métiers of the dandies. Notably lacking in anything large-scale, even in the dandy line—not to mention anything really serious, whether political or literary-critical." Yet between the wars writing travel books was not at all considered incompatible with a serious literary career. And who would not find *Sea and Sardinia* a better book than *The Plumed Serpent,* Forster's *Alexandria* a better book than *Maurice,* Ackerley's *Hindoo Holiday* better than the collected novels of Hugh Walpole? We can hardly condescend to the travel book when it is in that genre that Robert Byron wrote a masterpiece that (in England, at least) has outlived all but a half-dozen novels of its decade.

The problem for the critic is to resist the drowsy habit of laying aside his sharpest tools when he's dealing with things that don't seem to be fiction. It takes someone more like a common reader than a critic, someone like H. M. Tomlinson, to remind us of what's going on in these "non-fictional" genres. "We know that in the literature of travel our language is very rich," he writes; "yet as a rule we are satisfied with our certainty that these books exist. . . . We surmise vaguely that a book of travel must be nearly . . . all background. . . . We shrink from the threat of the vigilance it will exact; we shall have to keep all our wits about us." In short, "We have the idle way of allowing books of travel to pass without the test to which poetry must submit." That "test," we can assume, is the test both of a complicated coherence and of a subtle mediation between texture and form, data and significant shape. Like poems—and like any successful kind of literary performance—successful travel books effect a triumphant mediation between two different dimensions: the dimension of individual physical things, on the one hand, and the dimension of universal significance, on the other. The one is Coleridge's "particular"; the other, his "general." The travel book authenticates itself by the sanction of actualities—ships, trains, hotels, bizarre customs, odd people, crazy weather, startling architecture, curious food. At the same time it reaches in the opposite direction, most often to the generic convention that the traveling must be represented as something more than traveling, that it shall assume a meaning either metaphysical, psychological, artistic, religious, or political, but always ethical. A travel book is like a poem in giving universal significance to a local texture. The gross physicality of a travel book's texture should not lead us to patronize it, for the constant recourse to the locatable is its convention. Within that convention, as we have seen, there is ample room for the activities of the "fictionalizing" imagination. And an active, organic, and, if you will, "creative" mediation between fact and fiction is exactly the activity of the mind exhibited in the travel book, which Samuel Hynes has accurately perceived to be "a dual-plane work with a strong realistic surface, which is yet a parable." In the 30's, he understands correctly, two apparently separated modes of perception, reportage and fable, literal record and parable, tend to coalesce, and nowhere more interestingly than in the travel book. What distinguishes the travel books of the 30's from earlier classics like *Eothen* or even *Arabia Deserta* is the way, Hynes says, these writers between the wars "turned their travels into interior journeys and parables of their times, making landscape and incident [and, we must add, in Byron, architecture]— the factual materials of *reportage*—do the work of symbol and myth— the materials of fable." And since the journey is "the most insistent of 'thirties metaphors, . . . one might say that the travel books simply act out, in the real world, the basic trope of the generation." Acting out a trope, like perceiving the metaphor lodging always in the literal, is the essential act of poetry. It is also the essential act of both traveling and writing about it.

The End

"I do not expect to see many travel books in the near future," Waugh wrote in 1946, shocked and embittered by a war which, by destroying Europe and the Orient and multiplying controls on people and producing the jet aircraft engine, effectively ended travel in the old sense. "When I was a reviewer," Waugh says, travel books "used . . . to appear in batches of four or five a week, cram-full of charm and wit and enlarged Leica snapshots." But now, "in a world of 'displaced persons,'" travel seems wholly anomalous. "Never again, I suppose, shall we land on foreign soil with a letter of credit and passport (itself the first faint shadow of the great cloud that envelops us) and feel the world wide open before us." Never again "the years when Mr. Peter Fleming went to the Gobi Desert, Mr. Graham Greene to the Liberian hinterland; Robert Byron—vital today, as of old, in our memories; all his exuberant zest in the opportunities of our time now, alas! tragically and untimely quenched—to the ruins of Persia." They couldn't have traveled with such innocent enthusiasm if they'd known what Waugh knows now, if they'd known "that all that seeming-solid, patiently built, gorgeously ornamented structure of Western life was to melt overnight like an ice-castle, leaving only a puddle of mud." Then, and only then, between the wars, was the time *When the Going Was Good*. And looking back, Waugh perceived a pattern in his own travel books: "Each book, I found on re-reading, had a . . . slightly grimmer air, as, year by year, the shades of the prison-house closed." The gradually darkening tone of his travel books, and everyone else's, reflects the advance of the 30's to disaster.

In January, 1933, Hitler became Chancellor of Germany, and in the same year Osbert Sitwell, displaying remarkable prescience, began to feel that time for traveling was growing short. With Armageddon looming, "Whoever has the chance of seeing Angkor and doesn't is mad," he wrote. In 1934 Fleming records in *One's Company* ominous signs of Japanese national neurosis and militarism in noting the air-raid precautions in "Manchukuo," and something like a premonition of the end seems to lurk in *Waugh in Abyssinia* (1936), where we can witness the phenomenon of the comic travel book beginning to metamorphose into the war book. Returning to the place where five years earlier he'd enjoyed the levities of the anomalous coronation, he writes a comic-satiric passage which, as we look back on it now, seems to suggest more than it says:

> The triumphal arches that had been erected for the coronation had grown shabbier but they were still standing. The ambitious buildings in the European style with which Haile Selassie had intended to embellish his capital were still in the same rudimentary stage of construction; tufted now with vegetation like ruins in a drawing by Piranesi, they stood at every corner, reminders of an abortive modernism, a happy subject for the press photographers who hoped later to present them as the ravages of Italian bombardment.

In the same year as this excursus of Waugh's, there's another cloud no bigger than a man's hand. Penguin paperbacks began to appear, marking the beginning of the end for Cape's Travelers' Library. That year the Spanish War effectively ended travel to Spain, and the former Hispanic travel book turns perforce into the Spanish war book. Where before the opening chapter of a book about Spain might be titled "Journey to Seville," now, in Arthur Koestler's *Spanish Testament*

(1937), it is "Journey to Rebel Headquarters." Orwell's *Homage to Catalonia* (1938) seems to recall its paternity in the travel book, not least in the wonder and sense of strangeness with which Orwell regards the half-comic anomalies of life with the P.O.U.M.—its surprising defects of arms and equipment, and its flagrant indiscipline, with every order debated by the rank and file: "Any Public School O.T.C. is far more like a modern army than we were." When open warfare breaks out between the Left factions in Barcelona, Orwell views the wondrous events like a traveler from his hotel roof, where he used to sit for hours, "wondering at the folly of it all." Thus in the late 30's travel books are replaced on publishers' lists by works of political and military analysis, written by people who a few years before could pass for travelers but who now are identified as "foreign correspondents," like William L. Shirer, John Gunther, Negley Farson, Sisley Huddlestone, and Walter Duranty.

Henry Green's *Party Going*, published just before the war erupted, suggests the way things are changing. A group of gay young things, heading for the south of France, find themselves stuck at Victoria Station by a very British fog which has arrested all travel. Looking down on the crowd below from the station hotel, someone says, "What targets, . . . what targets for a bomb." Another of the aborted travelers, thinking of their sunny destination "so fantastically different from this," thinks, "Oh! . . . if only we could be there now." In a similar way Anthony Powell's just pre-war comic novel about the publishing business, *What's Become of Waring* (1939), seems to register a genuine and at the same time tongue-in-cheek conviction that the whole travel and travel-book era is at an end. The emblem of termination is the reported death in the south of France of the highly successful young romantic travel writer T. T. Waring. He closely resembles Peter Fleming, but fiction is now killing him off.

> "Is he really dead?" said Mrs. Pimley. "I read that one he wrote about the long walk he did in Asia. I enjoyed it very much."

No one, including his agent and his publisher, has ever seen him. He sends in his manuscripts from abroad. He is finally discovered, quite alive, living on the Riviera under the name of Robinson. Or Alec Pimley. Or Alec Mason. All Waring's travel books, which have delighted British readers for the past twenty years, prove to have been cribbed. He has never gone at all to his exotic locales but has worked up his books in libraries in the south of France. His travels have been nothing but a dream, and he has been nothing but a con man. There will be no more travel books from Waring, just as once the war begins there will be no more from anyone else.

In January, 1939, the traveling co-author (with MacNeice) of *Letters from Iceland* (1937) abandoned England for the United States, and two months later Auden published (with Isherwood) *Journey to a War*. That book's very title announces the capture of the travel book by events. On September 1, 1939, Germany invaded Poland; on the 3rd Britain declared war; and on the 8th the New Zealand journalist and traveler Hector Bolitho knew with sad intensity that travel was over. Listening to the exotic voices of the American war correspondents at the Savoy makes one feel, he writes in his diary, "less a prisoner on this little island, which we may not leave for many a long day." Six months later he solaces his imagination with still lively imagery of a travel world lost: "Gone are the holidays abroad, the scent of the pine trees in the Black Forest, the baskets of burning blue gentians on the steps in Vienna, the rafts of ice floating down the broad waters of the Danube." As he puts it a bit later, "One is reduced to nostalgic recollections of journeys one may never make again." But ironically, immobility brought its benefits, notably, Connolly's and Spender's monthly *Horizon*, which began in December, 1939. As Spender recalls, Peter Watson, "rich, passionately artistic but uncreative," came up with the money for the magazine. "He and Cyril had long discussed the idea of sponsoring a literature-and-arts magazine but had hesitated to do so, fearing that Cyril might tire of London and quickly forsake editing for wines and rock-pools in the South of France. The advantage of the war, from Peter's point of view, was that it would make Connolly stay put for the duration." But if the body could not flee abroad, the mind could. Hence the *Horizon* series "Where Shall John Go?"—essays considering various places abroad as alternatives to residence in an England widely regarded by *Horizon's* well-traveled readers as uninhabitable.

What made the war a constant source of wry irony for former travelers was its being, as journalism never tired of insisting, a "global war"—one had to "travel" to witness it. As the journalist Alaric Jacobs says in his significantly titled book *A Traveler's War: A Journey to the Wars in Africa, India, and Russia* (1944), the war has been "a global war. A war of globe-trotters. A traveler's war." And sometimes the war resembled real traveling, or did until you thought about it. Thus Graham Greene, proceeding south on a ship (but in convoy) to Africa: "Over and over again one forgets that this is war, looking forward to the south and the warm weather, then the sense of danger comes back like nausea." The sense of danger was always there, but for literary travelers perhaps never more so than when personal bad news arrived: the destruction of Robert Byron on his torpedoed destroyer, for example, or the sudden death of Roger Pettiward, Fleming's companion on the Brazil trip of 1932, killed while leading a commando group at Dieppe in 1942. Before the war was over, Monte Cassino, the setting of Maurice Magnus's and Lawrence's comical travel actions, would lie in ruins, surrounded by silent craters and graves. "Is Your Journey Really Necessary?" asked the poster of the British Railway Executive Authority.

All this seems foreshadowed by the travel books of the late 30's, which by contrast with earlier examples of the genre, will seem little more than repositories, often incoherent, of exhaustion, bitterness, and rabid ideology. "Preachy" is a good word for them, as Auden recognizes when, revising in 1973 the poems constituting part of *Journey to a War*, he sees that "the verse *Commentary* is . . . far too 'preachy' in manner. . . ." He knows that the other poems in the book are bad too, and even after his 1973 re-writing of most of them they remain strained and inert, some of Auden's very worst things, witnessing the sad sinking of their author's morale. Isherwood also recognizes now the unsatisfactoriness of his prose narrative, its self-consciousness and "excessive use of similes." We may agree with Waugh, who reviewed *Journey to a War* in the *Spectator*, that the dual authorship itself is a sign that all is not well. As Martin Stannard observes, to Waugh "it seemed the height of intellectual depravity . . . when it took two men . . . to write a book," a situation Waugh considered symptomatic of the collapse of aesthetics and workmanship in his time. It can be said that the unraveling and dissolving of forms, not just in *Journey to a War* but in *Letters from Iceland* two years earlier, marks the decadent stage in the course of the between-the-wars travel book. In both these books the narrative is disturbingly discontinuous, interrupted by

Christopher Isherwood and W. H. Auden off to China, January, 1938. (BBC Hulton Picture Library)

jokiness, nervousness over what literary mode is appropriate, and self-consciousness about the *travel book* genre itself. Both books give the unhappy impression of apologizing for themselves. In both, the narrative is eked out by poems that don't really belong, and nothing is rounded off: *Journey to a War* simply comes to a stop, for no particular reason, with the two travelers in Shanghai, baffled over what to make of it all: "Oh dear, things are so awful here—so complicated. One doesn't know where to start." It is all just a bit Camp, like the going-away party Julian Trevelyan gave Auden and Isherwood when they set off for China in January, 1938. "It was a large affair," says P. N. Furbank, "stage-managed by Rupert Doone. . . . [The] walls [were] decorated with collage pictures made from lumps of wool and frying-pans."

When Alec Waugh went around the world in 1929, a ship connoted nothing but delight—"At night, after dinner, on deck under the stars with the sound of music borne faintly from the saloon, I would let my book fall forward on my knees, my mind abroad." But to Isherwood in 1938, the ship conveying him and Auden from Marseilles to Hong Kong connotes nothing so much as some insidious terminal disease:

> This ship is like a hospital. Miles from land, home, love, sanity, we lie limp in our deck chairs, gazing out dully across a sea which is as boring and hopeless as an incurable spinal disease. . . . [T]he engines throb, deep down, like a fever. This voyage is our illness. As the long days pass, we grow peevish, apathetic, sullen; we no longer expect, or even wish, to recover.

And while Isherwood was writing that, Auden was working on a poem, "Passenger Shanty," recording that for him as well, ships have definitely lost their magic. Theirs, the French liner *Aramis*, is carrying them towards—note the order of the two items—

> . . . *the China War and the tropical sun.*

(Palm trees have also suffered demotion as romantic objects. The ones Isherwood sees in Ceylon are "weary . . . , like damp mops.") On the *Aramis*,

> *The passengers are rather triste,*

including the war photographer Robert Capa, now off to record disaster in China after "traveling" in Spain, where

> *He photographed Teruel Town in flames.*

The images that follow notate uselessness, dullness, frustration:

> *The idiot child stole a cigarette;*
> *The father looks at his wife with regret*
> *And thinks of that night at the Bal Musette.*

Even the pretty sailors and cabin-boys are useless:

> *The beautiful matelots and mousses*
> *Would be no disgrace to the Ballets Russes,*
> *But I can't see their presence is very much use.*

In short,

> *The sea is blau, the sea is tief,*
> *Parlez-vous*

The sea is blau, the sea is tief,
Parlez-vous
C'est le cimetière du Chateau d'If.
No doubt. But it's dull beyond belief.
Inky-pinky-parlez-vous.

If uncertainty and frustration compromise the travel performance of Auden and Isherwood, moral and political tendentiousness culminating in a fury almost disabling threatens end-of-the-period travel books like Waugh's *Robbery Under Law: The Mexican Object Lesson* (1939). His Mexican journey of 1938 notably lacks the purity—or the whimsicality—of motive implicit in the old-style travel book. It is sad to see the former ironic wit, the mock-dispassionate student of Port Said and the comic scourge of Boa Vista, reduced to a strident (and paid) doctrinaire. Waugh's and his wife's trip to Mexico on the *Bremen* was paid for by Clive Pearson, a British businessman whose extensive oil and railway holdings in Mexico had been expropriated by President Cardenas, to the wide approval of British socialists. Waugh originally wanted to title his book *Pickpocket Government*, but Pearson persuaded him that a slightly less inflammatory title might more readily advance the cause of private enterprise. The book was a failure, and it deserved to fail. Afterwards Waugh was uneasy about it, admitting that "it dealt little with travel and much with political questions," never his forte. In the book he was obliged to argue that the British companies in Mexico are the underdogs, a point whose absurdity would have delighted him a decade earlier; and if the book offers moments of the old sharp farcical observation, they are buried under the utterly solemn, self-righteous registrations of right-wing political outrage.

To the degree that *Robbery Under Law* forgoes the mode of earlier travel books for the sake of simply choosing sides and righting wrongs, it resembles another work of the same pre-war moment, Greene's *The Lawless Roads* (1939), also about the perfidy of the Mexican government, this time its persecutions of the Catholic Church. Just three years before, in West Africa, Greene had looked, accepted, and learned. Now he is angry and truculent—an attack of dysentery can't have helped—and like Waugh he plays the stock reformer pursuing his grievance unremittingly. His power of noticing nasty details is undiminished, but now it is enlisted in the service of a crude "point," and anomalies like the cock-fights and the "dead fleas dressed up as little people inside walnuts," as well as the constant "heat and flies, heat and flies," are deployed to dramatize the "useless cruelty" and pervasive anarchy which have provided a natural context for the extirpation of Christian institutions. What Greene notices in travel now is the "weariness and disappointment." What he concludes is simply that "I loathed Mexico." Under the strain of this hatred, Greene's style, never, perhaps, entirely secure, begins to break down. The writing is spotty, cliché-ridden, unpersuasively melodramatic, and occasionally illiterate: we hear of "a stigmata" and are told of a certain chapel interior that "it was all red velvet and gold: it gave an effect of being padded like some prayer books are." The Terrible Places of Byron and Fleming and early Waugh had been depicted with a certain joy and gusto: the seedy used to be fun. Now it is more like a nightmare, as Greene finds Villahermosa one evening:

> It was an awful night. The pavement outside the hotel was black with beetles. They lay on every stair up from the electric dynamo to the hotel; they detonated against the lamp and walls and fell with little plops like hailstones. Somewhere there was a storm, but the air in Villahermosa never cleared. I went to my bedroom and killed seven beetles; the corpses moved as rapidly as in life across the floor pushed by the swarms of ants

—a cause not of comedy or wonder but, as Greene says, of "the pathological hatred I began to feel for Mexico." And his hatred stays aflame when he returns, exhausted and depressed, to London. *The Lawless Roads* inverts—perverts might be a better word—the convention of previous travel books that the sour-comic I Hate It Here section appears at the beginning, as a half-fictional motivation for traveling. Here it appears at the end; one is not fleeing to something nicer, one is returning to something which travel has exposed as equally loathsome:

> The A.R.P. posters were new, as one jolted through the hideous iron tunnel at Vauxhall Bridge, under the Nine Elms depot and the sky-sign for Meux's beer. There is always a smell of gas at the traffic junction where the road is up and the trams wait; a Watney's poster, a crime of violence, Captain Coe's Finals. How could a world like this end in anything but war? I

wondered why I had disliked Mexico so much: *this* was home. One always expects something different.

We notice here the absence of subtlety or wit, the implicit self-pity, the blurring of distinctions, the instant leap from a little bit of data to frantic generalization, the mere positioning—no observation is required—of the received, standard symbols of the nasty. Actually, home is different: Mexico has no Watney's posters. But here, the activity of mind that might sense the meaning of the difference has been deformed by the anger and bitterness customarily attending "politics."

As the war approaches, emotional simplifications like this are not the only corrupters of the travel book. Others are more sinister, more suggestive of the world that has followed the war and been made by it. One of these worse corrupters can be studied in a book of Oriental travels by the journalist Mona Gardner, *Menacing Sun* (1939). The *sun* here is not at all the one treasured by the earlier British travel tradition, the one encouraging palm trees and nourishing a Lawrentian bodily well-being and enticing travelers to freedom in the south. It is an emblem of alarm, the Rising Sun of the expanding Japanese empire. Gardner has lived in Japan for twelve years before traveling in Indochina, Siam, the East Indies, India, and Malaya. Arriving in Singapore, she starts delivering a standard touristic appreciation of its varied exoticisms. Then, curiously, she turns to emphasize Singapore's utter invulnerability to land attack from the Malayan Peninsula, an odd subject, one would think, for a traveler in the old sense. Singapore, she assures us, is "one of the most formidable naval and military bases anywhere." Indeed,

> no outsider knows the actual extent of Singapore's military fortifications, or just how many units there are of the big land batteries with their 18-inch guns. All of this is kept very secret, as it should be. Until the formal opening of the base a year ago it was not even known that 18-inch naval guns had been dismounted from a warship and set up there as land batteries. Today officers will neither confirm nor deny their existence, but the certainty that these colossi are there is pretty well established.

Actually, this is entirely false. Singapore's armament consisted of no 18-inch guns at all but of 15-inch guns, and only five of them, emplaced

in concrete. They were flat-trajectory weapons and thus virtually useless as artillery in stopping an attack from the mainland. We can infer
with some certainty what has motivated Mona Gardner to interrupt
her travel account with this bit of specious propaganda. She has been
asked to put it in by the Foreign Office, or by Naval or Military Intelligence, as part of the British attempt to discourage Japanese attack
by exaggerating the strength of the defenses. The attempt recoiled,
and the loss of Singapore in 1942 was the result. As Colonel Masanobu
Tsuji, the architect of the Japanese land attack, writes, "The strength
of Singapore's position was purposely and extravagantly propagandized
without regard for the complacency which would be prompted among
the public and even among those responsible for its defense." The
legend of the invulnerability of Singapore, "created to fool the Japanese," says James Leasor, "fooled only the British." Poor General
A. E. Percival commented after the war (which he spent, having lost
Singapore, in a Japanese prison camp):

> From time to time exaggerated statements had appeared in the
> Press as to the strength of the Singapore defences. It is probable
> that, as a result of these statements, the public believed the de-
> fences were stronger than they really were. It is certain that the
> troops retiring from the mainland . . . were disappointed not to
> find the immensely strong defences which they had pictured.

Another who was disappointed—indeed, shocked—was Churchill. He
himself had been beguiled by these propaganda inserts in travel books
like Gardner's, or like R. H. Bruce Lockhart's *Return to Malaya*
(1936), where he would hear Lockhart designating Singapore "the
greatest citadel of the world" and descanting on its "vast military,
naval, and air defences . . . erected at enormous expense." Sometimes,
in fact, one doubts that any British travel book touching on Singapore
and Malaya from 1936 on retains its integrity uncompromised by these
secret official interpositions. And if we may suspect this of books about
southeast Asia, what about books recounting travels elsewhere, like
Egypt or Palestine? In the late 30's it became increasingly possible to
believe that adventurers and travelers were really spies, in accordance
with British folk-tradition dating back a century. When Forster traveled to South Africa in 1929, some naturally assumed he had gone on
some "hush-hush" work, just as T. E. Lawrence was widely believed

to be, as P. N. Furbank puts it, "Britain's top spy," in 1929 busy "fo-
menting a revolt in Afghanistan." In this atmosphere it was to be expected that rumor about the disappearance of Amelia Earhart and
Fred Noonan over the Pacific in 1937 would develop into a full-fledged
narrative of espionage. Their plane was shot or forced down, the story
went, by the Japanese on the fortified island of Saipan, which the fliers
were secretly scrutinizing while appearing to be merely adventuring.

Clearly not a world in which either travel or the travel book could
flourish. The going was good for only twenty years, and after the war
all that remained was jet tourism among the ruins, resulting in phenomena like the appalling pollution of the Mediterranean and the
Aegean. Claude Lévi-Strauss observes in 1974 that so full is the world
now of its own garbage that "journeys, those magic caskets full of
dreamlike promises, will never again yield up their treasures untar-
nished. . . . The first thing we see as we travel round the world is our
own filth, thrown into the face of mankind." Thus "the mad passion
for travel books" of the sort I've been considering. "They create the
illusion of something which no longer exists but still should exist."

The period between the wars opens with Eliot's "Burbank with a
Baedeker, Bleistein with a Cigar" (1919). It closes with both the
"Baedeker Raids" on cities formerly frequented by travelers and an
anti-Semitism grown cruel and murderous in a way unimaginable to
the conceiver of Bleistein twenty years earlier. The travel period ends
with the control of the Baedeker plant at Leipzig by totalitarians hostile to the very idea of travel. What we have now, as Lévi-Strauss perceives, is "monoculture." The acute sense of place that attended travel
between the wars has atrophied. Now apparently out of reach is the
sense of place that enabled Orwell, returning from Spain in 1938, to
register by contrast the English scene this way at the end of *Homage
to Catalonia*:

> Here it was still the England I had known in my childhood: the
> railway cuttings smothered in wild flowers, the deep meadows
> where the great shining horses browse and meditate, the slow-
> moving streams bordered by willows, the green bosoms of the
> elms, the larkspurs in the cottage gardens; and then the huge
> peaceful wilderness of outer London, the barges on the miry

river, the familiar streets, the posters telling of cricket matches and Royal weddings, the men in bowler hats, the pigeons in Trafalgar Square, the red buses, the blue policemen—all sleeping the deep, deep sleep of England, from which I sometimes fear that we shall never wake till we are jerked out of it by the roar of bombs.

The British did awake, but to a different world, one in which the idea of literary traveling must seem quaint and a book about it a kind of elegy.

Sources

Place of publication is London unless otherwise indicated.

ACKERLEY, J. R., *Hindoo Holiday: An Indian Journal* (1932).

ACTON, HAROLD, *Memoirs of an Aesthete* (1948).

——— *Nancy Mitford: A Memoir* (New York, 1975).

ALLEN, CHARLES, ed., *Plain Tales from the Raj: Images of British India in the Twentieth Century* (1975).

AMHERST, JEFFREY, *Wandering Abroad* (1976).

AMIS, KINGSLEY, *I Like It Here* (1958).

AUDEN, W. H., *The Dyer's Hand and Other Essays* (New York, 1962).

——— *The English Auden: Poems, Essays, and Dramatic Writings*, ed. Edward Mendelson (New York, 1977).

——— Interview with Michael Newman, *Writers at Work: Fourth Series*, ed. George Plimpton (New York, 1976).

AUDEN, W. H., and CHRISTOPHER ISHERWOOD, *Journey to a War* (1939; rev. ed., 1973).

——— *On the Frontier* (1938).

AUDEN, W. H., and LOUIS MACNEICE, *Letters from Iceland* (1937).

BAEDEKER, KARL, *Russia, with Teheran, Port Arthur, and Peking: Handbook for Travelers* (Leipzig, 1914).

BALFOUR, PATRICK, *Grand Tour: Diary of an Eastward Journey* (New York, 1935).

BARBUSSE, HENRI, *Under Fire (Le Feu)*, trans. W. Fitzwater Wray (1926).

BERGONZI, BERNARD, *Reading the Thirties: Texts and Contexts* (1978).

BENSON, STELLA, *The Little World* (1925).

BOLITHO, HECTOR, *War in the Strand: A Notebook of the First Two and a Half Years in London* (1942).

BOORSTIN, DANIEL J., *The Image: A Guide to Pseudo-Events in America* (New York, 1977).

BORGES, JORGE LUIS, Interview with Ronald Christ, *Writers at Work: Fourth Series*, ed., George Plimpton (New York, 1976).

BOSWELL, JAMES, *The Life of Samuel Johnson, LL.D.*, ed. George Birkbeck Hill and L. F. Powell (6 vols.; Oxford, 1934-1950).

BRAGG, MELVYN, *Speak for England* (New York, 1977).

BRENAN, GERALD, *A Life of One's Own: Childhood and Youth* (1962).

———— *Personal Records, 1920-1972* (New York, 1975).

BRERETON, LT.-COLONEL F. S., *Travel: An Account of Its Methods in Past and Present* (1931).

BRIEN, ALAN, "Tourist Angst," *Spectator*, July 31, 1959, p. 133.

BRINNIN, JOHN MALCOLM, *The Sway of the Grand Saloon: A Social History of the North Atlantic* (New York, 1971).

BRYDONE, PATRICK, *A Tour through Sicily and Malta* (2 vols.; 1773).

BUNTING, BASIL, *Collected Poems* (Oxford, 1978).

BURGESS, ANTHONY, Interview with John Cullinan, *Writers at Work: Fourth Series*, ed. George Plimpton (New York, 1976).

———— Introduction to *D. H. Lawrence and Italy* (New York, 1972).

BUTOR, MICHEL, "Travel and Writing," *Mosaic*, VIII (Fall, 1974), 1-16.

BYRON, ROBERT, *The Byzantine Achievement* (1929).

———— *An Essay on India* (1931).

———— *Europe in the Looking-Glass* (1926).

———— *First Russia, Then Tibet* (1933).

———— *How We Celebrate the Coronation: A Word to London's Visitors* (1937).

———— *The Road to Oxiana* (1937).

———— *The Station: Athos, Treasures and Men* (1928).

BYRON, ROBERT, and CHRISTOPHER SYKES, *Innocence and Design* (1935).

CAMPBELL, JOSEPH, *The Hero with a Thousand Faces* (2nd ed., Princeton, 1968).

CAREW, DUDLEY, *A Fragment of Friendship* (1974).

CARSON, ANTHONY, *Travels: Near and Far Out* (New York, 1962).

CARSWELL, JOHN, *Life and Letters: A. R. Orage, Beatrice Hastings, Katherine Mansfield, John Middleton Murry, S. S. Koteliansky, 1906-1957* (New York, 1978).

CAVITCH, DAVID, *D. H. Lawrence and The New World* (New York, 1969).

CHAPLIN, CHARLES, *My Autobiography* (New York, 1964).

CHAPMAN, GUY, *A Kind of Survivor*, Preface by Margaret Storm Jameson (1975).

CHATWIN, BRUCE, *In Patagonia* (1977).

CONNOLLY, CYRIL, *Enemies of Promise* (New York, 1948).

———— "Oxford in the Twenties," *The Evening Colonnade* (New York, 1975).

——— *Previous Convictions* (New York, 1963).

——— *The Rock Pool* (New York, 1936).

——— *A Romantic Friendship: The Letters of Cyril Connolly to Noël Blakiston* (1975).

COWLEY, MALCOLM, *Exile's Return: A Literary Odyssey of the 1920's* (New York, 1951).

CRANE, HART, *The Collected Poems of Hart Crane*, ed. Waldo Frank (New York, 1933).

CUNARD, NANCY, *Grand Man: Memories of Norman Douglas* (1954).

DAVIES, W. H., *The Autobiography of a Super-Tramp* (1908).

DELANY, PAUL, *D. H. Lawrence's Nightmare: The Writer and His Circle in the Years of the Great War* (New York, 1978).

DONALDSON, FRANCES, *Edward VIII* (Philadelphia, 1975).

DOS PASSOS, JOHN, *Journeys Between Wars* (New York, 1938).

DOUGLAS, NORMAN, *Alone* (1921).

——— *Experiments* (New York, 1925).

——— *Fountains in the Sand* (1912).

——— *How About Europe?* (1930).

——— *Late Harvest* (1946).

——— *Looking Back: An Autobiographical Excursion* (New York, 1933).

——— *Old Calabria* (1915).

——— *"One Day," Three of Them* (1929).

——— *Siren Land* (1911).

——— *Some Limericks* (Florence, 1928).

——— *South Wind* (1917).

——— *Together* (1923).

DRIBERG, TOM, *Ruling Passions* (1977).

DURRELL, LAWRENCE, *Spirit of Place*, ed. Alan G. Thomas (New York, 1969).

ECKERSLEY, ARTHUR, Review of *South Wind*, *English Review*, XXV (August, 1917), 189.

EDWARDS, A. S. G., "A Source for *A Handful of Dust*," *Modern Fiction Studies*, XXII (Summer, 1976), 242-44.

ELIOT, T. S., *Collected Poems, 1909-1935* (New York, 1936).

——— *Four Quartets* (New York, 1943).

——— *Selected Essays, 1917-1932* (New York, 1932).

EMPSON, WILLIAM, *Some Versions of Pastoral* (1935).

FERMOR, PATRICK LEIGH, A Time of Gifts (1977).

FINNEY, BRIAN, Christopher Isherwood: A Critical Biography (New York, 1979).

FLEMING, PETER, Brazilian Adventure (1933).

—— News from Tartary (1936).

—— One's Company: A Journey to China (1934).

FORD, HUGH, Published in Paris: American and British Writers, Printers, and Publishers in Paris, 1920-1939 (New York, 1975).

FORSTER, E. M., Alexandria: A History and Guide (1922).

—— Aspects of the Novel (1927).

—— "The Obelisk," The Life to Come and Other Short Stories (New York, 1976).

—— A Passage to India (1924).

—— Two Cheers for Democracy (New York, 1951).

FRANK, JOSEPH, "Spatial Form in Modern Literature," The Widening Gyre (Bloomington, Ind., 1968).

FREEDMAN, RALPH, Hermann Hesse: Pilgrim of Crisis (New York, 1979).

FREUD, SIGMUND, "A Disturbance of Memory on the Acropolis," Character and Culture, trans. James Strachey (New York, 1963).

FRYE, NORTHROP, Anatomy of Criticism: Four Essays (Princeton, 1957).

FRYER, JONATHAN, Isherwood (1977).

FURBANK, P. N., E. M. Forster: A Life (2 vols.; 1977).

FUSSELL, PAUL, "Patrick Brydone: The Eighteenth-Century Traveler as Representative Man," Literature as a Mode of Travel, ed. Warner G. Rice (New York, 1963).

GALTON, FRANCIS, The Art of Travel; or, Shifts and Contrivances Available in Wild Countries (1855).

GARDNER, MONA, Menacing Sun (1939).

GAY, JOHN, Poetry and Prose, ed. Vinton A. Dearing, with the assistance of Charles E. Beckwith (2 vols.; Oxford, 1974).

GOETHE, J. W., Italian Journey (1786-1788), trans. W. H. Auden and Elizabeth Mayer (New York, 1968).

GORER, GEOFFREY, Africa Dances: A Book about West African Negroes (1935).

GRABURN, NELSON H. H., "Tourism: The Sacred Journey," Hosts and Guests: The Anthropology of Tourism, ed. Valene L. Smith (Philadelphia, 1977).

GRAVES, ROBERT, Good-bye to All That (1929).

GRAVES, ROBERT, and ALAN HODGE, The Long Week-End: A Social History of Great Britain, 1918-1939 (1940).

GRAY, THOMAS, Correspondence of Thomas Gray, ed. Paget Toynbee and Leonard Whibley (3 vols.; Oxford, 1935).

GREEN, BOB, "Hong Kong," *Fodor's South-East Asia, 1978* (New York, 1978).

GREEN, HENRY, *Pack My Bag* (1940).

—— *Party Going* (1939).

GREEN, MARTIN, *Children of the Sun* (New York, 1976).

GREENE, GRAHAM, *England Made Me* (1935).

—— *In Search of a Character* (Harmondsworth, 1968).

—— *Journey Without Maps* (1936; 2nd ed., 1978).

—— *The Lawless Roads* (1939; 3rd ed., 1978).

—— *The Lost Childhood and Other Essays* (New York, 1951).

—— *Stamboul Train* (1932).

HALLIBURTON, RICHARD, *The Royal Road to Romance* (1925).

HARRISON, FREDERIC, "Regrets of a Veteran Traveler," *Memories and Thoughts: Men—Books—Cities—Art* (New York, 1906).

HART-DAVIS, DUFF, *Peter Fleming: A Biography* (1974).

HAZLITT, WILLIAM, "On Gusto," *The Round Table* (1817).

HEMINGWAY, ERNEST, *By-Line: Selected Articles and Dispatches of Four Decades,* ed. William White (New York, 1967).

—— *Death in the Afternoon* (New York, 1932).

—— *Green Hills of Africa* (New York, 1935).

—— *A Moveable Feast* (New York, 1964).

HEWISON, ROBERT, *Under Siege: Literary Life in London, 1939-1945* (1977).

HOLLIS, CHRISTOPHER, *Oxford in the Twenties: Recollections of Five Friends* (1976).

HOLLOWAY, MARK, *Norman Douglas: A Biography* (1976).

HOUSMAN, A. E., *The Collected Poems of A. E. Housman* (New York, 1945).

HOWARD, MICHAEL S., *Jonathan Cape, Publisher* (1971).

HOWARTH, PATRICK, *When the Riviera Was Ours* (1977).

HOWELL, SARAH, *The Seaside* (1974).

HURD, MICHAEL, *The Ordeal of Ivor Gurney* (1978).

HUSSEY, MAURICE, ed., *Poetry of the First World War* (1967).

HUXLEY, ALDOUS, *Beyond the Mexique Bay* (New York, 1934).

—— *The Olive Tree* (1936).

—— *Those Barren Leaves* (1925).

—— "Wordsworth in the Tropics," *Collected Essays* (New York, 1971).

HYNES, SAMUEL, *The Auden Generation: Literature and Politics in England in the 1930's* (1976).

ISHERWOOD, CHRISTOPHER, *All the Conspirators* (1928).
———— *Christopher and His Kind* (New York, 1976).
———— "Coming to London," *Exhumations: Stories, Articles, Verses* (New York, 1966).
———— Interview with W. I. Scobie, *Writers at Work: Fourth Series*, ed. George Plimpton (New York, 1976).
———— *The Memorial* (1932; 1977).
———— *Mr. Norris Changes Trains* (1935).
———— *The World in the Evening* (New York, 1954).

JACOBS, ALARIC, *A Traveler's War: A Journey to the Wars in Africa, India and Russia* (1944).
JAMES, CLIVE, "D. H. Lawrence in Transit," *D. H. Lawrence: Novelist, Poet, Prophet*, ed. Stephen Spender (1973).
JENKINS, ALAN, *The Thirties* (1976).
———— *The Twenties* (1974).
JOHNSON, SAMUEL, *The Letters of Samuel Johnson*, ed. R. W. Chapman (3 vols.; Oxford, 1952).

KARLIN, ALMA M., *The Odyssey of a Lonely Woman*, trans. Emile Burns (1933).
KEYSERLING, HERMANN, *The Travel Diary of a Philosopher*, trans. J. Holroyd Reece (2 vols.; New York, 1925).
KILVERT, FRANCIS, *Kilvert's Diary: Selections from the Diary of the Rev. Francis Kilvert*, ed. William Plomer (3 vols.; 1938-1940).
KOESTLER, ARTHUR, *Spanish Testament* (1937).
KRAMER, HILTON, "When the Going Was Good," *New York Times Book Review*, September 18, 1977, p. 48.

LAWRENCE, D. H., *Aaron's Rod* (1922).
———— *The Collected Letters of D. H. Lawrence*, ed. Harry T. Moore (2 vols.; New York, 1962).
———— *The Complete Poems of D. H. Lawrence*, ed. Vivian de Sola Pinto and Warren Roberts (2 vols.; New York, 1964).
———— *The Complete Short Stories* (3 vols.; New York, 1961).
———— *Etruscan Places* (1932).
———— *Kangaroo* (1923).
———— *Lady Chatterley's Lover* (Florence, 1928).

———— *The Letters of D. H. Lawrence*, ed. Aldous Huxley (New York, 1932).

———— *Mornings in Mexico* (1927).

———— *Phoenix: The Posthumous Papers of D. H. Lawrence*, ed. Edward D. McDonald (New York, 1936).

———— *Phoenix II: Uncollected, Unpublished, and Other Prose Works*, ed. Warren Roberts and Harry T. Moore (New York, 1970).

———— *The Plumed Serpent* (1926).

———— *Sea and Sardinia* (1921).

———— *Twilight in Italy* (1916).

———— *Women in Love* (1920).

LEASOR, JAMES, *Singapore: The Battle That Changed the World* (New York, 1968).

LÉVI-STRAUSS, CLAUDE, *Tristes Tropiques*, trans. John and Doreen Weightman (New York, 1974).

LOCKHART, R. H. BRUCE, *Return to Malaya* (New York, 1936).

LODGE, DAVID, "Modernism, Antimodernism, and Postmodernism," *The New Review*, IV, No. 38 (May, 1977), 39-44.

MACAULAY, ROSE, *Personal Pleasures* (New York, 1936).

MACCANNELL, DEAN, *The Tourist: A New Theory of the Leisure Class* (New York, 1976).

MACLEISH, ARCHIBALD, *Collected Poems* (Boston, 1952).

MACNEICE, LOUIS, *Autumn Journal* (1939).

———— *The Strings Are False* (New York, 1966).

MCPHEE, JOHN, "Templex," *The New Yorker*, January 6, 1968, pp. 32-66.

MAILER, NORMAN, Interview with Steven Marcus, *Writers at Work: Third Series*, ed. Alfred Kazin (New York, 1967).

MARSH, EDWARD, *Rupert Brooke: A Memoir* (1918).

MARSHALL, ARTHUR, "Many a Slip," *New Statesman*, January 19, 1979, p. 81.

MARTIN, JOHN SAYRE, *E. M. Forster: The Endless Journey* (Cambridge, 1976).

MASSINGHAM, HUGH and PAULINE, eds., *The Englishman Abroad* (1962).

MAUGHAM, ROBIN, *Escape from the Shadows* (1972).

MAUGHAM, W. SOMERSET, *The Narrow Corner* (1932).

———— *The Summing Up* (1938).

MINOGUE, KENNETH, in *My LSE*, ed. Joan Abse (1977).

MONTAGUE, C. E., *The Right Place: A Book of Pleasures* (1924).

MOORE, HARRY T., *The Priest of Love: A Life of D. H. Lawrence* (rev. ed., New York, 1974).

MORGAN, BRYAN, ed., *The Great Trains* (New York, 1973).

MORRIS, WRIGHT, lecture, Princeton University, December 2, 1971.

MORRISS, MARGARET, "Critical Response to *Labels* and *Remote People*," *Evelyn Waugh Newsletter*, Autumn, 1979, pp. 1-4.

MORTON, H. V., *In the Steps of the Master* (1934).

———— *In the Steps of St. Paul* (1936).

MOWAT, CHARLES LOCH, *Britain Between the Wars, 1918-1940* (Chicago, 1955).

MOYNIHAN, MICHAEL, *People at War, 1914-1918* (1973).

NABOKOV, VLADIMIR, *Pale Fire* (New York, 1962).

NICHOLS, BEVERLEY, *Twenty-Five* (1926).

ORWELL, GEORGE, *The Collected Essays, Journalism, and Letters of George Orwell*, ed. Sonia Orwell and Ian Angus (4 vols.; New York, 1968).

———— *Coming Up for Air* (1939).

———— *Homage to Catalonia* (1938).

———— *The Road to Wigan Pier* (1937).

PEARSON, JOHN, *The Sitwells: A Family's Biography* (New York, 1978).

PEARSON, J. P., *Railways and Scenery* (4 vols.; 1932).

PECKHAM, MORSE, "The Pleasures of the Po," *Texas Arts Journal*, I (1977), 2-12.

PERCIVAL, LT.-GENERAL A. E., *The War in Malaya* (1949).

PLOWMAN, MAX, *A Lap Full of Seed* (Oxford, 1917).

POST, EMILY, *Etiquette* (New York, 1922).

POUND, EZRA, *Jefferson and/or Mussolini* (1935).

———— *Literary Essays of Ezra Pound*, ed. T. S. Eliot (1954).

———— *Personae: The Collected Poems of Ezra Pound* (New York, 1926).

———— *Polite Essays* (Norfolk, Conn., 1937).

POWELL, ANTHONY, *Infants of the Spring* (1976).

———— *Messengers of Day* (1978).

———— *Venusberg* (1933).

———— *What's Become of Waring* (1939).

PRIESTLEY, J. B., *Delight* (New York, 1949).

PRITCHETT, V. S., *Marching Spain* (1928).

———— *Midnight Oil* (New York, 1972).

PRYCE-JONES, ALAN, *People in the South* (1932)

———— *The Spring Journey* (1931).

QUENNELL, PETER, *The Marble Foot* (New York, 1977).

———— *The Sign of the Fish* (1960).

———— *A Superficial Journey through Tokyo and Peking* (1932).

RABAN, JONATHAN, *Arabia through the Looking Glass* (1979).

———— "Stranger in the World," *The New Review*, III, No. 31 (September, 1976), 55-58.

RELPH, EDWARD, *Place and Placelessness* (1976).

RICE, DAVID TALBOT, and ROBERT BYRON, *The Birth of Western Painting* (1929).

RICHARDS, I. A., *Practical Criticism: A Study of Literary Judgment* (1929).

RICHARDSON, EMELINE, *The Etruscans: Their Art and Civilization* (Chicago, 1964).

ROLLIER, AUGUSTE, *Heliotherapy* (1923).

ROOSEVELT, THEODORE, "William Beebe's 'Jungle Peace,'" *New York Times Review of Books*, October 13, 1918, p. 1.

SANDHURST, FOURTH BARON, *From Day to Day, 1914-1915* (1918).

SASSOON, SIEGFRIED, *Collected Poems* (New York, 1949).

SCHORER, MARK, *D. H. Lawrence* (New York, 1968).

SHAW, GEORGE BERNARD, *The Adventures of the Black Girl in Her Search for God* (1932).

SIMMONS, LAURA, *The Crannied Wall* (Prairie City, Ill., n. d.).

SITWELL, OSBERT, *Discursions on Travel, Art and Life* (1925).

———— *The Four Continents* (1954).

———— *Great Morning!* (Boston, 1947).

———— *Winters of Content and Other Discursions on Mediterranean Art and Travel* (1950).

SLONIMSKY, NICOLAS, *Music Since 1900* (3rd ed., New York, 1949).

SMITH, VALENE L., ed., *Hosts and Guests: The Anthropology of Tourism* (Philadelphia, 1977).

SMOLLETT, TOBIAS, *Travels through France and Italy* (1766).

SONTAG, SUSAN, *On Photography* (New York, 1977).

SPENDER, STEPHEN, *Collected Poems, 1928-1953* (1955).

———— "Is It Serious?", *New Statesman*, January 27, 1978, pp. 126-27.

———— *The Thirties and After: Poetry, Politics, People, 1933-1970* (New York, 1978).

———— *World Within World* (1951).

STALLWORTHY, JON, *Wilfred Owen* (1974).

STANNARD, MARTIN, "Davie's Lamp," *The New Review*, III, No. 33 (December, 1976), 52-54.

STANSKY, PETER, and WILLIAM ABRAHAMS, *Journey to the Frontier: Two Roads to the Spanish Civil War* (New York, 1966).

———— *The Unknown Orwell* (New York, 1972).

STARK, FREYA, *Beyond Euphrates: Autobiography, 1928-1933* (1951).

———— *The Valleys of the Assassins* (1936).

STEVENSON, ROBERT LOUIS, *Travels with a Donkey* (1879).

STEWART, DESMOND, *T. E. Lawrence* (New York, 1977).

SWIFT, JONATHAN, *The Correspondence of Jonathan Swift*, ed. Harold Williams (5 vols.; Oxford, 1963-1965).

SWINGLEHURST, EDMUND, *The Romantic Journey: The Story of Thomas Cook and Victorian Travel* (New York, 1974).

SYKES, CHRISTOPHER, *Evelyn Waugh: A Biography* (Boston, 1975).

—— *Four Studies in Loyalty* (1946).

—— *Stranger Wonders: Tales of Travel* (1937).

SYKES, CHRISTOPHER, and ROBERT BYRON, *Innocence and Design* (1935).

SYMONDS, JOHN ADDINGTON, *Sketches in Italy* (Leipzig, 1883).

TAYLOR, A. J. P., *English History, 1914-1945* (Oxford, 1965).

THEROUX, PAUL, *The Great Railway Bazaar: By Train through Asia* (Boston, 1975).

—— *The Old Patagonian Express: By Train through the Americas* (New York, 1979).

—— "Round the World in 80 Clichés," *Sunday Times* (London), December 11, 1977, p. 41.

THOMSON, DAVID, *England in the Twentieth Century, 1914-1963* (1964).

TOMLINSON, H. M., *All Our Yesterdays* (1924).

—— *Norman Douglas* (1931).

—— "Some Hints for Those About to Travel," *The Face of the Earth* (New York, 1950).

—— *Tidemarks: Some Records of a Journey to the Beaches of the Moluccas and the Forest of Malaya in 1923* (1924).

TREGLOWN, JEREMY, "Gaol Bait," *New Statesman*, July 15, 1977, p. 91.

TSUJI, COLONEL MASANOBU, *Singapore: The Japanese Version* (New York, 1961).

TURNER, LOUIS, and JOHN ASH, *The Golden Hordes: International Tourism and the Pleasure Periphery* (1975).

UPWARD, EDWARD, *Journey to the Border* (1939).

WAUGH, ALEC, *The Early Years of Alec Waugh* (1962).

—— *Hot Countries* (New York, 1930).

—— "Just for Curiosity," *Traveler's Quest*, ed. M. A. Michael (1950).

—— *My Brother Evelyn and Other Profiles* (1967).

—— *A Year to Remember: A Reminiscence of 1931* (1975).

WAUGH, EVELYN, *The Diaries of Evelyn Waugh*, ed. Michael Davie (1976).

—— *A Handful of Dust* (1934).

—— Interview with Julian Jebb, *Writers at Work: Third Series*, ed. Alfred Kazin (New York, 1967).

—— *Labels: A Mediterranean Journal* (1930).

────── A Little Learning (1964).

────── A Little Order: A Selection from His Journalism, ed. Donat
        Gallagher (1977).

────── Ninety-Two Days: The Account of a Tropical Journey through
        British Guiana and Part of Brazil (1934).

────── The Ordeal of Gilbert Pinfold (Boston, 1957).

────── Remote People (1931).

────── Review of Peter Fleming, News from Tartary, Spectator, August 7,
        1936, p. 244.

────── Robbery Under Law: The Mexican Object-Lesson (1939).

────── Scoop: A Novel about Journalists (1938).

────── "This Sun-Bathing Business," Daily Mail, July 5, 1930, p. 8.

────── Tourist in Africa (Boston, 1960).

────── Vile Bodies (1930).

────── Waugh in Abyssinia (1936).

────── When the Going Was Good (Harmondsworth, 1946).

WEIGHTMAN, JOHN, "The Solar Revolution: Reflections on a Theme in
        French Literature," Encounter, December, 1970, pp. 9-18.

WELCH, DENTON, The Denton Welch Journals, ed. Jocelyn Brooke (1952).

WELSCH, ROGER L., Tall-Tale Postcards: A Pictorial History (1976).

WEST, REBECCA, Black Lamb and Grey Falcon: A Journey through Yugo-
        slavia (2 vols.; 1942).

────── Ending in Earnest: A Literary Log (1931).

WESTON, EDWARD, Daybooks, ed. Nancy Newhall (2 vols.; Rochester, 1961-
        1966).

WHITE, HAYDEN, "The Fictions of Factual Representation," The Literature
        of Fact: Selected Papers from The English Institute, ed. Angus
        Fletcher (New York, 1976).

WILLIAMS, JOHN, The Home Fronts: Britain, France and Germany, 1914-
        1918 (1972).

WILLIAMS, WILLIAM CARLOS, A Voyage to Pagany, Introduction by Harry
        Levin (New York, 1970).

WINTER, DENIS, Death's Men: Soldiers of the Great War (1978).

WOHL, ROBERT, The Generation of 1914 (Cambridge, Mass., 1979).

WOLFF, GEOFFREY, Black Sun: The Brief Transit and Violent Eclipse of
        Harry Crosby (New York, 1976).

WOOLF, VIRGINIA, Between the Acts (1941).

────── Collected Essays (4 vols.; 1966-1967).

YOUNG, G. M., Gibbon (New York, 1933).

YOXALL, H. W., MS. Diary in Imperial War Museum.

INDEX